Sustainable Development: OECD Policy Approaches for the 21st Century

EDITORIAL NOTE

This report was prepared by the OECD Task Force on Sustainable Development. Marilyn Yakowitz, Co-ordinator for Sustainable Development, served as general editor. It Is published under the responsibility of the Secretary-General of the OECD.

ORGANISATION FOR ECONOMIC CO-OPERATION AND DEVELOPMENT

ORGANISATION FOR ECONOMIC CO-OPERATION AND DEVELOPMENT

Pursuant to Article 1 of the Convention signed in Paris on 14th December 1960, and which came into force on 30th September 1961, the Organisation for Economic Co-operation and Development (OECD) shall promote policies designed:

- to achieve the highest sustainable economic growth and employment and a rising standard of living in Member countries, while maintaining financial stability, and thus to contribute to the development of the world economy;
- to contribute to sound economic expansion in Member as well as non-member countries in the process of economic development; and
- to contribute to the expansion of world trade on a multilateral, non-discriminatory basis in accordance with international obligations.

The original Member countries of the OECD are Austria, Belgium, Canada, Denmark, France, Germany, Greece, Iceland, Ireland, Italy, Luxembourg, the Netherlands, Norway, Portugal, Spain, Sweden, Switzerland, Turkey, the United Kingdom and the United States. The following countries became Members subsequently through accession at the dates indicated hereafter: Japan (28th April 1964), Finland (28th January 1969), Australia (7th June 1971), New Zealand (29th May 1973), Mexico (18th May 1994), the Czech Republic (21st December 1995), Hungary (7th May 1996), Poland (22nd November 1996) and the Republic of Korea (12th December 1996). The Commission of the European Communities takes part in the work of the OECD (Article 13 of the OECD Convention).

Publié en français sous le titre :

DÉVELOPPEMENT DURABLE : STRATÉGIES DE L'OCDE POUR LE XXIᵉ SIÈCLE

Reprinted 1998

FOREWORD

Unlike the pessimists to be found in some quarters of the sustainable development debate, I am a guarded optimist. My optimism is reinforced by economic trends in most regions, linked with the growing awareness that economic growth can no longer be credibly pursued without a much stronger concern for its sustainability. I am encouraged by the promise of globalisation and expanding linkages amongst OECD, developing countries, and economies in transition. My vision is based upon a ''paradigm'' integrating economic growth, social equity, and sound governance. The goal is a community of nations in which all citizens share in – and have a stake in – a decent standard of living, individual freedom, personal dignity and a healthy environment.

The phenomenon of globalisation weaves nations together, through open trade, foreign investment, and telecommunications, into a fabric of interdependence. We will need both the right policies, and wise and creative political leadership, if the dynamism of globalisation is to help move all nations together towards sustainable development. Enlightened decision-making to promote sustainable development depends upon a better grasp of the interactions among fiscal, economic, trade, energy, social and environmental policies. The OECD has increasingly turned its attention to interdisciplinary work to build up such knowledge, focusing particularly on the policies needed for sustainability.

This volume provides an overview and analysis of trends, of policies already established and of new policy directions related to many of the key socio-economic and sectoral issues of Agenda 21. It demonstrates how sustainability has emerged as an over-arching policy goal for the OECD and its 29 Member countries, since the Rio Earth Summit in 1992, and how progress hinges upon the integration of environmental and social goals with economic ones.

Environmental issues are becoming more complex, particularly at the interface between environment and economy. A new priority needs to be further ''decoupling'' pollutant releases, wastes, and resource inputs from economic output in all sectors. The sheer growth of OECD and other large country economies means that the aggregate effects of current patterns of consumption and production too often outpace improvements in technology and environmental protection measures. Progress has been made in OECD countries, but more is needed, and rapidly. Strategies for change must involve all stakeholders, and especially the private sector.

The government role in facilitating sustainable development must be joined by greater individual, civic and corporate responsibility. The OECD is working to this end with the OECD Business and Industry and Trade Union Advisory Committees, as well as deepening its interactions with NGOs.

The OECD's vision must be a global one. Sustainable development presents a special set of challenges for many poor countries that still have little access to the expanding volume of foreign direct investment and other private finance. In line with the partnership approach of the 1996 Statement on *Shaping the 21st Century,* the OECD recognises the clear need for external assistance to help promote the successful integration of these countries into the global trade and investment systems and to combat the constant challenge of extreme poverty.

OECD Ministers have resolved ''to work together to generate sustainable development and non-inflationary growth in the OECD and beyond by creating more jobs, reducing poverty and exclusion, protecting the environment, and increasing confidence''. They aim to translate these goals into action by pursuing the integration of environmental with economic and other policies.

I am firmly committed to the OECD taking a leading role in the development of innovative policy approaches for sustainable development. The twin challenges of sustainability and globalisation will require the diverse skills of the Secretariat, and the active support of our Member countries. These are challenges which I anticipate with enthusiasm.

Donald Johnston
Secretary-General

TABLE OF CONTENTS

INTRODUCTION

by

Marilyn Yakowitz

SCOPE OF THE BOOK

The special perspective of this volume is its integrated approach to economic, environmental, social, and development co-operation issues identified in Agenda 21, the Rio Earth Summit blueprint for sustainable development. Authors explore both positive trends pointing towards greater sustainability and areas where progress has proved more elusive. They identify policy gaps and trade-offs and suggest options for future policy directions. While the main focus is on the OECD region, expanding linkages – among all countries and regions – nevertheless, form an important part of the story.

At the OECD and its affiliated bodies[1] much recent attention has focused upon sustainable development as an increasingly important policy goal and guiding concept. The OECD has a long history of commitment to sustainable development both in the OECD area and world-wide. This commitment goes back to the foundation of the Organisation itself, when in 1961 the original Members agreed in the OECD Convention to promote policies to achieve sustainable economic growth in Member countries and to contribute to sound economic growth in countries beyond its membership.

This publication was developed by an OECD Secretariat Task Force on Sustainable Development, representing virtually all parts of the Organisation. It contributes in-depth analysis of many of the issues under review in the 1997 UN General Assembly Special Session – Earth Summit +5 – and in the Commission on Sustainable Development. It brings to bear the OECD's comparative advantages in subject matter expertise as well as its interdisciplinary approach.

Part I of this two-part volume is concentrated on socio-economic dimensions of Agenda 21 and means of implementation. Subjects include: the integration of economics and environment; trade and environment; changing consumption and production patterns; assessing environmental performance; development co-operation; and the evolution of aid agencies since Rio. **Part II** takes an in-depth look at nine sectoral issues: energy; transport; agriculture; toxic chemicals; climate change; nuclear energy; urbanisation; biotechnology; and education.

The selection of chapters reflects both current international priorities and particular OECD strengths with respect to sustainable development. Topics were chosen from among extensive OECD activities relevant to each of the 40 chapters of Agenda 21. Many other topics representing leading-edge research and policy development by the Organisation are drawn upon, for example: cleaner technologies; public and private financial resource flows; OECD peer review; and national reporting and statistical systems. All Rio Conventions and many related agreements, including the Desertification, Basel and Biological Diversity and Climate Change Conventions, command active OECD co-operation.

PART I: THEMES

Chapter 1: Integrating Environment and the Economy summarises the progress made thus far by OECD Governments in fostering better integration of economic and environmental decision-making through greater reliance on market mechanisms. It chronicles the growing use of charges and taxes, marketable permits or emissions trading and deposit-refund schemes, which are in practice complementary to regulatory instruments. OECD investigation of existing subsidy schemes and tax disincentives seeks to identify "win/win" solutions, in which both the environment and the economy can benefit from reform. This chapter emphasizes that the most powerful tool will still be the price mechanism, and the extent to which it gives the right signals to producers and consumers. This finding for the general case is consistent with that at the microeconomic level, as discussed in the chapters on transport and other sectors.

How is the development co-operation community meeting the challenge of transition from the Cold War era to the possibilities for a new era of shared human progress in the 21st century? What are the implications for Rio Summit and Agenda 21 follow-up? *Chapter 2: Shaping the 21st Century: the Contribution of Development Co-operation* focuses on a new Development Assistance Committee (DAC) strategy which sets out a vision of development co-operation as full partnership with developing countries and as an investment in a shared future. Consistent with Agenda 21 and other international conference outcomes, measurable goals are proposed for economic well-being and poverty-reduction, social development and environmental sustainability. The strategy also calls for measures to maximise development resources – domestic and foreign, private and public; improved co-ordination and efficiency in the use of official development assistance (ODA); and attention to mutual reinforcement of development co-operation and other policies affecting developing countries. *Chapter 5: Aid Agencies: Changing to Meet the Requirements of Rio* clearly shows how concepts have evolved into practice at the bilateral donor agencies and the implications for programmes, projects and resources. A *Survey of DAC Members' Activities in Support of Environmental Goals* (OECD, 1997) provided in-depth information which is the basis for this analysis.

Systematic monitoring and assessment of country performance, combining objective oversight and peer review, is a core function of the OECD. The peer review system results in regular country reporting in the fields of economics, environment, development assistance, and energy. For the OECD region, the Organisation is the key international supplier of relevant and timely statistical information, statistical standards, systems and classifications, in co-ordination with other international statistical agencies. The backbone of OECD analyses is numeric data, collected chiefly from Member governments, and increasingly from non-members, for example, on national accounts, labour force, foreign trade, prices, output, official development and private sector financial flows, the environment, and foreign direct investment.

Chapter 3: Assessing Environmental Performance documents the OECD approach, which has become a benchmark for country reports and indicators of performance. In addition, it provides a brief overview of the state of the environment in OECD countries, including achievements and problems. The environmental policies carried out in the 1980s and 1990s have clearly produced positive effects on the state of the environment. Despite fears to the contrary, analysis shows that they have not posed significant economic difficulties in OECD countries, nor created significant distortions in international trade or employment. Reviews of individual country domestic and international performance, particularly measured against country commitments, also indicate where much more progress is required to solve transfrontier, regional and global problems.

The OECD's key supporting role for efforts to change consumption and production patterns continues to deepen the analysis of the policy measures needed. *Chapter 4: Consumption and Production Patterns: Making the Change* documents progress in the international community towards a more constructive and forward-looking approach since Rio. It examines the origins of the issues, the implications of globalisation for sustainable consumption, the main concepts, the actors involved, the challenge of reaching the individual consumer and the role of government. Finally, it highlights three case studies concerning: *promotion of a sustainable paper cycle; total water cycle management; and the government as consumer – leading by example.*

In 1988, the current trade and environment debate was launched in the OECD with a systematic review of environment and trade policy links. But it was in 1991, in part supported by the momentum of the Rio Earth Summit preparations, that OECD Member countries established a collaborative effort to reflect on ways of achieving an appropriate balance between securing environmental objectives and preserving the open multilateral trading system. *Chapter 6: Trade and Environment in the OECD* documents the evolution of the themes and the dialogue involving policy making communities representing the different fields and NGOs, and looks at the challenges ahead.

PART II: THEMES

As energy is a critical input to the engine of economic growth, it will always be a commodity of central importance to nations. It is vital to meeting both basic and more sophisticated human needs and is a key factor in the globalisation process. At the same time, pressures have arisen to address the continued growth projected to occur in global energy demand and the patterns of energy production and consumption which underlie that growth. *Chapter 7: Energy Challenges and Opportunities for Action* elaborates the global energy situation and suggests various options for action consistent with sustainable development. *Nuclear Energy and Sustainability (Chapter 12)* presents the case for treating nuclear energy as a contributor to sustainable development and outlines necessary conditions to achieve this, including radiation protection, waste management, safety of plant management and economic competitively.

Striking the right balance between the benefits and costs of transport is very much at the heart of policy-making in OECD countries. *Chapter 8: Transport, Economic Development and Social Welfare* follows trends and policy responses not only in OECD Member, but also in non-member countries, for inland, air and maritime transport, and inter-modal considerations. It explores issues of efficiency, the role of markets and regulation, land use planning, road safety, transport of hazardous goods, and costs to welfare, notably in terms of accidents, pollution and degradation of ecosystems and landscapes. OECD governments have, on the whole, pursued a set of policies which have aimed to bring market forces to bear more strongly on transport sectors, particularly by promoting liberalisation and strengthening competition policy, while at the same time seeking ways to address more effectively environmental and safety issues.

Chapter 9: Sustainable Agriculture discusses what is necessary for the sector to become more sustainable, both in ecological and economic terms, and trade-offs that may be required. Reforming agricultural policies will help, but will often need to be combined with more targeted environmental measures. Authors examine issues related to regulatory matters, minimum standards, voluntary approaches and direct payments. While national approaches to promoting sustainable agriculture reflect different priorities, certain practices are identified as having a high potential for sustainability. Examples are provided of measures in OECD countries being formulated to address specific concerns of soil loss, nature conservation, nutrient imbalances, and pesticide use. OECD experience demonstrates a widening interest in and pursuit of sustainable agriculture and a greater understanding of its elements.

With regard to *Sound Management of Toxic Chemicals (Chapter 10)*, OECD has taken the lead in assisting countries in the development and co-ordination of environmental health and safety activities on an international basis. This chapter documents the expansion and acceleration of international assessment of chemical risks, harmonization of classification and labelling of chemicals, information exchange on toxic chemicals and chemical risks, and strengthening of national capabilities and capacities for management of chemicals. By sharing results internationally, the burden on each government and industry is reduced, while output is increased overall.

The issues and activities treated in the chapters on energy and transport also relate to work on climate change at the OECD, IEA, and ECMT. *Chapter 11: Climate Change: Options for OECD Countries* briefly summarises trends which indicate the current difficulties in achieving national targets for greenhouse gas (GHG) reductions. It focuses on: GHG mitigation strategies and policies, including the results of OECD and IEA economic analyses and modelling; the potential contribution of subsidy reform in the energy and transport sectors; and the implications of carbon/energy taxes, tradeable permits, voluntary agreements and energy efficiency standards. *Guidelines for National Greenhouse Gas Inventories*, developed by the OECD and the IEA and adopted officially by the Climate Change Convention Conference of the Parties, has been a major technical contribution for national reporting requirements.

Chapter 13: Urbanisation and Sustainability discusses problems ranging from congestion, brownfields, air and noise pollution, to urban travel and land use patterns. Despite considerable progress in terms of efficiency in resource use, equity in quality of life, and increasing understanding of the elements involved, some solutions to urban environmental problems are extremely difficult to implement, for example, those concerning urban travel. Partnerships and civic engagement are crucial to stimulate the innovation necessary for solutions to seemingly intractable problems. In turn, strong local government is required to implement policy. Integrative strategies are needed to create linkages between key policy areas and between levels of government. Engaging the private sector is essential to enhance employment and economic growth.

The diffusion and application of modern biotechnology, with implications for public policy, international significance or common interest, are addressed in *Chapter 14: Biotechnology and Sustainable Development*. The chapter focuses particularly on biotechnology and environmental protection, agriculture and the food system, and health care. The Organisation's wide-ranging interests in the field span emerging safety issues, regulatory oversight in biotechnology, intellectual property, technology transfer and genetic resources, scientific and technological advances in, for example, bioremediation of air, soil, and water quality, and many other issues. OECD has pioneered the review of environmental biosafety aspects of agro-food products. The OECD Website: *BioTrack On-Line* makes freely available information about major legislative developments, field trials, and commercialised products. OECD schemes for seed certification have been implemented by 45 Member and non-member countries across all continents. For developing country agriculture, the OECD Development Centre compares the advantages and disadvantages of imported biotechnology techniques, and/or products, versus local development.

Environmental Education and Sustainable Development: Trends in Member Countries (Chapter 15) identifies some of the major trends in environmental education in OECD Member countries. It foresees the powerful development of a new ''education market'' in the area of sustainable development. The chapter focuses particularly on the work of the Centre for Educational Research and Innovation of the OECD and the experience of the Environment and School Initiatives Network.

GENERAL FINDINGS

Even if it were possible, it was not the intention of this volume to look across the OECD region to produce a consolidated balance sheet concerning performance or a bottom line. Nevertheless, a number of broad findings can be drawn from this study. The evidence shows that a wide range of policies in

OECD Member countries increasingly integrate sustainable development as an important goal. Policy-making is also more likely to include long-term consequences as a consideration, as a result of emphasis on sustainability.

There is improved understanding of the elements necessary for sustainability and the trade-offs involved. More experience with the various policy measures available is leading to better informed and more cost-effective approaches.

A sense of urgency comes through in these chapters, reflecting the speed of change, particularly with regard to globalisation, economic growth, distributional or equity issues, and the burgeoning of knowledge-based technologies.

In the OECD region, both the accomplishments and the scope for further improvement are clear. For example, energy conservation measures and waste reduction technologies have led to considerable progress in reducing the pollution burden in the OECD area since the 1980s. In addition, across OECD countries, there is evidence, for certain key indicators, of a start to the decoupling of environmental pollution and resource use from economic growth.

One response to adverse trends has been the adoption, by Member country governments and industry of long-term performance objectives and increasingly, of quantitative targets for environmental performance. Ability to measure performance has become more important, as has the need to establish baseline measurements.

There is also growing acceptance of the fact that fulfilling sustainable development objectives requires policy coherence and policy integration. Throughout this book there are examples of the considerable efforts at OECD to experiment with procedures to enable policy-makers and actors from different parts of government, business and industry, and civil society to jointly address issues of common interest. In some cases, the co-operation of different ministries through work within the OECD is leading to their closer co-operation in capitals on specific tasks. In the pursuit of mutually supportive policies, Member countries are utilising the OECD to bring together diverse policy communities, in such areas as trade and environment, economics and environment, tax and environment, agriculture and environment, technology and environment, development assistance and environment, and energy and the environment.

Looking ahead, there is a need and commitment by the Organisation and its Members to work in partnership with countries outside of the OECD region, and to co-operate between regions. Similarly, collaboration with other international bodies is seen as the cost-effective and rational way to approach the issues. In this regard, the respective roles and responsibilities of the public and private sectors is increasingly germane.

RELATED OECD REPORTS

At the end of each chapter, readers will find many OECD references for further information about each of the various topics. In addition, four new, highly relevant reports are being released by the OECD to coincide with the Earth Summit +5: *Globalisation and the Environment; Environmental Taxes and Green Tax Reform; Sustainable Consumption and Production; and Environmental Regulatory Reform.*

NOTE

1. Components of the OECD and its Affiliated Bodies

OECD Departments
and Directorates:

– *Economics*
– *Environment*
– *Development Co-operation*
– *Trade*
– *Statistics*
– *Science, Technology and Industry*
– *Food, Agriculture and Fisheries*
– *Financial, Fiscal and Enterprise Affairs*
– *Education, Employment, Labour and Social Affairs*
– *Territorial Development*
– *Public Management, and the*
– *Advisory Unit on Multidisciplinary Issues.*

Independent Agencies
and Specialised Bodies:

– *International Energy Agency (IEA)*
– *Nuclear Energy Agency (NEA)*
– *European Conference of Ministers of Transport (ECMT)*
– *Development Centre*
– *Club du Sahel*
– *Centre for Educational Research and Innovation (CERI).*

Some 200 *specialised committees and subsidiary bodies* carry out the major part of OECD work, serviced by an international *Secretariat* (about 1 950 persons) headed by the *Secretary-General* of the Organisation. The *Council*, OECD's governing body, is composed of a Permanent Representative, having rank of Ambassador, from each of the 29 Member countries. Closer co-operation with non-member countries has been building steadily since 1989; it takes different forms, such as policy dialogues and participation in committee work, and concerns about 40 additional countries.

Part I

CROSS-SECTORAL ISSUES:
SOCIO-ECONOMIC DIMENSIONS

Chapter 1

INTEGRATING THE ENVIRONMENT AND THE ECONOMY

by

Michel Potier

Integrating economic and environmental decision-making constitutes a key challenge for governments in their quest for sustainable development. There are many ways to achieve a better integration of economic and environmental decision-making. This could be accomplished, for instance, through a more systematic use of cost-benefit analysis, an adjustment of the system of National Accounts, or the development of economic expertise in environment ministries, together with the development of environment expertise in sectoral or economic ministries.[1] The most powerful tool, however, will still be the price mechanism, and the extent to which it gives the right signals to producers and consumers. In turn, the role prices will play will depend ultimately upon the ability of governments to pursue an effective strategy of internalising environmental costs.

The focus of this chapter will be on summarising the progress made so far by OECD Governments in fostering better integration of the economic and environmental decision-making process generally, through greater reliance upon market mechanisms. The first section will examine the experience of OECD countries in their use of economic instruments followed by a discussion of the environmental benefits of a reduction or elimination of economic subsidies in the second section.

THE EXPERIENCE OF OECD COUNTRIES IN THEIR USE OF ECONOMIC INSTRUMENTS

Main Features in the Use of Economic Instruments by OECD Countries

The recent OECD survey on the role of economic instruments in Member countries highlights at least five important messages:

a) There is a Growing Use of Economic Instruments for Environmental Management

The OECD survey, which was carried out in 1987 and published in 1989, reported 150 cases of the use of economic instruments in 14 Member countries; of these 150 cases, 80 involved environmental charges, or taxes, 40 were related to subsidies, and the remainder concerned other instruments, such as deposit-refund systems and trading schemes. The subsequent survey (1994), which covered the period 1987/93, indicates that the increase in the number of economic instruments used is close to 50 per cent (subsidies excluded).

Although the number of instruments used does not provide much information about the impact of these instruments, as a first approximation it is indicative of the underlying trend. Compared with 1987 (for countries where we have more detailed information), the changes have been *extensive* in Finland, Norway, Sweden, and the US. They have been *moderate* in the Netherlands and *minor* in France, Germany and Italy.

b)   Product Charges and Deposit-Refund Systems Are now the Most Frequently Introduced Instruments

While emission charges seem to be used less frequently, the use of product charges and of deposit-refund schemes increased respectively by 35 and 100 per cent between 1987 and 1992/93. A number of product charges have particularly been introduced in the Scandinavian countries (on nickel, cadmium, mercury, lead batteries, packaging, etc.). One may wonder why. One reason is that the availability of data on production and transactions makes charges or taxes on products easier to implement than taxes on emissions, resulting in lower administrative costs. Another reason is probably the higher degree of acceptability of product taxes by the business community, which is often opposed to emission charges or taxes. In fact, it is often easier for industry to shift the burden of product taxes or charges downward than in the case of emission taxes, which usually fall on intermediate inputs, such as energy or raw materials.

The increased use of deposit-refund systems, particularly for packaging, reflects the growing concern among OECD countries about packaging waste problems. Packaging comprises one-quarter to one-half of all municipal waste volumes, which accounted for some 400 million tons per year in the late 1980s for OECD countries. Among the various deposit-refund systems in actual use, the one applied to plastic bottles has developed most remarkably, since it is applied now in at least eleven countries.

c)   The Revenue-Raising Function of Economic Instruments Prevails over Behaviour Modification

In theory the appropriate charge/tax rate should be set at the point where the marginal cost of reducing emissions equals the marginal damage cost. If set at this rate, the charge or the tax will give an appropriate signal to economic agents to change their behaviour, and will promote more efficient resource usage, as well as reducing waste volumes.

In 1993/92 (as in 1987) the financial function of charges/taxes still seems to prevail due to generally low levels of charges/taxes rates. However, there are indications that this may be changing. Recently, the rates of a number of incentive charges have increased quite substantially. Examples include CO_2 charges in Denmark, Norway and Sweden; Swedish NO_x and SO_x charges; the Danish waste disposal charge, and a number of product charges (*e.g.* on fertilisers in Sweden, on ozone depleting chemicals in the US, on packaging in Finland and Norway). Tax differentials on prices of new cars with catalytic convertors, and on unleaded petrol have also contributed to the rapid market penetration of these products.

d)   Environmental Taxes Are Being Combined More and More Often with Broader Fiscal Reforms

Fiscal reforms provide a good opportunity for "greening" the tax system. Increasing the total fiscal burden is quite unpopular, but the possibility of restructuring the existing tax system in a more environmentally-friendly way, while keeping the total fiscal burden unchanged, is attracting increased interest among a few OECD countries.

The idea that it would be better for society as a whole to tax "bads" rather than "goods' is progressing. Such a reform was introduced in Sweden in 1991, leading to a decrease in income taxes being compensated by the introduction of new taxes on CO_2, SO_x and NO_x. Norway and Denmark are also implementing similar reforms along the same lines.

Box 1. **Types of Economic Instruments**

1. **Charges and Taxes**
    - Environmental taxes are based on the environmental characteristics of the taxed item. The revenues go to the general budget. Environmental charges are payments made on the use of the environment; charge revenue is generally earmarked to specific environmental programmes;
    - **Emission charges or taxes** are calculated on the basis of the quantity and quality of the pollutant. They are payments on the discharge of pollutants into air, water, or on the soil, or on the generation of noise;
    - **User charges** are payments for the cost of collection and treatment services (solid waste, sewage water). They have, by definition, a revenue-raising purpose;
    - **Product charges and taxes** are levied on products that are harmful to the environment when used in production processes, consumed or disposed of (*e.g.* fuels, fertilisers, pesticides, detergents).

2. **Marketable permits or emission trading** are environmental quotas, allowances or ceilings on pollution levels that, once initially allocated by the appropriate authority, can be traded, subject to a set of prescribed rules. Trades may be external (between different enterprises) or internal (between different plants of the same firm).

3. **Deposit-refund systems** are systems where a deposit is paid on potentially-polluting products (*e.g.* beverage containers). When pollution is avoided by returning the products or their residuals, a refund of this deposit follows.

4. **Subsidies for environmental purposes** cover various forms of financial assistance (grants, soft loans, tax allowances), and act as an incentive for polluters to alter their behaviour.

e) *Economic Instruments Continue to be Used in Combination with Other Policy Instruments*

As already highlighted in the 1987 survey, economic instruments are not used as an *alternative* to other instruments, but in *combination* with them. This combination in fact offers several advantages. First, economic instruments can provide an additional incentive to direct regulations for compliance over and above the (regulated) standards. Second, economic instruments may facilitate the adjustment to new, regulatory conditions, particularly when the adoption of regulatory legislation is likely to be characterised by a lengthy process. Third, combining different types of economic instruments might create a powerful set of mutually-reinforcing incentives (*e.g.* a combination of a deposit-refund system and a product charge on non-returnable products). Finally, a combined approach may stimulate negotiations aimed at achieving voluntary agreements with industry for changing environmental behaviour. The actual combination of instruments used will, of course, vary not only according to the type of pollution, but also according to individual country conditions and their cultural traditions.

Issues Associated With the Implementation of Economic Instruments for Environmental Management

Member countries' experience shows that there are at least four broad sets of issues associated with the implementation of economic instruments: *i)* the design; *ii)* the acceptability of such instruments; *iii)* their distributive effects; and, *iv)* their international trade implications.

i) *Issues Associated With the Design of Economic Instruments*

The introduction of economic instruments raises a set of complicated issues for every kind of instrument.

- With *respect to charges and taxes*, the determination of the appropriate *charge or tax rate* requires a large amount of information, which is not generally available. Not only is marginal cost damage data very difficult to obtain, but information on the marginal costs of pollution abatement is also usually insufficient. As a consequence, public authorities are forced to adopt a second-best approach and to set the tax/charge rate according to a predetermined environmental target. Since it is generally not possible to set a high rate, at least initially, governments usually proceed with gradual increases over time. A pre-announcement of such increases will provide an opportunity for industry to make the necessary adaptations in terms of planning their investments. The definition of the *tax base* also poses difficult problems, particularly where it is difficult to measure pollution directly, as in the case of mobile or diffuse sources of pollution. When measuring actual emissions proves to be particularly hard, the use of proxies is one way to overcome the problem. For instance, instead of determining the tax base on the emissions of sulphur, or of carbon, it is determined on the sulphur or carbon content of the fuel. As mentioned earlier, the ease in *monitoring* emissions will also be a key factor in the choice between an emission charge and a product charge. To ensure that the incentive effect of a tax or of a charge is not eroded by inflation, there is also often a need to readjust periodically the tax rates, in order to reflect changes in the general price index.

- *With respect to emission trading schemes,* there are several technical conditions necessary for the development of a market. First, there is a need to identify a single good which is readily quantifiable, and with a clearly-defined unit. Second, there is a need for a sufficiently wide market. The trading schemes pioneered in California did not function very well because older sources of emissions were excluded from the market. By contrast, it was the possibility of transacting with all oil refineries in the US which largely accounted for the success of the lead emission trading scheme. Third, the possibility of banking the emission rights offers the possibility of widening the markets over time. Fourth, the system should be sufficiently simple and flexible. This means it would be unwise to amend the system too often, particularly to introduce changes to targets or to modify the rules for the allocation of rights because firms will be unwilling to invest in pollution reduction if they have no confidence in the stability of the market value of these assets. Fifth, the monitoring and compliance control procedures that need to be introduced to implement the trading system should be as uncomplicated as possible. Finally, it is necessary to have an efficient information and communication network between administrators responsible for the system and those participating in the market, in order to facilitate transactions.

ii)   *The Political Acceptability of Economic Instruments*

The political acceptability of economic instruments will depend upon which instruments we are referring to, *e.g.* charges, taxes, emission tradings, deposit-refund schemes or subsidies.

- *Charges and taxes* are very often challenged or opposed by *industry*. This stems from the fact that not only are their costs more transparent and visible than the costs of regulations, but also because the financial burden for industry will ultimately prove to be higher than with regulations as they capture part of the costs of residual damages. Industry will often also oppose environmental taxes because they suspect that the government will retain the tax over time even after the environmental objective has been reached. This distrust towards the government largely explains why industry tends to favour command and control instruments or voluntary agreements over economic instruments. The regulatory approach often provides industry with more room to influence environmental policy than economic approaches, such as taxation. This is what Prof. George J. Stigler called ''regulatory capture''. In fact, many special environmental regulations result from negotiations between the business community and government environmental administrators concerning the meaning of BAT (Best Available Technology).

Along the same lines, industry is now becoming more interested in *voluntary agreements.* Industry may benefit in a number of ways from voluntary agreements. First, by anticipating regulations (and thus gaining more time) the industrial sector will have a stronger hand in negotiations concerning the various aspects of environmental problems that it faces. It will therefore be able to influence the definition of environmental objectives and have more scope in deciding how it will achieve its commitments. Second, a voluntary agreement gives industry a certain degree of regulatory stability, and is thereby conducive to technological innovation. Lastly, such agreements tend to give to the public, and to environmental groups more specifically, a positive image of industry.

It is not only the business community which is opposed to the idea of environmental taxes or charges. In fact, the *general public* and the *environmental protection defence groups* have generally seen environmental taxes or charges as "licences to pollute", and have therefore resisted the idea on ethical grounds.

One way to increase the business community's acceptance of eco-taxes consists of developing redistributive charge schemes, such as the one in operation within the French river basin Agencies, or more generally, to "earmark" the revenues from taxes or charges for environmental expenditures. However, it is generally accepted that "earmarking" should be avoided, due to the risk that related expenditures may short-circuit normal processes of project or programme evaluation.

In another example, to gain acceptance of the NO_x charge introduced in Sweden in 1992, provisions were made to avoid discriminating against energy production in large boilers. Under this scheme, all income from the charge is refunded to the group of plants that initially pay it, in proportion to the relative energy efficiency in each plant. At the beginning of each year, emitters report their NO_x emissions and the amount of energy generated to the Swedish Environmental Protection Agency. The total revenue of the system and the refund per generated kW are then calculated. The charges for the emission and the revenues from the refund are netted out so that the boilers with relatively high NO_x emissions per energy unit generated are charged an additional cost, while boilers with relatively low NO_x emissions receive additional revenues. The system seems to work very well, since the NO_x emissions decreased by 35 per cent between 1990 and 1992 with a basically constant tax burden.

- *Emission-trading schemes,* which have been implemented mainly in the US, seem to have gained acceptability amongst the business community, at least to the extent that the initial allocations of permits is made on the basis of past emissions (*i.e.* "grandfathering").

It is becoming more apparent to business decision-makers that emission trading may generate substantial savings, relative to compliance with existing regulations. NGOs, which seemed to have reservations about the idea a few years ago, are now becoming more supportive of such schemes.

- **Subsidies:** Subsidies are often advocated by the business community as a way to help firms facing severe economic hardship to adjust to new environmental requirements. It is interesting to note that views expressed recently at one OECD consultation meeting with industry tended to go in the opposite direction. In general, participants at this meeting were opposed to any kind of financial assistance to pollution abatement and measures, such as favourable interest rate loans, accelerated depreciation, direct payments, etc. However there was still some sympathy for government subsidies for environmental research and development.

iii)   Distributive Implications of Economic Instruments

The implementation of economic instruments can result in different cost and distributional impacts, for various firms, sectors, regions and income groups.

Distributive impacts are at the centre of most policy debates surrounding the adoption of economic incentive programmes. For example, discussions of national carbon taxes often focus on whether the proposed tax would hurt the poor, put coal-miners out of work, or derail export industries. These considerations were key in the adoption of the Swedish carbon tax, and are still central elements of the energy-carbon tax being proposed by the European Commission.

Distributive issues have also been a key element in discussions about emission trading programmes in the US, although here the discussions tend to focus on who gains, as well as on who might be harmed. For example, the formula to allocate initial allowances was one of the most contentious issues in the debate about the acid rain provisions of the 1990 Clean Air Act. A similar debate took place in the Los Angeles Basin in California when this region developed a trading programme to deal with urban smog. Both small business and labour groups were concerned that the programme would hurt them. These concerns subsequently led to proposals to modify the programmes, in order to avoid such losses.

Relatively few empirical analyses have been done of the distributive impacts of environmental programmes, and even fewer have been done for economic instruments. Nevertheless, the results of a few studies show that some environmental taxes (in particular, energy-related taxes) tend to be slightly regressive.

Indeed, offsetting measures and compensatory measures may both be needed to ensure the political acceptance of economic instruments. However, in the case of a tax, revenues will be generated which could be used to compensate those most affected. Such measures should be designed as much as possible in a way that will not erode the original incentive effect of the tax.

iv)   International Trade Implications of Economic Instruments

International trade implications also vary with the economic instruments in question.

Environmental charges and taxes are generally opposed by industry, due to concerns about the loss in international competitiveness. Although the introduction of an environmental charge or tax is often claimed to negatively affect (at least in the short term) the international competitiveness of individual firms, empirical analysis of the level of environmental expenditure by OECD countries and its impact on competitiveness suggest that there is little systematic relationship between higher environmental standards and competitiveness in the trade of environmentally-sensitive goods. Historically, OECD countries with a high level of environment expenditures have both gained and lost competitiveness in environmentally-sensitive industries.

However, the opposition of industry to such a tax, particularly in the energy field, has led many governments to introduce various exemptions or rebates which eventually erode the incentive effect of the original tax, and thereby undermine the achievement of the environmental objectives.

Although there is limited practical experience with *emission trading systems*, these can potentially function in a way that deters either domestic or foreign investment. If initial emission rights are grandfathered to existing firms, these firms will receive an advantage compared to new entrants, both domestic and foreign, who try to enter the system. Depending on how these systems are designed and operated, emission trading can therefore potentially discriminate against new investors.

In the case of *deposit-refund schemes* trade impacts lie not so much with the financial incentive measures of the system, (*i.e.* the deposit charge or the subsequent refund), but rather with the additional requirements and costs imposed by participating in the scheme. Deposit-refund schemes can potentially act as non-tariff barriers to trade and give competitive advantages to domestic products, either intentionally or unintentionally. For example, in the case of beverage containers, foreign suppliers may be placed at a comparative disadvantage relative to domestic suppliers who can more easily create or purchase facilities or services in storing, recycling and/or reusing the containers in question. By participating in the original design of the scheme, domestic suppliers may also discriminate against foreign suppliers, depending upon the types of containers and the market share of the types of containers that are included in the deposit-refund scheme.

Subsidies are likely to cause distortions in international trade. According to OECD rules, financial assistance schemes are subject to special conditions because they are contrary to the Polluter-Pays Principle (PPP) adopted in 1972 by OECD countries. The granting of assistance is limited to the following conditions: *i)* it should be selective, and restricted to those parts of the economy where severe economic difficulties would otherwise occur; *ii)* it should be limited to well-defined transitional periods laid down in advance, and adapted to the specific socio-economic problems associated with the implementation of a country's environmental programme; and, *iii)* it should not create significant distortions in international trade and investment.

Financial Assistance schemes are monitored by the Organisation periodically. Four surveys have been conducted: 1975, 1978/79, 1981/82, 1987, and another is under way. The difficulties in drawing firm conclusions from these surveys include incomplete responses; lack of data at the industry level; no evidence on enforcement; and difficulty regarding assistance for environmental protection from, say, programmes for employment or regional development. Recognising these limitations, the latest survey found that financial assistance to the private sector for environmental protection as a percentage of GDP ranged between 0.006 and 0.105 per cent for those OECD countries that acknowledged some assistance and for which the statistics could be calculated. The new survey which is currently under way should enable OECD to monitor whether non-member countries are actually implementing the PPP.

The Performance of Economic Instruments

Little Systematic Evaluation of the Performance of Economic Instruments Has Been Conducted

The number of explicit evaluations identified in the course of OECD work has been very limited, compared with the increasing number of economic instruments used in OECD Member countries' environmental policies and the interest these instruments are generating among policy-makers. There are a number of reasons for this. First, there is little or no tradition in many countries to evaluate government policies in general, and the lack of evaluation of economic instruments is no exception. Second, even when such evaluations are conducted, the division of policy responsibility between different government departments makes the evaluation much more difficult to set up – this is particularly true when the departments which are most interested in the effectiveness and efficiency of economic instruments are not responsible for their implementation. Third, since some economic instruments have only recently been introduced in OECD Member countries, it is too soon to assess their impact on the effectiveness and efficiency of environmental policy, particularly with regard to their effects on long-term incentive.

Evaluations Are Limited by Both Conceptual and Practical Difficulties

One of the greatest difficulties is to specify clearly the alternatives to which the performance of the economic instrument is being compared (''baseline'' issue) – in other words, to establish what would have happened if the economic instrument under review had not been introduced. It is not enough to compare the pollution levels before the instrument was introduced with pollution levels after its introduction, because the reduction in pollution levels may not be related to the introduction of the economic instrument but, for example, due to a change in the available technologies, or to a decline in the general level of economic activities.

A second difficulty lies in disentangling the specific contribution of an economic instrument when it is used in combination or as part of a package of policy instruments. Therefore, in practice, it will be necessary to accept some limitations in the ability to reach conclusions about the economic instrument alone.

Finally, the lack of suitable data constitutes a major obstacle to the evaluation of the performance of economic instruments. Data are needed before and after the introduction of a new instrument to assess the difference that this instrument has made. Unfortunately, for the reasons mentioned above, the necessary data are not generally collected beforehand, which makes retrospective evaluation very difficult. This lack of data, (of *cost* data in particular), made the task of a Norwegian interdepartmental committee extremely difficult when it started to evaluate the performance of policy environmental instruments in Norway at the end of 1992.

Ex ante *Versus* ex post *Evidence*

While the efficiency and effectiveness of economic instruments is proven by theory and confirmed by *ex ante* calculations, as mentioned above, little *ex post* evaluation of the actual achievements of economic instruments has been carried out. Available evidence, however, suggests the satisfactory performance of such instruments. For instance, charging and taxation measures have not simply been totally absorbed as a cost by polluters, but have generally led to some changes in emission levels. Cost savings attributed to emission trading programmes appear to be impressive, although it has proven impossible to determine how much, if any, of the perceived improvements in air quality can be attributed to such programmes. Deposit refund systems generally appear to have been successful, with rates of return reaching 30 to 100 per cent, according to the type of container. There are also a few cases where poor performance has resulted in the withdrawal or substantial redesign of the original economic instrument.

More analysis needs to be done to get a more comprehensive picture of the actual performance of economic instruments in OECD countries. This would imply that appropriate data needs to be systematically recorded whenever a policy instrument is developed or implemented. Therefore, the OECD, in its work on the performance of economic instruments, has proposed a framework for a ''built-in'' evaluation process.

CAN THE ELIMINATION OR THE REDUCTION OF ECONOMIC SUBSIDIES BE BENEFICIAL FOR THE ENVIRONMENT?

Another important element of promoting sustainable development is to ensure that existing government policies do not give inappropriate signals to producers and consumers about pollution costs and/or natural resource scarcities. Many subsidy schemes or tax concession programmes in OECD countries can be placed in that category: they are suspected of encouraging polluters or users not to pay the full social costs of their activities. If this proves to be true, their reduction, (if not their elimination), could result not only in environmental improvements, but also in a more efficient use of economic resources. Such clear cut ''win/win'' situations may in reality be much more complicated, to the extent that economic subsidies may generate either positive or negative environmental and/or economic effects. Consequently, the net effect of reducing or eliminating subsidies or tax concessions will not necessarily lead to an improvement of the environment or the economy. The actual effects of any reform will depend on the context in which the subsidies were granted in the first place, and on the specific way in which they are eventually reduced.

All these issues are currently being investigated by the OECD in response to a request made by both Environment and Finance Ministers in 1996 asking the Organisation ''to carry out a wide ranging analysis of the effects of subsidies and tax disincentives on sound environmental practices in various economic sectors and the costs and benefits of their elimination or reform''.

Undertaking such analysis implies several steps:

- first, to agree on the concept of subsidy and tax concessions:
- second, to review available evidence concerning the concept of subsidies which has been adopted;
- third, to explore the linkages between the level of subsidies and their impact on the environment.

What Definition of Subsidies to Adopt?

In OECD countries, there are a variety of subsidies or tax treatments which have an impact on the environment. The most important examples of *explicit* subsidies are below-market pricing of natural resources (*e.g.* agricultural water use and infrastructure), below-market financing costs for some electricity infrastructure, tax preferences for oil and mineral extraction, agricultural commodity price programmes and tax preferences for private vehicle transport, relative to other transport modes. There are also a number of incentives in place to protect the environment, such as deductibility or tax credit for cleaner technologies. Current OECD work on subsidies and environment is concentrating on economic subsidies or tax treatments which can have *negative* impacts on the environment, and not to consider subsidies which *improve* environmental conditions as part of the programme.

Another question is whether the *implicit* subsidies arising from the non-internalisation of environmental costs should be included. The assessment of implicit subsidies confronts the analyst with the problem how to quantify *ex ante* the environmental externalities involved. In the face of such challenges, it was considered more practical to focus in OECD work on explicit subsidies, than on subsidies that arise from distortions in the non-internalisation of environmental damages.

What Does Available Evidence on Subsidies or Tax Treatments Reveal?

In the *transport sector,* for example, road transport has been heavily subsidised through the building of highway infrastructures, resulting in over supply and over use of this mode of transport and, from an environmental standpoint, in increased air and noise pollution. It has been estimated that in the United States road transport pays for only 79 per cent of its total costs through taxes and tolls paid by road users, the remaining costs being borne by the government in what amounts to a direct subsidy to road transport[2] (excluding environmental externalities). Moreover, if similar subsidies granted by cities for the construction of parking facilities are included, these figures could be twice as high. The same study found lower subsidies in France than in the US. The lower volume of subsidy in France is no doubt explained by the fact that petrol prices and road tolls are higher there than in the US.

In the *energy* sector, annual coal subsidies in eight OECD countries amount to $10 billion. *Agricultural* subsidies in OECD countries are estimated to amount to $350 billion annually (about 2 per cent of OECD GDP). Subsidies to the *fisheries* sector amount to $50 billion in OECD countries (see Box 2).

Box 2. Environmental impacts of subsidies: some examples

Examples of subsidies	...and their environmental impacts
Agriculture	$350 billion annually in OECD countries; roughly 2 per cent of OECD GDP.	Depending on environmental and economic circumstances. Parts of these subsidies have severe negative impacts on the environment (*e.g.* pesticide and fertiliser use, erosion, desiccation).
Industry	The net cost to government of *industrial support* activities averaged $66 billion annually over the period 1986-1989; this was about 2.5 per cent of total manufacturing value-added in the 22 OECD countries reviewed. 28 per cent of this total was for *direct investment* support. *R&D, Regional Development and Export Promotion* accounted for a further 12 per cent, 22 per cent and 20 per cent, respectively. Depletion allowances *in excess of* total development and extraction costs in some *extraction industries (e.g. mining)* amount to more than $1 billion per year in the US.	Especially when raw materials processing and energy use are subsidized, a considerable negative impact on recycling and (by consequence) a very strong negative impact on all kinds of emissions and waste. (Roughly 75 per cent of all emissions and waste is generated by raw materials and energy processing).
Electricity	Annual coal subsidies in eight OECD countries amount to more than $10 billion. Electricity subsidies in the US cost at least $5 billion (1991).	Subsidies in the energy sector generally favour "black" energy uses over "green" ones.
Traffic	Only 79 per cent of *road* infrastructure investment costs in the US are directly borne by road users. The remainder (approximately $15 billion in 1991) comes from the general taxpayer. Significant income transfers in favour of trucking in most other countries.	Stimulates road traffic, which is more polluting than railways or using waterways (too many pollutants to be enumerated).
Water use in industry and agriculture	*Irrigation water* in US costs more than $1 billion per year, only 25 per cent of which is recovered in user fees. In addition, fewer than 6 per cent of farmers receive more than 50 per cent of the total benefits.	Desiccation, erosion, exhaustion of a natural resource.
Fisheries	$50 billion in OECD countries.	Exhaustion of fish stocks. Lower catches in the past would have allowed for significantly higher catches today.

Similarly, certain forms of tax treatment or concessions can have either positive or negative impacts on the environment. Among those suspected of leading to perverse environment implications are the many tax provisions in the field of transport. For instance, the preferential taxation of company cars and the tax deductibility of commuting expenses both induce an overuse of private cars and lead to additional congestion, pollution, noise and accidents. The lower taxation of diesel fuel for motor-vehicles induces the over-development of road transport and an increase in the number of diesel automobiles, both of which contribute significantly to local air pollution and noise (see Box 3).

Box 3. **Examples of environmentally-detrimental tax provisions**

Surface transport

Parking Space	Free (or reduced costs of) parking space provided by employers is often not included as taxable income (benefit in kind).
Company Cars	The use of company cars for commuting to the place of work is in some countries not considered a taxable benefit.
Deductibility of Commuting Expenses	The costs of commuting may be deductible from taxable income and there is in many countries no distinction made between the use of public transport and private cars.
Reimbursement of Commuting Expenses	Tax-free reimbursement of commuting expenses (whether by car or by public transport) is possible in a number of OECD countries where reimbursement by the employer (based on home to work distance) to an employee travelling in his or her own car is allowed free of income taxation.

Aviation

Fuel	No taxes on kerosene (note that the price elasticity for flying cost is estimated at -0.8 to -2.0; hence a potential strong effect of an increased price of kerosene).

The Linkages Between Economic Subsidies, Tax Concessions and the Environment

As already mentioned, it is a very complicated task to assess the environmental implications of a reduction of an economic subsidy, or of the modification of a tax concession. The environmental effects of subsidies depend not only upon the type of subsidies granted but also on how the receiving environmental medium reacts to the pollution generated by the activity concerned.

According to a preliminary analysis conducted by the OECD, it seems that the point of incidence of a subsidy or a tax concession will be a key element for assessing the environmental impact. Three kinds of subsidies can be identified according to this criteria: inputs, market support and direct income support. Input subsidies include, for example, subsidies to energy or irrigation water, to agrochemicals, or to labour or capital. Subsidies in the form of market support include price regulations – by setting minimum prices above the market level, price regulations generate subsidies from consumers to producers. Direct income support may take various forms, such as cash payments or special rates of taxation. Preliminary results tend to show that input subsidies are much more environmentally-damaging than the other two forms of subsidies. Conversely, direct income support would appear to be the least-environmentally-damaging form of subsidy.

CONCLUSIONS

- By harnessing the power of the market, economic instruments contribute to the integration of environmental concerns into economic policies by bringing market signals closer to their socially desirable levels – a necessary condition for sustainable development.

- There is a continuing trend towards an increased use of economic instruments (charges, taxes, emission trading schemes, deposit refund systems), although economic instruments in practice have not replaced regulations.

- Economic instruments have been generally introduced as supplements to regulations, with a view to collecting revenues rather than to changing the environmental behaviour of economic agents.

- There is little systematic evaluation of the performance of economic instruments and of the various policy instruments more generally on environmental policy.

- Another important element of promoting sustainable development is ensuring that existing government policies do not encourage unsustainable behaviour. A review of existing subsidy schemes and tax disincentives to sound environmental practices will contribute to this endeavour. A key challenge for this undertaking will be to identify clear cases for ''win/win'' situations, in which both the environment and the economy can benefit from subsidy reform.

NOTES

1. See for instance, *Integrating Environment and Economy – Progress in the 1990s*, (OECD, 1996), 60 p.
2. J.J. MacKenzie, R.C. Dower and D.D.T. Chen, *The Going Rate, What it Really Costs to Drive.* World Resources Institute, Washington DC, 1992.

BIBLIOGRAPHY

OECD, (1996) *Evaluating Economic Instruments for Environmental Policy,* Paris.

OECD, (1996) *Implementation Strategies for Environmental Taxes,* Paris.

OECD, (1995) *Environment Taxes in OECD Countries,* Paris.

OECD, (1994) *Managing the Environment: The Role of Economic Instruments,* Paris.

OECD, (1994) *The Distributive Effects of Economic Instruments for Environmental Policy,* Paris.

OECD, (1993) *Environmental Policies and Industrial Competitiveness,* Paris.

OECD, (1991) *Taxation and the Environment: Complementary Policies,* Paris.

OECD, (1991), *Environmental Policy: How to Apply Economic Instruments,* Paris.

OECD, (1989) *Economic Instruments for Environmental Protection,* Paris.

Chapter 2

SHAPING THE 21st CENTURY
THE CONTRIBUTION OF DEVELOPMENT CO-OPERATION

by

James H. Michel

TOWARD GLOBAL INTEGRATION AND PEOPLE-CENTRED DEVELOPMENT

The first half of the present decade has marked the passage from the Cold War era to what can become a new era of shared human progress in the 21st century. The development community is well on its way through the period of transition, to the new era that is taking shape, based upon an increasingly clear vision of partnership – of mutual interests and mutual responsibilities.

Over the past several years the perception of the nature and context of international development co-operation has certainly evolved. The end of the Cold War removed a traditional and well understood security rationale for development co-operation, while also creating new and largely unanticipated demands. As a result, increased opportunities for productive collaboration were being threatened by a reduced sense of urgency, manifested by a diminished commitment of both political will and related financial resources.

The risk was that declining resources could produce a downward spiral of disappointing results and diminished expectations. The remedy was to build on the growing consensus view of development as an integrated process, based on political will, capacity, and public support within each developing country and supported by genuine international partnerships to advance shared interests. The stakes for future generations throughout the world in increased human security through sustainable development would become the new focal point of political motivation. Improved measures of results would provide evidence of effectiveness and justification for increased investment of public resources in development co-operation.

By 1995, these broad notions had begun to take definite shape. The OECD Development Co-operation Report for that year placed greater emphasis on the two salient themes of development co-operation in the 1990s:

- the clear recognition that people are the subjects of development and that an improved quality of life for all is its objective; and
- the need for developing countries to participate in, and to benefit from, the unprecedented expansion in the global movement of goods, services, capital and technology.

These themes of people-centred development and economic globalisation provided the backdrop for the path-setting statement, *Development Partnerships in the New Global Context,* adopted by the DAC at its High Level Meeting of 3-4 May 1995. The DAC's 1995 policy statement was especially noteworthy in two fundamental aspects:

- First, it reinforced the need for integrated development strategies that incorporate certain key elements:
  - a sound policy framework encouraging stable, growing economies with full scope for a vigorous private sector and an adequate fiscal base;

- investment in social development, especially education, primary health care, and population activities;
- enhanced participation of all people, and notably women, in economic and political life and the reduction of social inequalities;
- good governance and public management, democratic accountability, the protection of human rights and the rule of law;
- sustainable environmental practices;
- addressing root causes of potential conflict, limiting military expenditures, and targeting reconstruction and peace-building efforts toward longer-term reconciliation and development.

- Second, it recognised the need for a division of labour which respects the primary responsibility (including financial responsibility) of governments, institutions and people of the developing countries for these key elements of integrated development strategies, and looks to the external actors to support the strengthening of local capacities, provide needed complementary resources, and carry out co-ordinated and coherent policies supportive of development in a true spirit of partnership.

The 1995 *Development Partnerships* statement built upon the work of the DAC in its 1989 policy statement on development co-operation in the 1990s. In particular, it reiterated the importance of a combination of broadly-based economic growth, participation and environmental sustainability. In this regard, *Development Partnerships* was consciously intended as a mid-decade review, specifically addressing the needs of the second half of the 1990s. In a final sentence, however, the Members of the DAC reaffirmed their commitment to work together ''to implement the directions outlined here for this decade ...and to help prepare strategies looking to the next century''.

In 1996 the DAC has built upon these agreed principles of people-centred development, local ownership, global integration and international partnership in an extraordinary exercise. Rather than commission experts to prepare studies, analyses and recommendations in order to give effect to their commitment ''to help prepare strategies looking to the next century'', the development ministers and aid agency heads of DAC Members decided themselves to fashion and describe the forward-looking strategies anticipated by their *Development Partnerships* statement.

Their collaboration continued throughout a full year. The outcome was a succinct report entitled *Shaping the 21st Century: The Contribution of Development Co-operation.* This report was adopted at the DAC's High Level Meeting of 6-7 May 1996, and was endorsed by the OECD Council at Ministerial Level at its annual meeting held on 21-22 May 1996.

This new development-partnerships strategy is intended as a basis for dialogue and concerted action, working with developing countries to achieve demonstrable progress in furtherance of agreed objectives. It aims to act upon an existing broad agreement on the need for a genuine partnership to combat poverty, expand opportunity, preserve the environment and, generally, to enhance human security and well-being on a sustainable basis. It is intended to contribute to the ongoing dialogue and broad range of efforts under way in the international community. It has no pretensions of exclusivity or of displacing other initiatives.

The principal task now is to define the vision more concretely, and to translate it into reality. That will be far more difficult and complex than the process of conceptualising which has led to the articulation of this new strategy. As the strategy document predicts, ''we will need to change how we think and how we operate, in a far more co-ordinated effort than we have known until now''. But it will also be an invigorating challenge to collaborate in implementing changes in development co-operation thinking and practice so as to contribute more surely to an improved quality of life for all.

DEFINING THE VISION

Measurable Goals

The outstanding feature of the DAC's new development partnerships strategy is its bold proposal for a global effort to achieve a limited number of specific, obviously worthwhile goals within a foreseeable time. Based on the experience of many years and the conclusions reached at a series of global conferences, these selected goals seek to give concrete meaning to the improved quality of life that is the ultimate aim of sustainable development. The quantitative goals identified in the strategy are few in number, but they are of profound significance for the kind of world that future generations will inhabit.

The goals fall into three interrelated categories:

a) *Economic well-being*: The first, and undoubtedly the most ambitious, goal is to reduce by at least one-half by 2015 the proportion of people living in extreme poverty in the developing countries. Based on a standard of $370 per capita annual income, the World Bank has estimated that 30 per cent of the population in developing countries – more than 1.3 billion people – live in extreme poverty. Reducing that number to 15 per cent would be a major step toward the aspiration of eradicating poverty which the 1995 Copenhagen Declaration identified as "an ethical, social, political and economic imperative of humankind".

b) *Social development*: The strategy identifies goals for progress in four areas of social development – primary education, gender equality, basic health care and family planning. All of these goals are based upon commitments agreed to at the 1994 Cairo Conference on Population and Development, the 1995 Copenhagen Summit on Social Development and the 1995 Beijing Conference on Women:

- universal primary education in all countries by 2015;
- elimination of gender disparity in primary and secondary education by 2005;
- reduction of infant and child mortality rates by two-thirds the 1990 level and reduction of maternal mortality by three-fourths, all by 2015;
- access through the primary health-care system to reproductive health services for all individuals of appropriate ages, including safe and reliable family planning methods, by 2015.

c) *Environmental sustainability and regeneration*: The third measure of progress identified in the strategy is to have national strategies for sustainable development in operation in all countries by 2005, so as to ensure a reversal of current trends in the loss of environmental resources by 2015. National sustainable development strategies were called for by the 1992 Rio Conference on the Environment and Development.

The Limits of Measurement and Qualitative Factors

The selection of the above-described measurable goals involved considerable thought and many judgements. For example:

- The DAC could have chosen just one or two objectives, or it could have chosen a great many more than it did. These particular goals were chosen as being representative of a coherent and understandable vision of human progress, as well as a standard of accountability for development co-operation efforts. Their selection is in no way intended to diminish the importance of other development goals or other areas of international co-operation.
- The DAC could have sought to identify independently new goals for economic well-being, social development and environmental sustainability, or it could look to goals already identified

by the international community. The decision taken was to rely upon the conclusions of major international conferences in which developing countries had actively participated. In some cases, the DAC has attempted to express the goals with greater specificity, but it has not proposed the weakening of any existing agreed standard.

The goals are not intended as a prescription, but as a proposal. The basic approach reflected in the DAC strategy is one of partnership for locally-owned, participatory and sustainable development. No outside party can set the goals for any developing country, and no single, global set of goals could adequately address the enormous variety of challenges that is faced by very different countries in very different circumstances. Therefore, the goals set out in the DAC strategy can offer no more than a global framework for dialogue, while recognising that each country must set its own goals and that successful development strategies must be based on local ownership and local capacity.

It cannot be overstated that the measurable goals set forth in the DAC's new development partnerships strategy are representative of a vision, and do not by themselves present a comprehensive description of that vision. Indeed, some of these key elements in development are exceedingly difficult, if not impossible, to measure. In particular, issues of democratic accountability, the protection of human rights and the rule of law are increasingly recognised as important to sustainable development. The DAC strategy reaffirms the conviction that these qualitative aspects of development are essential to the attainment of the more measurable goals and that they must remain a part of the agenda for development co-operation.

Working as Partners

The DAC strategy places stronger emphasis than ever on the developing country itself as the starting point for development co-operation efforts that reflect local circumstances, encourage local commitment and participation, and foster the strengthening of local capacities. It suggests that locally-owned country development strategies and targets should emerge from dialogue by local authorities with their people and with their external partners. Rather than a situation in which each donor and multilateral agency has its own development strategy for a particular country, the ideal should be a locally-owned development strategy which external partners can all support.

The approach to effective partnerships advocated by the new DAC strategy places a premium on knowledge of local circumstances and the freedom to act flexibly in a manner that is responsive to local conditions. Growing budget constraints on many donors are making it increasingly difficult for them to maintain a field presence and to delegate authority at just the time when those capabilities are most needed. While the emphasis is now on capacities in developing countries, the strategy assumes that DAC Members and the multilateral agencies, as well as other external partners, will also have the capacity to carry out their part of the partnership compact.

Adequate Resources, Effective Co-ordination and Coherent Policies

Beyond the immediate question of the capacity by donors to operate in a decentralised manner, there lies a more fundamental issue of the credibility of a new strategy that sets ambitious goals and calls for greater efforts in a time of declining levels of official development assistance. Making aid work better and bringing our policies together are the final subjects treated in the new strategy.

Total resource flows to developing countries are continuing to grow. However, within this aggregate total there are two very different kinds of flows – an increasing volume of private flows to growing and dynamic economies and a diminishing volume of official flows to poor countries that are not yet able to attract private capital. A continuation of that trend could be fatal to the achievement of development goals which will require the greatest progress in the poorest countries.

The new DAC strategy calls for four kinds of measures to deal with the need for resources:

- First of all, it calls for a stronger effort to sustain and increase official development assistance (ODA) in order to help reverse the growing marginalisation of the poor and achieve progress toward realistic goals of human development. This will involve efforts to increase ODA budgets in DAC Member countries, a stronger effort to concentrate available ODA resources on countries that have the greatest need and the capacity for effective use of those resources, and expanding the base of development partnerships – in particular, by a greater involvement of more countries, institutions and individuals who can share their own experiences in successful development.

- Second, the strategy calls for increased efficiency in the use of ODA. This will involve, among other things, enhanced co-ordination among donors (both bilateral and multilateral) on the ground, as well as in international fora such as Consultative Groups and Round Tables. It will also involve strengthened monitoring and evaluation to inform and improve ongoing efforts.

- Third, the strategy calls attention to the increasingly diversified composition of development finance and the importance of domestic savings, efficient local financial systems, sound economic policies and private foreign investment in the experience of the fast-growing developing economies. It calls for the use of concessional resources in ways that help countries build their capacities to create and mobilise domestic resources, attract private capital and become less dependent on aid.

- Finally, the strategy recognises that the policies of the industrialised countries in areas other than development co-operation can have profound implications for development objectives. It calls for the integration of development co-operation resources and expertise into coherent policy frameworks in a concerted effort to assure that the entire range of policies of industrialised countries will be consistent with and supportive of development.

TRANSLATING THE VISION INTO REALITY

Definition

The implementation of the new strategy is expected to be built upon a growing number of national experiences. A continuing process of country-by-country dialogue should help to specify and clarify concrete national goals of economic well-being, social development and environmental sustainability. The dialogue should help to identify specific measures to attain those goals and ways in which international co-operation can support those measures, always with an emphasis on local capacity and sustainability.

Generally, we can anticipate that the definition of development partnerships will involve the promotion of growth and integration into the global economy, combined with the fostering of participation and increased opportunities for people. We can assume that issues of access to capital, markets and technology, capacity development, good governance and sustainability will all feature prominently. We can also anticipate that issues with respect to regional co-operation will take on increased prominence.

However, the central point remains that the strategy is intended to foster local ownership and participation and to help strengthen local capacities for managing development plans and their implementation. Even though we can anticipate the likelihood of needs for special attention to particular elements of integrated development strategies, we must avoid the trap of allowing our expectations to lead us into a top-down, donor-driven approach that would be self defeating.

Co-ordination

A number of existing international mechanisms can contribute to the process of dialogue to define and implement the strategy at national and regional levels. Consultative Groups (normally organised by the World Bank) and Round Tables (organised by the United Nations Development Programme) already bring national and international actors together on a periodic basis. Much could be achieved by increased and systematic emphasis in these fora on locally-owned, integrated development strategies (including support for capacity development), the selection of measurable national goals for economic well-being, social development and environmental sustainability, the identification of measures to further those goals and the co-ordination of coherent support by external partners for those measures.

Even more important than co-ordination at these occasional international meetings is the ability of partners to work together on a continuing basis at the local level in their day-to-day activities. It is at this level that it will be determined whether the notion of coherent international support for locally-owned strategies through effective partnerships has more than rhetorical commitment.

A strategy that sets forth measurable goals demands a workable system for measuring progress. A great deal of relevant information is already being collected by UNDP, UNICEF, the World Bank and other multilateral organisations. The DAC will work with those data collection and reporting systems, in order to assure that adequate, current and reliable data are being assembled in a manner that fosters local capacity and minimises undue administrative burden or duplication of effort. Finding the most appropriate means for tracking national and global progress against the goals of the development partnerships strategy will require intensive consultations among experts and a strong commitment to co-ordination on the part of all the agencies concerned.

A particular undertaking where close co-ordination will be pursued is the effort by the United Nations to follow up on the entire range of commitments made in the major international conferences since 1990. A set of inter-agency task forces has been established:

- the task force on basic social services for all, chaired by UNFPA;
- the task force on full employment and sustainable livelihoods, chaired by ILO;
- the task force on the enabling environment for people-centred sustainable development, chaired by the World Bank; and
- the committee on empowerment and advancement of women, chaired by the Secretary-General's Special Advisor on Gender.

These task forces, and a related inter-agency committee on sustainable development already in place to follow up on the Rio Conference, are intended to assure effective support from the United Nations System for pursuit of the conference goals and commitments.

Monitoring and Evaluation

There is also a need for public reporting on the progress of developing countries toward the goals of the strategy. We cannot just wait for 20 years to see if those goals are attained and then announce the results. We will have to take stock repeatedly, make adjustments where necessary, and keep the public informed as to whether and how active partnerships are making a difference.

Evaluation presents a complex set of questions. Timely evaluation of the partnerships as they evolve will be essential for confident implementation of the strategy on a broader basis. How quickly professional judgements can be made and what conditions will best contribute to reliable evaluation and usable feedback will require study and advice by experts.

Vision or Mirage?

The new development partnerships strategy is in many ways more evolutionary than revolutionary in its thinking. It draws upon what we have learned in a half century of development co-operation, and it reflects the changes that have occurred in the world during that period. It is, at its core, a pragmatic and realistic approach to expanding and deepening the recognition that there exists a global community of shared interests, and that there is a need for solidarity and concerted action in order to advance those shared interests in the coming millennium.

More revolutionary are the demands of the new strategy upon the actual conduct of development co-operation. There remain deeply entrenched gaps between theory and practice. These contradictions contribute to the uncertainty and ambivalence in public and political support for development co-operation efforts. If they are not overcome, the prospects for existing patterns of co-operation will become increasingly bleak. We do not have the option of preserving the *status quo* in development co-operation in a changing world. The changing situation demands changes in how we act and, in particular, proof that we take development seriously:

- Both developing countries and external partners acknowledge the value of local ownership and capacity; yet patterns of donor activism and recipient passivity continue to be found, characterised more by paternalism than by relations of partnership.
- Donors proclaim the importance of development; yet, many have resorted disproportionately to cuts in already reduced development assistance budgets in their policies of fiscal restraint. On the other hand, concerns about the aggregate aid effort need to focus on both the volume of aid and its effectiveness in contributing to development outcomes.
- It is increasingly evident that a comprehensive approach employing coherent policies is essential; yet, officials in aid agencies and trade ministries (for example) often act independently of each other as if aid and trade were independent, or even competing, alternative policy instruments.
- All agree on the need for better co-ordination; yet the principal focus, too often, remains inward, concentrating on one's own projects and programmes.
- Efficiency is universally demanded in the expenditure of public funds; yet, practices like tied aid continue even as international competition in government procurement has otherwise become the norm.

The new development strategy seeks to change the incentives in ways that can influence behaviour and moderate these anomalies. Its vision is that of a more prosperous, stable, secure, just and sustainable world in the 21st century. It is a vision of hope and of opportunity. By identifying some measurable goals of human progress and by encouraging all who are concerned with development co-operation to pursue partnerships designed to advance those goals, it poses a challenge.

Will the international community respond to the challenge by demonstrating that it regards these development goals as important? Will it invest the financial resources and the effort to rationalise policies so as to give those goals priority? The answers to these questions will be revealed as the process of implementing the strategy unfolds.

If, as partners, we can exercise the disciplined will to address the contradictions and to implement the strategy, its vision will come to be seen as a realistic prediction of a better future. If we do not make the effort, it will become equally apparent that the strategy projects no more than a cruel mirage of what might have been. The adoption of the strategy will make it even more difficult to justify inaction and deferred decision. This new strategy declares that we have thought about these questions, that we know what to do and how to do it, and that the time for action has arrived.

A Strong Compact for Effective Partnership

Joint responsibilities

- Create the conditions conducive to generating adequate resources for development
- Pursue policies that minimise the risks of violent conflict
- Strengthen protections at the domestic and international levels against corruption and illicit practices
- Widen the scope for effective development contributions from throughout civil society
- Enlist the support of rapidly developing countries and regional development mechanisms

Developing country responsibilities

- Adhere to appropriate macroeconomic policies
- Commit to basic objectives of social development and increased participation, including gender equality
- Foster accountable government and the rule of law
- Strengthen human and institutional capacity
- Create a climate favourable to enterprise and the mobilisation of local savings for investment
- Carry out sound financial management, including efficient tax systems and productive public expenditure
- Maintain stable and co-operative relations with neighbours

External partner responsibilities

- Provide reliable and appropriate assistance both to meet priority needs and to facilitate the mobilisation of additional resources to help achieve agreed performance targets
- Contribute to international trade and investment systems in ways that permit full opportunities to developing countries
- Adhere to agreed international guidelines for effective aid, and monitoring for continuous improvement
- Support strengthened capacities and increased participation in the developing country, avoiding the creation of aid-dependency
- Support access to information, technology and know-how
- Support coherent policies in other aspects of relations, including consistency in policies affecting human rights and the risks of violent conflict
- Work for better co-ordination of the international aid system among external partners, in support of developing countries' own strategies.

Chapter 3

ASSESSING ENVIRONMENTAL PERFORMANCE

by

Christian P. Avérous

For the past 20 years, the OECD has kept under review the ''state of the environment'' in its Member countries. In 1989-91, the OECD received mandates[1] to design and conduct a programme of supplementary assessments of the environmental performance of its Member countries. It has since done so through *i)* the development and use of environmental indicators and *ii)* systematic peer reviews of each individual country's environmental performance.

There is now an unprecedented range of domestic and international environmental commitments. The environmental performance question, *i.e.* the question of the actual fulfilment of these commitments, was and is central to the environmental credibility of governments *vis-à-vis* their own public opinion, other governments, and the international community. Have you done what you said you were going to do? This question is even more pressing now because environmental policies have to be implemented under domestic and international conditions often characterised by short-term time horizons, underpricing of natural resources, concerns over budgets and cumulated public deficits, and structural economic changes, as well as increased globalisation and international economic interdependencies.

THE CONCEPT OF ENVIRONMENTAL PERFORMANCE

Achieving Objectives

Whether policy objectives and commitments are in fact being met is the essence of appraising environmental performance. Performance refers to three main questions relating to the achievement of domestic objectives or the compliance with international commitments:

- *To what extent are the objectives achieved?* A clear distinction needs to be made between intentions, actions and results, an emphasis on results being central to assessing performance.

> **HIERARCHY OF PERFORMANCE**
> - intentions
> - actions
> - results

- *Are the objectives ambitious or modest?* In other words, how do these objectives relate to the country-specific context, *i.e.* to the past and current state of the environment, natural resource endowment, economic structure and development levels, and demographic trends?

- Are the objectives achieved in a *durable and cost-effective* way?

By building on the answers to these questions, recommendations can be formulated on how to improve performance in the future.

Following Strategic Orientations

The unprecedented range of domestic and international environmental commitments of the late 1980s-early 1990s have induced OECD Environment Ministers to define strategic orientations, which are central to environmental performance analysis:

- The *cost-effectiveness of environmental policies* for reducing the overall pollution burden and ensuring sustainable development and use of natural resources; here environmental management is related to a country's absolute environmental quality; environmental performance is measured with respect to a country's objectives in air, water and waste management, nature conservation and natural resource management.
- The *integration of environmental considerations into all other policies;* here environmental management is related to a country's overall decision-making process; environmental performance is measured with respect to a country's capacity to take account of environmental considerations in economic and sectoral decision making, to avoid unsustainable patterns of development and to achieve efficiently related objectives.
- The *effectiveness of co-operation with the international community;* here environmental management is related to a country's relations with its neighbours and the international community; environmental performance is measured with respect to bilateral, regional and multilateral commitments.

INDICATORS OF ENVIRONMENTAL PERFORMANCE

The OECD Approach

In order to establish a sound, factual basis, the OECD adopted, with its Member countries, a pragmatic approach requiring environmental indicators to be policy relevant, analytically sound and measurable: in brief, operational. The OECD work has led to:

- a common terminology and conceptual framework;
- the development of and agreement on core indicators;
- the measurement and publication of indicators;
- their regular use in OECD analytical work and environmental performance reviews

A Common Conceptual Framework

The Pressure-State-Response Model

A first dimension of the conceptual framework structuring the OECD's work on environmental indicators is the pressure-state-response (PSR) model. This framework is now widely used nationally and internationally, probably because it is policy relevant, linking the environment with economic activities and agents, as well as readable and robust.

- *Indicators of environmental pressures* describe pressures from human activities exerted on the environment, including on natural resources.
- *Indicators of environmental conditions* relate to the quality of the environment and the quality and quantity of natural resources. As such, they reflect the ultimate objective of environmental policies. Indicators of environmental conditions are designed to give an overview of the situation (the state) of the environment and its development over time.

◆ Figure 1. **The PSR model**

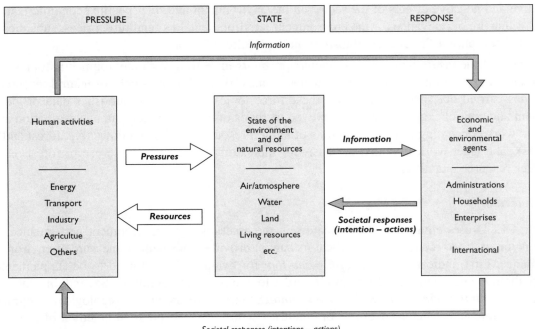

Source: OECD.

- *Indicators of societal responses* show the extent to which society is responding to environmental changes and concerns. They refer to individual and collective actions *i)* to mitigate, adapt to, or prevent human-induced negative impacts on the environment, *ii)* to halt or reverse environmental damage already inflicted, and *iii)* to preserve and conserve nature and natural resources.

Major Issues of Common Concern

The second dimension of the conceptual framework is given by 13 major environmental issues of common concern in OECD countries: climate change, ozone layer depletion, water quality, acidification, toxic contamination, urban environmental quality, biodiversity/landscapes, waste, water resources, forest resources, fish resources and soil degradation (desertification and erosion).

Output

The OECD has developed: a *"core set"* of environmental indicators common to Member countries; *"sectoral indicators"* to integrate environmental concerns in sectors such as energy, transport and agriculture; and indicators derived from *environmental accounting*.

The OECD *"core set"* of environmental indicators is published regularly and provides a first mechanism to *track environmental progress* for OECD countries. It is based on environmental data collected regularly by the OECD Secretariat from national authorities and harmonized among countries. It also includes economic data to track pressures on the environment and responses by governments, industry and households to these pressures.

"Sectoral indicators" were developed to *promote the integration of environmental concerns in sectoral policies and practices.* They describe *i)* trends of environmental significance in the sector; *ii)* positive and negative effects of the sector on the environment and; *iii)* specific economic features of the sector that are of relevance for the environment (environmental expenditure, prices, subsidies, etc.). Focus has been put on the energy, transport and agriculture sectors.

In view of the insufficiencies of *economic accounts* in dealing with environmental topics such as environmental expenditure, environmental damage and variations in the stocks of natural resources, the OECD has carried out special studies on these three topics. It regularly publishes data on pollution abatement and control expenditure, has surveyed methods of environmental damage estimation and has reviewed work concerning physical accounts of natural resource stocks and flows (*e.g.* forest and water accounts). The latter work provided the basis for indicators of the sustainable use of forest resources and water resource quantities.

Using Indicators

The OECD uses environmental indicators in the assessment of environment performance. However, it is important to recognise that indicators cannot provide a mechanical measure of environmental performance. First, indicators provide *only one tool* for evaluations and need to be supplemented by other qualitative and scientific information in order to avoid misinterpretation. Second, indicators must be reported and *interpreted in the appropriate context,* taking into account the ecological, geographical, social, economic and structural features of countries. Third, there is no single method of standardization: when comparing indicators across countries, the outcome of assessment will depend on the chosen denominator (GDP, population, land area) as well as on national definitions and measurement methodologies; nevertheless, standardization is needed to facilitate inter-country comparisons.

The methodology and a number of the core indicators are being used nationally and internationally, in co-operative work with Member countries, as well as with several international organisations.

REVIEWING ENVIRONMENTAL PERFORMANCE

The review of trends, policies and countries' performances, as well as the use of peer pressure to improve them is a very basic OECD function. It was extended in the early 1990s to the environment, through the programmes on environmental performance reviews. The OECD has now completed 20 such environmental examinations. These concern, among its Member countries: Austria, Canada, Finland, France, Germany, Iceland, Italy, Japan, Korea, Netherlands, New Zealand, Norway, Poland, Portugal, Spain, Sweden, United Kingdom and United States. They also include reviews of Bulgaria and Belarus.

Aims

The principal aim of these reviews is to check whether domestic objectives and international commitments are actually translated into concrete actions and whether results are achieved. In addition, these reviews *i)* help individual governments judge and make progress by establishing baseline conditions, trends, policy commitments, institutional arrangements and routine capabilities for carrying out national evaluations; *ii)* promote a continuous policy dialogue among Member countries through the transfer of information on policies, approaches and experiences of reviewed countries; and *iii)* stimulate greater accountability from Member countries' governments towards public opinion and other countries. They thus help Member countries improve their individual and collective performance in environmental management and trace a path towards sustainable development.

Peer Review Process

The OECD environmental performance reviews build on a four-stage process:

- a *preparatory stage* including the identification of major issues for the review, the compilation of facts and figures, and a first identification of national objectives and commitments;

- a *review mission* during which a team of experts from reviewing countries and from the OECD Secretariat meets with government and non-government representatives of the country under review; discussions focus on the evaluation of environmental performance and provide direct input to the analysis made by the team of experts; an early draft of the review prepared during the mission is consolidated and harmonised through further consultation within the OECD and with all reviewing country experts;

> **AN OECD SPECIALITY**
>
> Improving the individual and collective performances of Member countries through **peer pressure:**
> - Helping governments judge and make progress
> - Promoting policy dialogue
> - Stimulating accountability

- a *peer review meeting*[2] where a full day is allocated to the examination of a given country, with all OECD countries participating in the debate, and the reviewing countries taking the lead in opening the debate about specific parts of the review; the independence of the review itself and of the policy dialogue is ensured through a free and frank exchange of views and the final approval of the review's conclusions by the group of peers.

- the *publication and dissemination* stage, used by reviewed countries to bring the evaluation and its conclusions to the attention of a wider audience within the country itself and abroad.

A Strong Factual Base

Each review of the first OECD cycle of reviews includes:

- a factual description of the country's environmental state and trends, and of the factors having a bearing on them (*e.g.* direct and indirect pressures);
- a factual description of the country's responses, *i.e.* those of administrations, enterprises and households; this surveys relevant environmental and economic policies and programmes and highlights policy objectives (aims, goals, targets) and responses (measures taken);
- an evaluation of the results achieved and of the areas where progress is needed.

Recommendations and Peer Pressure

Each review addresses around 60 recommendations to the reviewed country to help it consolidate achievements and make further progress. Although OECD countries are bound together by a shared commitment to democratic ideals, pluralistic institutions and market-oriented economies, they also exhibit a wide diversity of physical, economic, social, cultural and environmental conditions that need to be taken into account when specifying these recommendations. For all countries, recommendations are made on the topics of air, water, waste management, integration of environmental and economic decision-making and implementation of international commitments. In addition, special chapters and recommendations concern topics chosen according to the country, such as nature, agriculture, energy, transport, tourism, fisheries, forestry and the chemical industry.

The publication of these reviews and the reaction given them by governments (*e.g.* formal government responses), by the news media or by decision makers (*e.g.* in governments, Parliaments, the private sector) contribute to their *influence*. It is expected that a second cycle of OECD reviews will help follow up on the implementation of the recommendations adopted several years before. There is also much for other countries to learn from the experience, strengths and weaknesses of each reviewed country.

EXTENDING PERFORMANCE REVIEWS INTERNATIONALLY

Interest has also been expressed in environmental performance reviews outside the OECD, by non-member countries or other international organisations. The Czech Republic, Hungary, Korea and Mexico, now new OECD Member countries, have, during their accession process, asked to be reviewed. The reviews of these countries have been completed or are planned. The Russian Federation has also formally asked the OECD to review its environmental performance.

Building on the 1993 "Environment for Europe" Conference of Environment Ministers at Lucerne, the OECD has co-operated with the UN Economic Commission for Europe in jointly carrying out reviews of Poland, Bulgaria and Belarus, and the UN-ECE has undertaken additional reviews in central and eastern Europe (*e.g.* Estonia, Slovenia).

The OECD favours these extensions of the review process. It has responded to these requests and supported these developments by sharing methodology and expertise.

LESSONS LEARNED: THE ENVIRONMENTAL PERFORMANCE OF OECD COUNTRIES[3]

It is possible to draw certain important lessons from the collective experience of OECD countries in addressing environmental issues over the course of the past twenty years, and particularly during the first half of the 1990s, based upon OECD environmental indicators and the results of OECD environmental performance reviews.

The environmental policies carried out in the 1980s and the first half of the 1990s have clearly shown positive effects on the state of the environment. Moreover, these policies have not in themselves posed significant economic difficulties in Member countries, nor did they create significant distortions in international trade or cause detrimental effects on employment. *To meet current and future environmental commitments,* however, it will be imperative to step up *integration* of environmental and economic policies in the near future, especially in the energy, transport and agriculture sectors, and to provide *price signals* that reflect social and environmental costs and are not biased by environmentally damaging subsidies. In addition, *international co-operation* must be greatly strengthened, and *environmental policies* will need adjustment towards increased emphasis on pollution prevention and on cost-effectiveness, openness, accountability, implementation and enforcement.

Towards Sustainable Development: Fostering the Integration of Government Policies

Meeting environmental commitments to ensure the well-being of present and future generations will necessitate much stronger integration of sectoral and environmental government policies than has been achieved so far by Member countries, and wider adoption of *result-oriented* policies, *i.e.* policies explicitly aimed at achieving specified improvements to the environment. Progress requires broad strategies that fully take into account both economic and environmental dimensions and that incorporate environmental requirements from the outset. To make full use of dynamic forces in the economy and society, Member countries should draw up *long-term plans* to meet the challenges of the next

◆ Figure 2. **Major protected areas, OECD countries**

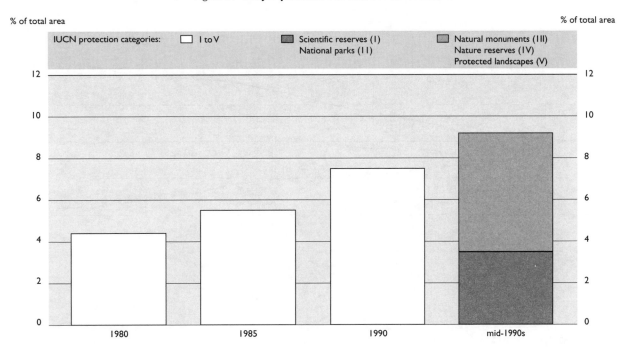

Source: IUCN; OECD.

century, *clarify environmental goals* and *set targets* for actions to be undertaken in relation to the environment. This approach requires close dialogue between relevant ministries, leading to a more structured integration of government activities. Other stakeholders, industry, and the general public must be fully engaged.

Energy, transport and agriculture policies need to be modified to better take account of environmental constraints and to avoid unsustainable patterns of development. Ever-growing *use of fossil fuels* cannot continue if Member countries are to meet their commitments, and, more important, if health risks and risks associated with climate change are to be mitigated. The likelihood that a number of Member countries will not meet commitments concerning CO_2 emissions by 2000 is a source of concern and requires urgent action. Additional road building and further increases in vehicle use are likely to be very damaging environmentally in most Member countries. Further intensification of *agriculture* without appropriate offsetting measures would have negative environmental effects, which must be prevented. Overuse of natural resources, *e.g.* depletion of green space, fish stocks and old growth forests, must also be controlled.

Stronger co-operation among the various levels of government must be pursued. Monitoring of environmental performance of subnational authorities, especially when they have considerable autonomy in carrying out their environmental policies, would help maintain a level playing-field, inform citizens about the state of their environment, and promote a democratic debate on environment.

Progress towards sustainable development will require significant changes in *production and consumption patterns.* These can be promoted by increasing consumer awareness and expanding use of approaches such as life-cycle analysis of products and extended producer responsibility. Governments can show the way to more sustainable policies by *"greening" their own operations.* This implies not

◆ Figure 3. *Air emissions, OECD countries*

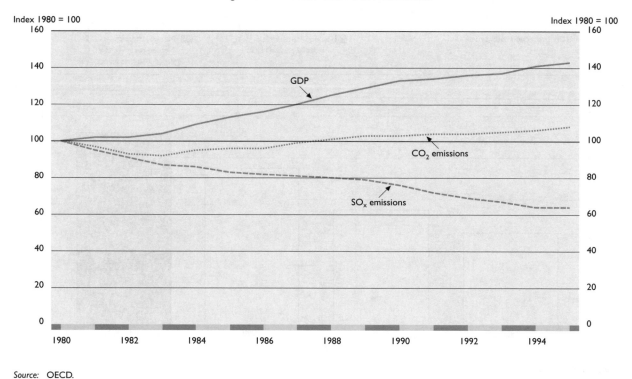

Source: OECD.

only assessing the environmental implications of policy decisions, but also reducing the environmental impact of government activities and promoting the use of "green" products by public authorities.

Towards Sustainable Development: a Greater Role for Market Forces

Another consistent finding that emerges from the OECD Environmental Performance Reviews is that meeting environmental commitments demands strategies aimed at ensuring sustainable development in the context of market-based economies. This implies that greatest use will be made of the market through *removal of distortions caused by externalities and subsidies* that affect the environment adversely. To combat environmental degradation and overuse of natural resources, it is essential to provide the *right price signals,* to promote internalisation of externalities by applying the *polluter pays principle* and the *user pays principle* and by introducing economic instruments, and to remove as far as possible subsidies that have negative effects on the economy and on the environment. Fiscal and environmental policies should be seen as mutually supportive. Wider use of *economic instruments* and other societal instruments, such as education and consumer information, will help in mobilising social and economic sectors to reach new, ambitious environmental goals cost-effectively while reducing demand for goods and services that cause environmental degradation. Such instruments can also help in financing environmental protection activities. The private sector should, in this context, be given sufficient lead-time to adapt itself to new environmental requirements, to seek cost-effective approaches and to develop innovations in the *technology* it uses and the products and services it delivers.

Meeting International Commitments

Much more progress is also required to solve transfrontier, regional and global problems. Globalisation of the economy, of trade, and of environmental issues means that linkages among the activities and interests of nations are tightening, and that avoiding conflicts and optimising benefits will require more solidarity on "spaceship earth". As for the major challenges, the need to mitigate *climate change* has not yet been adequately faced and the provision of *environmental aid* and technical assistance to less developed countries is falling short of what is required. Member countries, with their large economic resources, could do much more than they are doing at present to solve global environmental problems for which they bear a large degree of responsibility, *e.g.* by meeting their commitments on further financial assistance to developing countries; they could also strengthen their support to central and eastern European countries in actions to protect the environment. International co-operation can also be strengthened in a number of areas without major new expenditures: in particular, environmental capacity building initiatives in developing countries (*e.g.* cleaner-technology centres) could be further promoted, international environmental law could be further developed and many issues of responsibility and liability could be addressed more open-mindedly. Similarly, progress could be made by reconciling trade and environment policies.

The OECD review series demonstrates the need for Member countries to strengthen their co-operation on regional issues to define joint strategies and common policies that are at least as effective as those used for domestic issues. Close integration and interdependence of the economies of regional groups of Member countries (*e.g.* European Union, North American Free Trade Agreement) is likely to lead to novel approaches in environmental co-operation, reflecting closer economic integration.

Improving Cost-Effectiveness, Openness and Accountability of Environmental Policies

Finally, a common feature of the OECD environmental performance reviews is an assessment of how OECD Member countries are responding to the need to improve the cost-effectiveness, openness and accountability of environmental policies. The reviews reveal that, over the past five years, there has been an intensifying search within Member countries for more cost-effective approaches to coping with environmental issues. Several countries have moved or are moving from *process-oriented environmental policies to result-oriented policies,* and many Member countries have introduced a *mix of instruments* (regulatory, economic and societal instruments) to deal with difficult environmental issues. Further emphasis is also needed on preventive approaches, integrated pollution control, and place-based and ecosystem management, while making full use of voluntary agreements.

Difficult decisions that will have to be taken in coming years will need to be supported by well thought out, broad-based consultative and awareness-raising activities. To be successful, environmental strategies will require openness in decision-making as well as a high quality assessment process. Openness will require full access for all players to environmental information, more meaningful consultation with and participation by the public, and a continuing dialogue with stakeholders (*e.g.* industry, trade unions, non-governmental organisations, local communities).

The availability of meaningful environmental data and indicators and well-synthesised information should lead to a better democratic debate, and to better accountability of public authorities and the various actors. Improved assessment and policy planning will require better databases, broader use of environmental impact assessment to deal with programmes and policies, and evaluation of cost-effectiveness and cost-benefit comparison. Regarding the latter, work on the valuation of benefits will need to be increased to ensure that a proper balance is maintained, given the recent emphasis in some Member countries on quantifying the cost of environmental protection.

CONCLUSIONS

In an age of pressing environmental problems coupled with the search for transparency and cost-effectiveness, the OECD has developed and implemented innovative programmes on environmental indicators and environmental performance reviews, which have proven to be powerful tools to track and chart environmental progress.

Indeed, building capacity for systematic monitoring and assessment of environmental performance, with objective oversight and peer review, deserves a high priority by all governments for a number of good reasons. In particular, participating countries:

- learn about themselves and other countries;
- give explicit account of progress against their national environmental objectives and international commitments;
- promote cost-effectiveness through more results-oriented strategies.

Therefore, all governments may want to think about the importance of, and means for, keeping environmental performance under review.

NOTES

1. The mandates for the OECD programmes concerning environmental indicators and environmental performance reviews derive from agreements by the OECD Council at its Ministerial level meetings in June 1989 and June 1991; and communiqués by Heads of State and Government at the Paris, Houston and London G-7 economic summits in 1989, 1990 and 1991.

2. Held by the OECD Group on Environmental Performance (GEP).

3. Based on ''Environmental Performance in OECD countries: Progress in the 1990s'', OECD, Paris, 1996.

BIBLIOGRAPHY

OECD (1997) *Environmental Indicators,* OECD Core Set [also 1991, 1994].

OECD (1997) *OECD Environmental Data, Compendium 1997* [also 1985, 1987, 1989, 1991, 1993, 1995].

OECD (1997) *OECD Pollution Abatement and Control Expenditure Data* [also 1991, 1993].

OECD (1996) *Environmental Performance in OECD Countries: Progress in the 1990s.*

OECD *Environmental Performance Reviews:*

Germany	(1993)	English, French, German
Iceland	(1993)	English, French
Norway	(1993)	English, French
Portugal	(1993)	English, French
Japan	(1994)	English, French, Japanese
United Kingdom	(1994)	English, French
Italy	(1994)	English, French, Italian
Netherlands	(1995)	English, French
Poland	(1995)	English, French, Polish
Canada	(1995)	English, French
Austria	(1995)	English, French, German
United States	(1996)	English, French, Spanish
Bulgaria	(1996)	English, French
Sweden	(1996)	English, French
New Zealand	(1996)	English, French
France	(1997)	English, French
Spain	(1997)	English, French, Spanish
Korea	(1997, forthcoming)	English, French
Finland	(1997, forthcoming)	English, French

ANNEXES

Annex I. SELECTED ENVIRONMENTAL DATA[1]

	CAN	MEX	USA	JPN	KOR	AUS	NZL	AUT	BEL	CZ.R	DNK	FIN	FRA	DEU*	GRC	HUN	ISL	IRL	ITA	LUX	NLD	NOR	POL	PRT	ESP	SWE	CHE	TUR	UKD*	OECD***
LAND																														
Total area (1 000 km²)[2]	9976	1958	9809	378	99	7713	270	84	31	79	43	338	552	357	132	93	104	70	301	3	37	324	313	92	505	450	41	779	245	34593
Major protected areas (% of total area)[3]	8.9	5.0	10.6	7.3	7.0	7.7	22.8	23.9	2.5	13.5	32.2	8.1	9.7	25.8	1.7	6.2	8.8	0.7	7.6	13.9	10.2	14.3	9.8	6.3	8.4	6.6	17.7	1.1	20.3	9.1
Nitrogenous fertiliser use (t/sq.km of arable land)	3.1	4.5	5.7	13.2	23.1	1.3	25.4	8.1	21.5	7.7	12.4	7.7	11.9	15.3	9.6	4.9	9.3	46.5	7.4		39.8	12.4	5.7	4.3	4.7	7.0	12.8	3.7	21.4	5.9
FOREST																														
Forest area (% of land area)	45.1	25.5	31.1	67.0	65.4	19.4	28.2	46.9	20.2	34.0	10.5	76.4	27.7	29.9	20.3	19.1	1.4	5.7	23.0	34.4	10.3	38.9	28.9	35.3	32.3	68.3	31.7	26.2	10.1	32.7
Use of forest resources (harvest/growth)	0.6	0.2	0.6	0.3	..	..	0.7	0.6	0.5	0.6	0.6	0.6	0.7	0.7	0.5	0.5	..	..	..	0.7	0.5	0.6	0.5	1.1	0.5	0.6	0.8	0.8	0.5	0.6
Tropical wood imports (US$/cap.)[4]	0.6	..	1.5	20.1	6.6	6.6	1.9	1.5	11.0	..	3.2	2.9	6.9	4.7	3.5	..	1.9	8.5	7.6	"	18.4	4.7	..	16.0	6.0	1.2	0.6	0.6	3.8	6.3
THREATENED SPECIES[5]																														
Mammals (% of species known)	7.8	31.8	10.5	7.4	14.5	13.8	100.0	37.5	21.5	29.9	24.0	11.9	20.2	51.0	37.1	69.9	–	16.1	32.2	53.2	44.8	8.0	6.5	17.2	16.8	18.2	26.5	10.2	45.2	..
Birds (% of species known)	4.5	29.5	7.2	8.1	5.3	5.9	29.5	28.1	29.0	28.2	12.9	6.8	14.7	44.0	11.8	94.2	13.3	24.7	30.9	19.3	32.6	10.4	7.5	34.9	11.6	7.8	40.7	8.7	22.5	..
Fish (% of species known)	4.4	3.5	2.4	7.5	7.5	0.4	37.0	42.5	..	23.9	18.2	11.7	6.3	70.0	36.9	34.6	–	..	28.6	38.2	43.5	–	2.6	18.6	23.5	4.3	18.5	3.9	12.2	26.3
WATER																														
Water withdrawal (% of gross annual availability)	1.6	18.7	18.9	20.9	34.0	4.3	0.6	2.8	..	15.8	10.0	2.0	21.3	28.2	..	5.7	0.1	..	32.1	5.2	8.6	..	19.5	10.1	26.3	1.7	2.2	14.3	15.5	11.1
Fish catches (% of world catches)	0.9	1.1	5.4	6.7	2.5	0.2	0.5	–	..	–	1.7	0.2	0.8	0.2	0.2	–	1.4	0.3	0.5	–	0.5	2.3	0.4	0.2	1.3	0.4	–	0.6	0.9	26.3
Public waste water treatment (% of population served)	63	22	71	50	45	..	..	72	..	56	98	77	77	86	11	32	4	..	61	88	97	57	42	21	59	95	91	6	87	60
AIR																														
Emissions of sulphur oxides (kg/cap.)	106.2	..	73.5	7.1	34.2	..	..	8.9	42.1	124.8	30.4	21.5	17.4	36.8	50.2	72.2	29.4	53.4	29.6	26.0	9.4	8.3	67.6	27.4	52.8	11.0	4.8	29.2	46.5	41.5
(kg/1 000 US$ GDP)[6]	5.8	..	3.0	0.4	2.8	..	..	0.5	2.5	14.4	1.7	1.4	0.9	2.2	5.2	12.2	1.7	4.5	1.8	1.1	0.6	0.4	14.4	2.7	4.2	0.7	0.2	6.4	2.9	2.4
Emissions of nitrogen oxides (kg/cap.)	67.9	..	81.5	11.9	25.7	..	43.4	22.8	30.1	36.3	51.5	53.8	25.8	27.1	33.3	18.3	80.9	36.5	36.0	..	34.9	53.1	28.7	25.5	31.3	44.6	19.2	9.3	38.0	40.1
(kg/1 000 US$ GDP)[6]	3.7	..	3.3	0.6	2.1	..	3.1	1.3	1.8	4.2	2.9	3.4	1.4	1.6	3.5	3.1	4.6	3.1	2.1	2.0	2.0	2.7	6.1	2.5	2.5	2.7	0.9	2.1	2.3	2.4
Emissions of carbon dioxide (t./cap.)[7]	16.0	3.9	19.9	9.2	7.9	16.6	7.9	7.1	11.8	11.6	11.8	13.2	6.1	10.7	7.3	5.6	9.1	9.8	7.4	21.5	11.8	6.6	8.4	5.0	6.4	6.1	5.9	2.5	9.6	11.2
(t./1 000 US$ GDP)[6]	0.83	0.84	0.80	0.48	0.65	0.93	0.55	0.39	0.66	1.34	0.63	0.84	0.33	0.61	0.74	0.93	0.51	0.66	0.42	0.78	0.68	0.32	1.68	0.48	0.49	0.36	0.28	0.49	0.58	0.64
WASTE GENERATED																														
Industrial waste (kg/1 000 US$ GDP)[6,8]	..	70	142	61	67	125	..	41	171	..	20	206	48	59	44	573	9	..	34	164	32	39	122	..	28	89	9	86	61	87
Municipal waste (kg/cap.)	630	320	730	410	390	..	..	480	470	400	520	410	560	360	310	420	660	..	470	530	540	620	260	350	370	360	380	390	350	510
Nuclear waste (t./Mtoe of TPES)[9]	7.4	0.1	0.9	1.5	1.6	–	–	–	1.9	1.1	–	2.2	5.1	1.9	–	..	–	..	..	–	0.2	–	..	..	1.8	4.2	2.8	–	5.8	1.8
NOISE																														
Population exposed to leq > 65dB(A) (million inh.)[10]	..	..	17.2	38.0	..	..	..	1.2	1.2	1.5	0.5	0.2	9.4	9.5	2.0	..	..	..	..	0.6	0.6	0.5	..	3.0	8.9	0.3	0.8	..	5.7	124.0

.. Not available. – Nil or negligible.

* Figures in italics include: for Germany: western Germany only; for United Kingdom: threatened species and public waste water treatment: Great Britain only; water withdrawal: England and Wales only.

** Figures underlined do not include Mexico.

a) Data for Luxembourg are included under Belgium.

1. Data refer to 1995 or to the latest available year. They include provisional figures and Secretariat estimates. Varying definitions can limit comparability across countries. Total refers to the 25 OECD Member countries as of November 1995.
2. NLD: excluding Lake IJssel (1 708 km²) and internal waters (Wadden Sea and North Sea: 2 473 km²).
3. Data refer to IUCN categories I to V.
4. Total imports of cork and wood from tropical countries.
5. NZL: data refer to indigenous species only (mammals: 5 species).

6. GDP at 1991 prices and purchasing power parities.
7. CO2 from energy use only; international marine bunkers are excluded.
8. Waste from manufacturing industries (ISIC 3).
9. Waste from spent fuel arising in nuclear power plants, in tonnes of heavy metal, per million tonnes of oil equivalent of total primary energy supply.
10. Road traffic noise.

Source: OECD Environmental Data, Compendium 1995.

Annex II. SELECTED ECONOMIC DATA AND TRENDS[1]

	CAN	MEX	USA	JPN	KOR	AUS	NZL	AUT	BEL	CZ.R	DNK	FIN	FRA	DEU*	GRC	HUN	ISL	IRL	ITA	LUX	NLD	NOR	POL	PRT	ESP	SWE	CHE	TUR	UKD	OECD**
TOTAL AREA (1 000 km^2)[2]	9976	1958	9809	378	99	7713	270	84	31	79	43	338	552	357	132	93	104	70	301	3	37	324	313	92	505	450	41	779	245	34593
POPULATION																														
Total population, 1995 (100 000 inh.)	296	948	2631	1253	449	181	36	80	101	103	52	51	581	817	105	102	3	36	573	4	155	44	386	99	392	88	71	616	586	9798
% change (1980-1995)	20.4	36.1	15.5	7.2	17.6	22.9	13.9	6.6	2.9	0.0	2.0	6.9	7.9	4.3	8.5	-4.5	17.1	5.3	1.5	13.2	9.2	6.7	8.5	1.0	4.9	6.2	10.9	38.7	4.1	13.0
Population density, 1995 (inh./km^2)	3.0	48.4	26.8	331.5	451.9	2.3	13.3	96.0	332.2	131.0	121.3	15.1	105.4	228.8	79.2	110.0	2.6	50.9	190.1	159.7	414.1	13.5	123.3	107.8	77.7	19.6	171.5	79.1	239.4	28.3
GROSS DOMESTIC PRODUCT[3]																														
GDP, 1995 (billion US$)	573	437	6563	2431	546	321	51	145	180	89	98	81	1087	1437	103	62	5	53	1015	11	268	91	194	104	517	149	148	319	974	17164
% change (1980-1995)	43.4	21.7	46.2	57.9	241.3	56.5	39.0	36.7	28.9	..	35.2	31.4	33.5	36.3	24.3	..	36.8	81.3	31.8	101.4	37.8	49.8	..	42.3	43.5	24.5	22.9	94.9	37.8	43.4
Per capita, 1995 (1 000 US$/cap.)	19.4	4.6	24.9	19.4	12.2	17.8	14.3	18.1	17.8	8.6	18.7	15.8	18.7	17.6	9.9	6.0	17.8	14.9	17.7	27.7	17.4	20.8	5.0	10.5	13.2	16.9	20.9	5.2	16.6	17.5
INDUSTRY[4]																														
Value added in industry, (% of GDP)	26	29	28	38	44	28	26	34	27	41	24	30	27	36	21	31	23	35	31	34	27	35	32	33	33	28	34	33	27	30
Industrial production % change (1980-1994)	31	..	40	42	308	48	..	36	16	..	45	43	11	19	6	..	..	146	10	19	19	91	..	47	18	26	32	..	27	31
AGRICULTURE																														
Value added in agriculture, (% of GDP)[5]	2	7	2	2	7	3	9	2	2	6	3	5	2	1	13	6	10	7	3	3	3	3	6	4	4	2	3	16	2	2
ENERGY SUPPLY																														
Total supply, 1995 (Mtoe)	234	149	2078	495	146	98	15	26	53	38	21	32	240	337	24	24	2	11	163	3	73	24	91	19	101	50	25	62	220	4555
% change (1980-1995)	21.0	52.6	15.4	42.6	251.4	39.2	67.4	13.0	14.5	..	6.4	28.3	26.1	-6.2	47.3	-16.9	38.7	33.9	17.1	-8.5	12.4	25.3	-26.7	83.6	47.3	21.6	20.3	97.8	9.1	19.6
Energy intensity, 1995 (Toe/1 000 US$)	0.41	0.34	0.32	0.20	0.27	0.31	0.30	0.18	0.29	0.43	0.21	0.40	0.22	0.23	0.23	0.38	0.42	0.21	0.16	0.29	0.27	0.26	0.47	0.18	0.20	0.33	0.17	0.19	0.23	0.27
% change (1980-1995)	-15.6	25.3	-21.1	-9.7	3.0	-11.0	20.5	-17.3	-11.1	..	-21.3	-2.3	-5.5	..	18.4	1.4	62.3	-26.1	-11.2	-54.6	-18.4	-16.4	..	29.1	2.6	-2.3	-2.1	-1.5	-20.8	..
Structure of energy supply, 1994 (%)[6]																														
Solid fuels	14.7	8.8	26.5	17.2	20.7	46.1	13.5	23.2	19.0	57.4	43.3	37.5	11.3	29.3	38.9	20.2	3.3	28.9	8.4	27.1	13.3	9.1	76.3	24.5	20.6	18.7	5.5	41.5	22.6	23.0
Oil	33.1	65.4	38.8	55.9	61.9	36.1	32.8	43.2	41.6	19.4	43.5	32.7	35.1	40.3	59.9	30.1	34.4	50.8	60.3	58.1	37.2	33.8	15.2	70.2	55.3	31.7	50.0	45.9	39.2	42.5
Gas	28.0	20.5	24.1	10.6	5.7	16.3	27.2	22.0	18.8	14.5	12.7	9.5	11.6	18.2	0.2	34.6	–	19.6	26.8	14.5	48.0	15.2	8.3	–	6.6	1.3	7.6	–	27.5	20.6
Nuclear	12.1	0.8	8.7	14.6	11.5	–	–	–	20.6	8.4	–	16.9	39.2	11.7	–	15.0	–	–	–	–	1.5	–	–	–	15.0	38.2	24.2	–	10.5	11.0
Hydro, etc.	12.1	4.6	1.9	1.7	0.3	1.6	26.5	11.6	0.1	0.3	0.5	3.4	2.8	0.5	0.9	–	62.3	0.7	4.5	0.3	–	41.9	0.2	5.3	2.5	10.2	12.8	4.8	0.2	3.0
ROAD TRANSPORT[7]																														
Road traffic volumes, 1994																														
Billion veh.-km	254	56	3753	708	48	143	26	52	60	..	40	42	451	575	48	27	2	28	442	4	98	29	113	43	133	68	55	31	413	7553
% change (1980-1994)	23.7	..	55.2	81.9	456.0	24.4	54.7	46.3	30.8	..	51.7	56.0	52.3	55.2	136.6	41.4	69.2	52.1	95.0	85.8	40.0	76.4	153.4	102.4	88.1	52.4	50.1	111.6	71.0	58.5
Per capita (1 000 veh.-km/cap.)	8.7	0.6	14.4	5.7	1.1	8.0	7.3	6.5	5.9	..	7.7	8.2	7.8	7.1	4.6	2.6	7.5	7.9	7.7	10.3	6.4	6.7	2.9	4.4	3.4	7.7	7.9	0.5	7.1	7.8
Road vehicle stock, 1994																														
10 000 vehicles	1744	1230	19547	6359	740	1052	195	377	462	319	195	213	3004	4197	295	246	13	118	3258	24	650	202	858	324	1661	391	344	380	2485	48720
% change (1980-1994)	32.0	111.1	25.5	71.6	1303.1	44.8	24.6	54.6	32.9	64.9	18.0	53.9	38.4	52.6	133.3	108.9	37.9	47.1	70.4	66.3	34.5	44.5	179.9	169.1	85.8	27.1	41.6	225.0	43.4	43.0
Per capita (veh./100 inh.)	60	13	75	51	17	59	55	47	46	31	37	42	52	52	28	24	49	33	57	59	42	47	22	33	42	45	49	6	43	50

.. : Not available. – : Nil or negligible.
* Figures in italics include western Germany only.
** Figures underlined do not include Mexico.
1. Data may include provisional figures and Secretariat estimates. Total refers to the 25 OECD Member countries as of November 1995.
2. NLD: excluding Lake IJssel (1 708 km²) and internal waters (Wadden Sea and North Sea: 2 473 km²).
3. GDP at 1991 prices and purchasing power parities.
4. Value added: includes mining and quarrying (ISIC 3), manufacturing (ISIC 2), gas, electricity and water (ISIC 4), and construction (ISIC 5); production: ISIC 2 to 4.
5. Agriculture, forestry, hunting, fishery, etc.
6. Breakdown excludes electricity trade.
7. Refers to motor vehicles with four or more wheels, except for Japan and Italy, which include three-wheeled goods vehicles.
Source: OECD Environmental Data, Compendium 1995.

Annex III. **SELECTED MULTILATERAL AGREEMENTS (WORLDWIDE)**

Y = in force S = signed R = ratified D = denounced

Year	City	Agreement	Y	CAN	MEX	USA	JPN	KOR	AUS	NZL	AUT	BEL	CZ.R	DNK	FIN	FRA	DEU	GRC	HUN	ISL	IRL	ITA	LUX	NLD	NOR	POL	PRT	ESP	SWE	CHE	TUR	UKD	EC
1946	Washington	Conv. – Regulation of whaling	Y	D	R	R	R		R	R	R	R		D	R	R	R			D	R	R		R	R			R	R	R		R	R
1956	Washington	Protocol	Y	R	R	R	R		R	R	R	R		R	R	R	R			R	R	R		R	R			R	R	R		R	R
1949	Geneva	Conv. – Road traffic	Y	R	R	R	R		R	R	R	R	R	R	R	R		R	R	R	R	R	R	R	R	R	R	R	R	S	R	R	R
1957	Brussels	Conv. – Limitation of the liability of owners of sea-going ships	Y				D	D			D			D	D	D	D			R		S	R	D	D		R	R	D	R		D	
1979	Brussels	Protocol	Y			D	R				R	R		R	S	D	S			R		S	R	D	R		R	R	R	R		D	
1958	Geneva	Conv. – Fishing and conservation of the living resources of the high seas	Y	R		R	R		R	S	R	R		R	R	R		R		S	S			R	R	R	R	S		R		R	
1962	Brussels	Conv. – Liability of operators of nuclear ships	Y								S	S					S			S	S			R			R	S		R		S	
1963	Vienna	Conv. – Civil liability for nuclear damage	Y		R						R		R				S	R	R	S					R	R			R		S	S	
1988	Vienna	Joint protocol relating to the application of the Vienna Convention and the Paris Convention	Y																														
1963	Moscow	Treaty – Banning nuclear weapon tests in the atmosphere, in outer space and under water	Y	R	R	R	R		R	R	R	R	R	R	R	S	S	S	R	R	R	R	R	R	R	R	R	R	R	R	R	R	
1964	Copenhagen	Conv. – International council for the exploration of the sea	Y	R		R	R		R		R	R		R	R	R	R	R		R	R	R		R	R	R	R	R	R	R	R	R	
1970	Copenhagen	Protocol	Y	R		R	R		R		R	R		R	R	R	R	R		R	R	R		R	R	R	R	R	R	R	R	R	
1969	Brussels	Conv. – Intervention on the high seas in cases of oil pollution casualties (INTERVENTION)	Y	R		R	R	S	R	R		R		R	R	R	R	S		R	R	R	R	R	R		R	R	R	R		R	
1973	London	Protocol (pollution by substances other than oil)	Y	R		R	R		R	S		R		R	R	R	R			R	R	R		R	R		R	R	R	R		R	
1969	Brussels	Conv. – Civil liability for oil pollution damage (CLC)	Y	R		S	R	R	R	R		R		R	R	R	R	R		R	R	R	R	R	R	S	R	R	R	R		R	
1976	London	Protocol	Y	R		R	R	R	R	R		R		R	R	R	R	R		R	R	R	R	R	R	S	R	R	R	R		R	
1992	London	Protocol	Y	R								R		R	S	R	R	R				R			R		R	R	R			R	
1971	Bern	Conv. – Transport of goods by rail (CIM)	Y								R	R	R			R	R	R	R			R	R					R		R	R		
1971	Brussels	Conv. – International fund for compensation for oil pollution damage (FUND)	Y	R			R	S	R	R		R		R	R	R	R	R		R	R	R	R	R	R	R	R	R	R	S		R	
1976	London	Protocol	Y	R		R	R		R			R		R	R	R	R	R		R	R	R		R	R	S	R	R	R	R		R	
1992	London	Protocol	Y	R		R	R		R			R		R	R	R	R	R		R	R	R		R	R	S	R	R	R	R		R	
1971	Brussels	Conv. – Civil liability in maritime carriage of nuclear material	Y											R	R	R				R	R	R		R	R		S	R	R	R		S	
1971	London, Moscow, Washington	Conv. – Prohib. emplacement of nuclear and mass destruct. weapons on sea-bed, ocean floor and subsoil	Y	R	R	R	R	R	R	R	R	R	R	R	R	R	R	R	R	R	R	R	R	R	R	R	R	R	R	R	R	R	
1971	Ramsar	Conv. – Wetlands of international importance especially as waterfowl habitat	Y	R	R	R	R		R	R	R	R	R	R	R	R	R	R	R	R	R	R	S	R	R	R	R	R	R	S	R	R	
1982	Paris	Protocol	Y	R	R	R	R		R	R	R	R	R	R	S	R	R	R	R	R	R	R	S	R	R	R	R	R	R	S	R	R	
1971	Geneva	Conv. – Protection against hazards of poisoning arising from benzene (ILO 136)	Y									R	R		R	R	R	R				R					R			R			
1972	London, Mexico, Moscow, Washington	Conv. – Prevention of marine pollution by dumping of wastes and other matter (LC)	Y	R	R	R	R	R	R	R		R		R	R	R	R	R		R	R	R		R	R		R		R	R		R	
1978	..	Amendments to Annexes (incineration at sea)	Y	R	R	R	R	R	R	R		R		R	R	R	R	R		R	R	R		R	R		S		R	R		R	
1978	..	Amendments to convention (settlement of disputes)		R		R						R	R	R	R	R	R	R		R		R		R	R		R		R	R		R	
1980	..	Amendments (annexes)	Y	R	R	R	R		R	R		R		R	R	R	R	R		R	R	R	S	R	R		R		R	R		R	
1972	Geneva	Conv. – Safe container (CSC)	Y	R	R	R	R		R	R		R	R	R	S	R	R	R		R	R	R		R	R		R		R	S	S	R	
1972	London, Moscow, Washington	Conv. – International liability for damage caused by space objects	Y	R	R	R	R		R	R		R		R	R	R	R	R		S		R		R	S	R	R	R	R	R		R	
1972	Paris	Conv. – Protection of the world cultural and natural heritage	Y	R	R	R	R		R	R		R	R	R	R	R	R	R		R	R	R	R	R	R	R	R	R	R	R	R	R	R

Annex III. **SELECTED MULTILATERAL AGREEMENTS (WORLDWIDE)** *(cont.)*

Y = in force   S = signed   R = ratified   D = denounced

Year	Place	Agreement		CAN	MEX	USA	JPN	KOR	AUS	NZL	AUT	BEL	CZ.R	DNK	FIN	FRA	DEU	GRC	HUN	ISL	IRL	ITA	LUX	NLD	NOR	POL	PRT	ESP	SWE	CHE	TUR	UKD	EC
1978	London	Protocol – Prevention of pollution from ships (MARPOL PROT)	Y	R	R	R	R	R	R	R	R	R	R	R	R	R	R	R	R	R	R	R	R	R	R	R	R	R	R	R	R	R	
1978	London	Annex III	Y	R	R	R	R	R	R	R	R	R	R	R	R	R	R	R	R	R	R	R	R	R	R	R	R	R	R	R	R	R	
1978	London	Annex IV	Y		R		R		R		R	R	R	R	R	R	R	R	R	R	R	R	R	R	R	R	R	R	R	R	R		
1978	London	Annex V	Y	R	R	R	R	R	R	R	R	R	R	R	R	R	R	R	R	R	R	R	R	R	R	R	R	R	R	R	R	R	
1973	Washington	Conv. – International trade in endangered species of wild fauna and flora (CITES)	Y	R	R	R	R	R	R	R	R	R	R	R	R	R	R	R	R	S	R	R	R	R	R	R	R	R	R	R	R	R	
1974	Geneva	Conv. – Prev. and control of occup. hazards caused by carcinog. subst. and agents (ILO 139)	Y				R					R		R	R	R	R					R		R	R		R	R	R	R		R	
1976	London	Conv. – Limitation of liability for maritime claims (LLMC)	Y		R		R		R	R	R	R	R	R	R	R	R			R	R	R	R	R			R	R	R	R		R	
1977	Geneva	Conv. – Protec. of workers against occup. hazards in the working env. due to air poll., noise and vibrat. (ILO 148)	Y											R	R	R	R											R					
1979	Bonn	Conv. – Conservation of migratory species of wild animals	Y						R		R	R	R	R	R	R	R	R	R		R	R	R	R	R	R	R	R	R	R		R	R
1991	London	Agreem. – Conservation of Bats in Europe	Y								R	R	R	R	S	S	R	R	R		R	R	R	R	R	S	S	R	R			R	R
1992	New York	Agreem. – Conservation of Small Cetaceans of the Baltic and the North Seas	Y						S		S	S		S	S	S	R					S		R	R	S		S	S	S		R	S
1982	Montego Bay	Conv. – Law of the sea	Y	S	R	S	S	S	R	S	S	S	R	R	R	R	R	S	R	R	S	R	S	S	R	S	S	S	S	S	R	R	S
1994	New York	Agreem. – relating to the implementation of part XI of the convention	Y	R	R	R	R	R	R	R	R	R		R	R	R	R	R	R	S	R	R	R	R	R	R	R	S	R	R	R	R	R
1983	Geneva	Agreem. – Tropical timber	Y	R		R	R	R	R	R	R	R	R	R	R	R	R	R	R	R	R	R	R	R	R	R	R	S	R	R	R	R	R
1994	New York	Revised agreem.	Y	S		R	R	R	R	R	R	R	R	R	R	S	R	R	R	R	R	R	R	R	R	S	R	S	R	S	R	R	R
1985	Vienna	Conv. – Protection of the ozone layer	Y	R	R	R	R	R	R	R	R	R	R	R	R	R	R	R	R	R	R	R	R	R	R	R	R	S	R	R	R	R	R
1987	Montreal	Protocol (substances that deplete the ozone layer)	Y	R	R	R	R	R	R	R	R	R	R	R	R	R	R	R	R	R	R	R	R	R	R	R	R	R	R	R	R	R	R
1990	London	Amendment to protocol	Y	R		R	R	R	R	R	R	R	R	R	R	R	R	R	R	R	R	R	R	R	R	R	R	R	R	R	R	R	R
1992	Copenhagen	Amendment to protocol	Y	R		R	R	R	R	R	R	R	R	R	R	R	R	R	R		R	R	R	R	R	R	R	R	R	R	R	R	R
1986	Vienna	Conv. – Early notification of a nuclear accident	Y	R		R	R	R	R	R	R	S	R	R	R	R	R	R	R	R	R	R	S	R	R	R	R	R	R	R	R	R	
1986	Vienna	Conv. – Assistance in the case of a nuclear accident or radiological emergency	Y	S		R	R	R	R	R	R	S	R	S	R	R	R	R	R	R	R	R	S	R	R	S	R	R	R	R	R	R	
1989	Basel	Conv. – Control of transboundary movements of hazardous wastes and their disposal	Y	R	S	S	R	R	R	R	R	R	R	R	R	R	R	R	R	R	R	R	R	R	R	S	R	S	R	R	R	R	R
1989	London	Conv. – Salvage	Y	R	R	R	R		R	R	R	R	R	R	R	S	S	R		R	R	S	R	S	S	S		S	R		R	R	
1990	London	Conv. – Oil pollution preparedness, response and co-operation (OPPRC)	Y	R	R	R	R	R	R	R	R			R	R	R	R	R	R	R	R	S		R	R	S	R	R	R	R	R	R	
1990	..	Conv. – establishing a marine scientific organization for the North Pacific Region (PICES)	Y	R		R	R	R	R																								
1992	Rio de Janeiro	Conv. – Biological diversity	Y	R	R	R	R	R	R	R	R	R	R	R	R	R	R	R	R	R	R	R	R	R	R	R	R	R	R	R	S	R	R
1992	New York	Conv. – Framework convention on climate change	Y	R	R	R	R	R	R	R	R	R	R	R	R	R	R	R	R	R	R	R	R	R	R	R	R	R	R	R	R	R	R
1993	Paris	Conv. – Prohibition of the development, production, stockpiling and use of chemical weapons and their destruction	Y	R	R	R	R	R	R	R	R	R	R	R	R	R	R	R	R	R	R	R	R	R	R	R	R	R	R	R	R	R	
1993	Geneva	Conv. – Prevention of major industrial accidents (ILO 174)																											R				
1993	..	Agreem. – Promote compliance with international conservation and management measures by fishing vessels on the high seas		R			R				S			S		S	S	S	S	S	S	S		S	R		R	R	R		S	S	R
1994	Vienna	Conv. – Nuclear safety		S	S	S	S	S	S		S	S	S	R	S	S	S	S		S	S	S		S	S	S	S	S	S		S	S	S
1994	Paris	Conv. – Combat desertification in those countries experiencing serious drought and/or desertification, particularly in Africa		S	S	S	S	S	S		S	S	S	R	R	S	S	S		S	S	S		S	S	S	S	S	S		S	S	S

Source: IUCN; OECD.

Chapter 4

CONSUMPTION AND PRODUCTION PATTERNS: MAKING THE CHANGE

by

Elaine Geyer-Allély and Jeremy Eppel

THE ORIGINS OF THE ISSUE

Twenty-five years ago the issue of sustainable consumption was at the centre of a scientific and political debate about limits to the Earth's non-renewable resources and its ability to accommodate an ever growing population and expansion in economic production. Although many of the theories and scenarios developed during that period have since been discredited, elements of the debate have endured. As a result, while today there is cause for optimism that technological improvements could allow great increases in efficiency in the use of natural resources and reductions in the negative environmental impacts of production and consumption patterns, there is also a widely shared recognition that trends in many current levels and patterns of consumption and production are unsustainable.

In addition to these environmental considerations, concerns about the *equity* of modern consumption levels and patterns also underlie the international debate about which measures should be taken, and where, to reverse unsustainable trends. Although resource-intensive lifestyles are spreading across the globe, OECD Member countries remain the principal consumers of the world's natural resources. Thus, while Principle 8 of the Rio Declaration strikes a balance between the need to *"reduce and eliminate unsustainable patterns of production and consumption and promote appropriate demographic policies"*, Agenda 21 clearly looks to the industrialised countries to lead the initiative to achieve sustainable consumption patterns.

GLOBALISATION AND SUSTAINABLE CONSUMPTION

Consumption patterns among middle- and upper-income groups across the globe appear to be converging. This is in part a consequence of globalisation – the process through which the structure of economic markets, technologies, and communication patterns becomes progressively more complex and more international over time. OECD's recent work on economic globalisation and the environment[1] identifies a series of general trends in the links between globalisation and environmental quality of relevance to sustainable consumption and production. In terms of *production patterns*, three trends are discernible in OECD countries: *i)* a movement away from environmentally-intensive outputs and/or factors of production – services now account for an increasing share of GDP (in contrast, some developing countries are experiencing a shift from agriculture to heavy industry); *ii)* a certain "dematerialisation" of economic activity through the reduced use of some environmental resources per unit of GDP; and, *iii)* falling levels of pollution per unit of GDP.

Although these trends are likely to be reinforced by the process of globalisation, the full picture may not be as positive. The negative *scale* effects of globalisation (*e.g.* the overall environmental impact from the expansion of world economic output) may turn out to be very large, effectively swamping any positive technological and/or structural effects. Despite encouraging reductions in the *average* intensities of pollution loads and resource usage, the *total* burden on the environment may therefore be higher in a more globalised economy than it is today. In addition, the trends towards depollution and dematerialisation are being observed primarily in the industrialised countries, and not as yet in many developing countries (particularly in the rapidly developing countries).

In terms of global *consumption* patterns, the deepening and widening of market structures as part of the globalisation process may lead to more uniform consumer tastes, influenced by transnational mass media imagery and advertising. Improvements in transportation and communication systems may also encourage some suppliers to locate their activities further away from their consumers.

The work on globalisation prompts a number of additional questions in relation to trends in *consumption patterns*, in particular:

a) Will globalisation be accompanied by a parallel "globalisation" of environmental protection and quality considerations related to products?

b) Consumer tastes, at least among middle- and upper-income groups, appear to be becoming more uniform globally. What shape will this "global consumption" take in the future?

c) How will the components of consumption change as improvements in transportation and communications allow any individual market to be supplied by producers from across the globe?

d) What impact will globalisation have on wealth generation and distribution, and how will these factors influence consumption and production trends?

e) What would globalisation imply for calculating the "ecological footprints" of consumption patterns?

A common theme in much of the international work on sustainable consumption and production has been the recognition and mapping out of the range of links between trade, technology and lifestyles across the globe.[2] The links between changing consumption patterns in the industrialised world and potential impacts on developing countries have been of particular interest.

Since Rio, there have been important shifts in thinking in both industrialised and developing countries, which have reduced the geopolitical tension that emanated from the *consumption versus population* debates of the preceding two decades. In the industrialised world, a growing number of countries have acknowledged that rethinking ways in which environmental resources are utilised to meet human needs is both a moral obligation and in their enlightened self-interest. In the developing world, the widespread adoption of export-led development strategies has lessened the earlier pressure by developing country governments for changes in industrialised country consumption patterns to provide the global "environmental space" in which they can grow. A new caution has emerged, based on fears that a cleaner and more efficient pattern of consumption in OECD countries could either depress demand for exports of energy, industrial raw materials, and agricultural commodities, and/or lead to the raising of "green protectionist" trade barriers to developing country exports through ever-more demanding consumer preferences and regulatory requirements. At the same time, although a large proportion of developing countries are still struggling to meet basic needs, rapid economic growth and trade liberalisation in several Asian, Latin American and African countries is leading to a "consumption explosion" among higher-income groups.

These policy shifts and global trends suggest that, over the next quarter of a century, the tensions and policy challenges stemming from the sustainable consumption agenda are increasingly likely to straddle "North" and "South", and to deal with issues common to both. While the burden of reform lies first and foremost with the industrialised countries, achieving more sustainable patterns of consumption will become less and less exclusively the responsibility of these countries. At the same time, while the goals, driving forces, and range of economic sectors and actors involved in patterns of consumption are generally constant, the consumption patterns themselves and their environmental implications vary widely both between and within countries in the OECD and the non-member Economies (NMEs).

Increasing globalisation and ''linkage-intensive'' development imply at least three areas of focus important to achieving sustainable consumption globally:

a) *The Geopolitical Dimension:* Although there has been a lessening of the geopolitical confrontation since Rio, visible, concerted efforts by the industrialised countries to improve the sustainability of their consumption patterns remain critical to maintaining a constructive and progressive dialogue and to stimulating change in both OECD countries and NMEs.

b) *Consumption ''Footprints'':* Globalisation has prompted growing attention to the environmental and resource content of trade between nations, and the ''ecological footprints'' over the planet left by the consumption and production patterns in OECD countries. Rapid growth in some developing countries is also generating concern about the environmental consequences of increasing the flow of resources to these countries. The range of issues relating to the environment and resource content of trade must be examined (through environmental indicators, green national income accounting) for any comprehensive picture of the sustainability of consumption patterns to be drawn.

c) *Consumption Patterns:* With sales of consumer goods rising by 10-20 per cent in fast-growing NMEs, there is an increasing convergence, particularly for middle- and upper-income groups, towards the consumption levels and patterns in OECD countries. In the process, the traditional ''North-South'' consumption divide is blurring: globalisation appears to be producing ''a collection of highly segmented clusters of consumers sharing a common lifestyle despite being separated by great distances''. This convergence suggests not only the need for heightened attention to the transboundary and global environmental impacts caused by consumption patterns in both OECD and non-member Economies, but also that there are ample opportunities for collaborative efforts to identify effective policy instruments and measures and scope for common action.

RESPONDING TO RIO: THE OECD APPROACH

Within this global context, and in response to the issues raised in Rio, OECD Ministers decided in June 1993 to ask the OECD Secretariat to examine the relationship between consumption and production patterns and sustainable development. The willingness of OECD countries to confront the challenge of changing consumption and production was a product of several converging factors:

• the emerging long-term perspective for analysis and planning demanded by the sustainable development model;

• the continued growth of environmental problems – and associated risks to human health and natural ecosystems – despite heavy investments by OECD nations in counter measures over the past three decades; and

• the recognition of many positive trends (*e.g.* the decoupling of economic growth from energy demand in certain countries, the continuing move to closed-cycle industrial processes, and growing consumer support for recycling, eco-labelling and other ''environmental'' initiatives), which suggested that commitments and new strategies to induce major changes in consumption and production patterns could be pursued successfully.

The OECD has focused its analysis on *consumption issues and demand-side management,* since substantial progress has already been made in OECD countries to control and reduce the environmental impacts of *production* processes. This also reflects the trend in both public policy and corporate strategy to develop a more integrated approach to environmental management – one that seeks to reduce environmental impacts throughout the life-cycle of goods and services. Many of the initiatives examined in the OECD's work are relatively recent or are in the early phase of design or implementation. Nevertheless, some trends are emerging in both the approaches already taken, or those seen to be necessary, to address unsustainable consumption and production patterns. The following paragraphs provide an overview of some of the key issues which have emerged to date.

FRAMING THE PROBLEM: ASSESSING CONSUMPTION PATTERNS

The sustainable consumption agenda implies some notion of environmental limits within which consumption can take place – although this ''carrying capacity'' is usually difficult to define at the level(s) at which consumption patterns have an impact. This has created the need to talk about a trajectory towards ''more sustainability'' rather than some absolute end-point.

Similarly, the discussion of ''consumption patterns'' has tended to remain at a relatively superficial level, in part because ''consumption'' is in many ways like non-point source pollution, but also because it is difficult to piece together in a comprehensible framework all the influences which shape what and how societies consume. There is, as a result, only a limited concrete basis for government efforts to refine their policies to change environmentally damaging consumption patterns. *Better knowledge* of present consumption patterns is needed to develop effective policies to influence them.

Case Study 1.   **Strategies to Promote a Sustainable Paper Cycle**[3]

Global paper consumption has increased by a factor of twenty this century, and by a factor of three in the past three decades alone. Average per capita consumption varies widely internationally – ranging from 333 kg/person in the US, to 160 kg/person in Western Europe and 12 kg/person on average in the developing world. The cycle of paper production and consumption illustrates the importance of a life-cycle analysis for identifying the most important points of leverage for improving the sustainability of consumption patterns. Thus, although the generation of waste associated with short-lived paper products is of concern, the most critical environmental impacts are not in fact within the control of final consumers, but occur higher in the production and use chain – in forest management, pulp and paper production, and the intermediate use of paper for packaging. There is now the beginning of an evolution in government policy away from a focus on promoting recycled paper, to a more comprehensive life-cycle-based approach, including product standards and extended producer responsibility.

Although the upstream environmental impacts in the paper cycle are the most critical, there is nevertheless significant room for reducing *end-use* inefficiencies. Examples of efforts to improve the efficiency of paper consumption highlight some key messages:

  a) there is no "science" of how materials such as paper are actually used, and consequently little understanding of what happens after a product is made and before it is disposed of;

  b) traditional approaches to changing paper consumption have tended to stress recycling to the exclusion of efforts to improve efficiency;

  c) the primary driving forces for efficiency innovations for paper as an intermediate input (*e.g.* for packaging) are market competition, cost control, and, increasingly, environmental concerns; and

  d) innovations are needed in both technology and social behaviour to modify the way paper is produced and used.

There are, of course, examples where consumption patterns are well understood. Environmental quality standards and water delivery and treatment costs have forced industries in many countries to carefully examine how they use water in their production processes. In contrast, however, government agencies rarely measure their water consumption or evaluate their use patterns or total consumption. Similarly, in the case of paper, there is no ''science of material use'', which seeks to clearly understand how paper products, for instance in office settings, are used between the time they are delivered and when they end up in recycling facilities, landfills or incinerators. For certain culturally significant goods – those which having access to or not has the power to change lifestyles – like water, telecommunications or the car – *understanding the full range of primary and secondary uses* which those goods serve is critical. The level(s) at which this analysis takes place will vary with the scope of the problem and the required response: international (climate, biodiversity); regional (water resources; transport); or local (transport, water, and wherever local behaviour leads to local effects).

Developing effective and efficient policies to encourage behaviour change requires a better understanding of the various facets of consumption patterns, and their environmental impacts, in order to pinpoint: 1) where consumption patterns are susceptible to change; 2) where in the product life-cycle is the best point, or points, of intervention; and 3) which actors in the network, including government, are likely to be the most effective agents of change. (See *Case Study 1: Strategies to Promote a Sustainable Paper Cycle*).

SETTING GOALS

From an environmental point of view, the broad objective of policies for sustainable consumption and production is to bring consumption patterns, primarily in the industrialised countries (but increasingly in developing nations as well), into line with the environment's carrying capacity. Working as they must with loose definitions and important uncertainties regarding the earth's limits, governments have concentrated on reducing the visible stress points, primarily focusing on the production side of the consumption-production equation.

The consumption element, however, introduces a new and more difficult dynamic – one which opens up a different, interlinking set of problems and considerations which governments are less experienced in addressing. This may explain much of the enthusiasm with which the concept of ''eco-efficiency'' has been embraced as a potential guiding framework for policies to achieve more sustainable consumption patterns. However, neither eco-efficiency nor eco-space (which, although a useful concept for highlighting the social equity dimensions of consumption patterns, cannot be practically implemented) is the vision, or the end-point, for the sustainable consumption agenda. Although a number of concepts have been advanced to effect changes in levels and patterns of consumption and production (See Table 1), *a framework and set of goals has not yet been defined* by governments to comprehensively address consumption issues and to evaluate potential policy responses.

Defining a set of goals for sustainable consumption and production implies the construction of a wider vision of welfare in which the satisfaction of needs, rather than consumption *per se,* is the aim. It also implies clarifying the environmental, social and economic indicators of what is considered ''more sustainable''. Governments have an important responsibility in *stimulating public debate* on these issues.

Table 1.   **Sustainable Consumption and Production – Key Concepts**[a]

Carrying Capacity	A quantitative concept that assumes limits, though often difficult to define, to the capacity of natural ecosystems to support continued growth in resource consumption and pollution. Key factors include population numbers and density, affluence and technology (including the ability to "expand" carrying capacity). Concerns focus on depletion rates of renewable and non-renewable resources and the build-up of hazardous wastes in the environment.
Steady State Economy	A concept based on the premise that the human economy is "an open sub-system of the earth ecosystem, which is finite, non-growing and materially closed". The steady state economy is thus a non-growth economy in biophysical equilibrium, where *a) stocks* are maintained at a level sufficient for an abundant life for the present generation and ecologically sustainable for a long (but not indefinite) future; *b) service* is maximised given the constant stock; and *c) throughput* is minimised.
Ecospace	A concept based on quantitative limits (carrying capacity and critical loads) set on the basis of scientific analysis and political evaluation of the risks associated with exceeding such limits. Some proponents add a resource distribution component, which suggests allocated ecospace at a national, regional or per capita level (global "fair shares").
Ecological Footprints/ Ecological Rucksacks	Measures of consumption which estimate the natural capital requirements of an economy, based on an interpretation of carrying capacity that takes into account the impacts of technological development and trade. As wealth and consumption levels increase, so do the area of productive land (EF) and throughput of material (ER) required to support every individual. A key assumption is that technology and trade do not expand the earth's carrying capacity in the long-term, only displace geographically the effects of increased consumption levels.
Natural Resource Accounting/ Green GDP	Natural resource accounting is seen as a tool to demonstrate linkages between the environment and the economy to correct distortions in standard measures of national "growth" and "welfare". Green GDP measures are based on quantitative indicators of national performance based on data relating to the availability and use of natural and environmental resources (stocks and flows) and incorporating qualitative judgements as to what constitutes economic, environmental and, sometimes, social welfare.
Eco-Efficiency	A management strategy based on quantitative input-output measures which seeks to maximise the productivity of energy and material inputs in order to reduce resource consumption and pollution/waste per unit output, and to generate cost savings and competitive advantage. Eco-efficiency is also seen by some as a framework for redirecting the goals and assumptions driving corporate, and potentially government and household, behaviour.

a) Drawn from *Final Report: OECD Workshop on Sustainable Consumption and Production: Clarifying the Concepts,* OECD *Proceedings Series,* (forthcoming, 1997).

CONSIDERING LIFESTYLES

The growing importance being attached to sustainable consumption and production is perhaps in part a recognition by governments that sustainable development demands a strategic and long-term approach which attempts to tackle and reform the underlying causes of environmental damage. Spurred by successes in reducing the impacts of production processes, there is a greater willingness to begin to look at how the more difficult question of consumption can be addressed. This is evident in the willingness to begin to re-examine some formerly "taboo" consumption patterns and lifestyles: in some areas, governments are shifting away from an objective of stretching resources to meet ever increasing demand towards a strategy of drawing demand into line with available supply. Water is an example: although water has a long history as a social good, it is increasingly recognised that water-intensive consumption and production is not a social right. Similarly, but to a much lesser degree, there are signs of a growing willingness to question whether private motorised transport is essential for a satisfactory quality of life.

Although it is challenging to tread into the territory of lifestyles and "welfare" – as discussions about consumption patterns inevitably do – policy-makers probably have more room for action than they currently believe. A growing body of expertise indicates that "needs" and lifestyles (and thus relative perceptions of welfare) evolve in response to a variety of influences. They are as much a function of habit and circumstance as of any underlying values fundamentally linked to a sense of well-being. This suggests that *policies to change consumption patterns can start with practical measures* to bring about changes in habits and real and perceived options to change consumption behaviour, without attempting to influence deeply held values. It will also be important for such policies to stress the *positive* aspects of change.

INFLUENCING THE DRIVING FORCES

A network of actors and influences shape consumption patterns: a short list includes elements such as the price of goods and services, stock of physical infrastructure (*e.g.* for housing, energy, transportation and waste management), individual and firm time budgets and activity patterns, and lifestyle choices. The layering of influences and interconnections in these networks highlights critical considerations for government policy to effect change. (See also *Case Study 2: Total Water Cycle Management*):

a) Attention must be placed on *defining the critical points in the lifecycle of a product or service* where the greatest leverage can be exerted over: *i)* environmental impacts, or *ii)* consumption behaviour. For some goods, such as paper, private individual consumers may not be the most effective point of change because the environmental impact of their combined actions is relatively small. For others, such as transport, individual "consumers" are a valid point of focus, but actions targeted at changing their behaviour must also be combined with *action to change the context* within which individual consumption decisions are made.

b) The existing pattern of land-use planning and infrastructure provision can have a major impact on the current range of options open to individual consumers to modify their consumption patterns. For example, land-use patterns affecting the location of residential areas, commercial zones, and workplaces, and past investment in different modes of transport infrastructure (*e.g.* roads, rail, walking/cycling paths) have created conditions in parts of many OECD countries where the private car is the only viable option for short-distance mobility. Similarly, past investments in water supply and waste-water treatment facilities and land-use planning decisions concerning zoning of land for industrial or agricultural use have significantly affected water consumption patterns in many countries. Land-use planning policies and patterns of infrastructure investment present perhaps two of the most challenging issues to be addressed in order to significantly shift the underlying potential for more sustainable consumption and production patterns. This is due to both the constraints which past decisions impose on efforts to shift current behaviour, and the crucial importance of new policies in these areas for shaping consumption and production patterns in the future.

c) Government actions must be designed to address the wide set of factors which influence consumption patterns. Although using economic instruments to ensure that prices of goods and services consumed fully reflect their true environmental costs remains fundamental to changing consumption patterns, price is only one variable influencing those patterns, and in some cases may not be the most important. It is critical in many cases, such as water, to overcome the political and institutional hurdles to full-cost pricing, but it is likely to take more than just sharper economic instruments to get the average commuter seriously to consider an alternative to the car. Similarly, *information and awareness-raising campaigns not only need to be better targeted, but must also be linked to opportunities to put new information to use.* Governments can also improve their dialogue with the public by drawing on expertise from a wider range of disciplines (particularly the non-economic social sciences), as well as on private sector expertise in marketing and advertising.

d) The growing trend for central government to seek *partnerships* with other actors – private sector, local governments, NGOs, communities, – is likely to be even more fruitful for influencing *consumption* patterns than it already has been for finding innovative solutions to the environmental impacts of *production*. The high priority now attached to the consumption issue by leaders in business (for instance in the World Business Council for Sustainable Development (WBCSD), as well as by local authorities and NGOs), is thus an encouraging sign that governments are likely to find willing partners to tackle the issue with them.

Case Study 2.   **Total Water Cycle Management**[4]

Countries are increasingly recognising, and acting on, the need to influence the network of economic, technological, institutional, and social influences which shape water consumption patterns. A better understanding of the network of factors influencing consumption patterns is essential to policies to modify consumption behaviour. Underpinning this development is the concept of *total water cycle management,* which considers both production and demand side pressures, and has the multiple objectives to: minimise waste; maximise the efficiency of water use; maximise water availability by limiting degradation of water supplies, and through re-use; optimise water allocation to competing users; and limit access to sustainable levels. The optimal allocation of water resources requires full recognition of the environment as a "user", and the ability to identify the minimum water requirements to support ecological systems.

The mix of government policies and instruments to promote sustainable water resources management will vary between countries and will depend on the social, economic and technological status of the country as well as the specific end-use patterns in question. There are nevertheless some common imperatives. Strategies to implement integrated water cycle management must include an improved *information base* on available water resources, environmental pressures, and present and future demand and more appropriate *institutional structures,* functions and responsibilities(including allocation policies and mechanisms). Greater involvement of *water users,* including private sector firms and communities, is another critical element and requires explicit mechanisms to promote user "ownership" of water issues, and involvement and responsibility in water policy planning and implementation (*e.g.* partnerships in setting objectives and joint implementation).

Equally important, total water cycle management requires *appropriate water pricing regimes* that over time reflect the full costs of supplying water, preserving water quality and maintaining the resource base. The exact structure of water pricing regimes will vary according to the capital, operating, environmental and social costs of supplying water in each region, but a first area of focus in most countries is the removal of direct and indirect subsidies to water. In the transition to full-cost pricing, adequate provision will have to be made in many countries to guarantee that water requirements for basic needs are met in low-income groups. There is also a need to employ mechanisms to promote a faster and wider diffusion of already available water efficient *technologies* in the industrial, agricultural and commercial/residential sectors. This will include identifying economic, technical and social barriers to the uptake of technology.

Finally, more effective *social instruments* are required to modify user behaviour in order to increase efficiency and to conserve water. Education, information, and partnership strategies are needed which foster user ownership and responsibility in water resources management *and* allow users to put new information to use, such as: institutional arrangements providing for user involvement in water policy planning and implementation; information on, and demonstration of, more efficient water delivery technologies; and, metering to give households direct feedback on their water consumption.

REACHING THE INDIVIDUAL CONSUMER

One of the biggest challenges for central government is providing policy direction which has the intent of influencing individual consumers. Informed and empowered consumers, however, can be a major driving force behind less environmentally stressful patterns of consumption and production. A central message is developing from the results of OECD work in this area: there are merits in *decentralising problem analysis and the development of responses* to the regional and/or local level wherever the environmental impacts of consumption patterns are likely to be most felt at those levels. A number of examples have been identified of local or regional level initiatives which have been successful at drawing individual consumers and communities into the planning process to find innovative solutions to consumption-related problems (*e.g.* the US ISTEA framework for community participation in transport planning; the Central Scotland ''All Change!'' process of intensive community consultation which has led to a radical change in transport spending; and involvement of water user associations in water resources management in France).

Similarly, a growing number of non-governmental initiatives aimed directly at changing household consumption patterns are showing encouraging results, such as the Global Action Plan's work on household electricity and water consumption, waste production, transportation, and goods and services consumption, and the work by *Social Data* in Germany to change household travel behaviour. A key reason for the success of these efforts appears to be that they help individuals perceive new options *and* give them the opportunity and encouragement to try them out. A striking feature of both initiatives mentioned is their *low-cost* and *simplicity*. Questions remain about whether the behaviour change resulting from initiatives of this type is enough to affect environmental outcomes, and whether the behaviour change is sustained: simple steps, however, appear to count. In the light of the direct impact they have on the individual consumer, not only in changing specific consumption habits, but also in widening the individual's perception of his impact on the quality of his community's environment, more needs to be known about *how local and even central governments can support these efforts.*

MACRO-MICRO CONNECTIONS

The discussion of sustainable consumption and production puts a particular focus on the economic system as a whole, and on the need to take a systems view of both the microeconomic influences on firms and households, as well as the macroeconomic influences on the structure of the economy. Changes in consumption patterns will inevitably influence the structure and/or volume of demand through price and substitution effects. Such potential macro-economic effects need to be analysed. Other links, *e.g.* between investment, sector activities and structural changes, infrastructure, land-use patterns, and technological change should also be investigated.

Structural changes will be facilitated by the use of economic instruments and ''green tax reforms'', in particular removing existing distortionary taxes and subsidies and shifting the tax burden *e.g.* away from labour and capital to the consumption of polluting goods and activities. Although the body of evidence on the effectiveness of these tax reforms is still limited, experience in a few OECD countries is beginning to show that these strategies can be effective and efficient means of improving environmental protection and improving economic efficiency by reducing distortions in the economy.[5]

Nevertheless, the majority of OECD countries have been more conservative in their application of economic instruments and there are still significant economic and political barriers to implementing a wider macro-economic approach which could bring about a broad-based change in consumer behaviour. Further analysis is needed to identify both market and government failures which result in ''overconsumption'' of certain natural resources or particular goods and services and where corrective measures need to be taken.

THE ROLE OF GOVERNMENT

Continuing efforts are needed to document and analyse the growing number of initiatives in both OECD and non-OECD countries to modify unsustainable patterns of consumption and production, and to clarify the implications of such policies, particularly their impacts on consumer welfare, employment and competitiveness. There is also a clear need to identify where the existing array of policy tools (*e.g.* subsidy removal, green tax reform, voluntary agreements, product policies, education and information, land-use planning, investment, incentives to innovation, and technology policy) could be strengthened, or new measures designed, to address consumption and production patterns identified as unsustainable. Government leadership, not least through actions to ''green'' their own consumption patterns, is an essential factor for encouraging change by other economic actors. (See also *Case Study 3: Government as a Consumer: Leading by Example*).

Priorities for government policy development include:

- Sharpening the understanding of essential issues in the ''sustainable consumption and production'' debate, including the related concepts of ''eco-efficiency'' and ''dematerialisation'', and analysing their potential to provide a more meaningful frame of reference for governments, the private sector and households.
- Generating a wider debate in society on sustainable consumption and production and its implications for broader societal objectives, economic development and social progress. A spectrum of environmental, economic, and social issues are likely to be affected by changes in consumption patterns. Thus, systematic mechanisms are needed to promote active participation and dialogue amongst the multiple stakeholders within nations (governments, industry, labour, local communities, NGOs), as well as amongst OECD and non-OECD countries.

Case Study 3.   **Government as a Consumer – Leading by Example**[6]

In several OECD countries, the government is the single largest consumer of goods and services, accounting for approximately 20-25 per cent of GDP. This underlines the government's potential impact on the environment, whether positive or negative. In 1996, OECD Environment Ministers agreed on a Council Recommendation on *Improving the Environmental Performance of Government,*[7] to spur governments to reduce the environmental impacts of their own operations and to improve their decision-making processes.

Progress has been made through numerous "greening" initiatives. Advances have been made in a majority of OECD countries, for instance, to green government procurement polices, and a number of countries have set quantitative targets, in areas such as reducing energy and water consumption, and waste generation. More tentative efforts have been made in applying environmental management systems in government-owned or -operated facilities. OECD Member countries have also instituted a variety of mechanisms to improve the integration of environmental considerations in government *decision-making processes.* These mechanisms are designed to help spread the responsibility for environmental "stewardship" across the government. Regional and local governments are active on environmental issues related to their own administrations – and in many cases are more progressive than the central government. Activity at the local level in some countries is linked to "Local Agenda 21s", and involves close collaboration with, and motivation from, the local community. Central government can facilitate action at the regional and local level, including through mechanisms to reduce set-up costs for "greening" initiatives, financial assistance, information exchange, and by transmitting best practices.

The OECD will also host an Internet site[8] to facilitate information exchange between countries on actions to improve government environmental performance. Originally created by the Canadian Government, the site is being restructured to reflect the major elements of the OECD Council Recommendation, and will be located on the OECD Internet Homepage in mid-1997, at: [*http://www.oecd.org/env/*].

- Identifying more clearly the most effective mix of policy instruments for particular sectors or issues. In some fields (*e.g.* water resources management), the steps needed to address unsustainable patterns have already been clearly outlined (*e.g.* full-cost pricing; institutional reform; allocation policies; public information and participation). In such cases, more emphasis needs to be given to the design of effective transitional arrangements to smooth the shift to new patterns.

THE WAY FORWARD

The international community has made important progress in the debate on sustainable consumption and production since Rio; and, as noted earlier, the ongoing dialogue at the international, regional and bilateral levels is today more constructive and forward-looking. One of the benefits has been the spread of a common vocabulary and set of reference points between OECD and non-OECD countries. This dialogue needs to continue, with an emphasis on identifying and analysing consumption and production trends of common concern, as well as the international implications of changing consumption and production patterns, for instance in the area of trade.

OECD countries need to remain committed to addressing the call in Agenda 21 to reduce the pressures of industrialisation and consumerism on the world environment and to share their experience and policy tools with others. There is a tremendous scope for international co-operation to move forward in this area through the sharing of best practices, technology diffusion, and parallel implementation of a number of different strategies. The OECD will continue to play an active supporting role in this process, by deepening its analysis of the policy measures needed to promote more sustainable consumption and production patterns, by monitoring Member country progress, and by contributing to further exploration of the global dimensions of change.

NOTES

1. (OECD, 1997), *Economic Globalisation and the Environment.*

2. See Robins and Roberts, *"Linkages II and Sustainable Consumption Patterns", IIED,* (Draft of September 1996) – an input to the OECD reports *Globalisation and Linkages to 2020: Challenges and Opportunities for OECD Countries ("Linkages II"),* (OECD, forthcoming, 1997) and *Towards a New Global Age: Challenges and Opportunities.*

3. Thise example is developed from material in: Robins and Roberts, *Rethinking Paper Consumption,* Discussion Paper, (IIED, September 1996) and Robins and Roberts, *Rethinking Paper Consumption: Report of the Oslo Workshop* (OECD, General Distribution Document, forthcoming).

4. *Report from the OECD Experts Workshop on Sustainable Water Consumption,* (OECD, forthcoming, 1997).

5. OECD (1997), *Environmental Taxes and Green Tax Reform.*

6. Project documents include, *Final Report: OECD Meeting on Improving the Environmental Performance of Government,* (OECD, forthcoming 1997).

7. C(96)39/Final. An OECD Council Recommendation is not a binding legal instrument, but represents a policy commitment by the governments of Member countries.

8. The site is presently at **http://www.globalx.net/envcan/index.html**. The address leads to a dialogue box. Type (Username): **envcan** [tab]**Note: Do not use return**, then (Password): **green**. This procedure brings you to a general information page. Click on the **Français** or **English** buttons to move on to the matrix. Click on any subject area for Canada to see additional information. You can also access the matrix page directly by using the adress: **http://www.globalx.net/envcan/qx.html.**

BIBLIOGRAPHY

Environmental Resources Management Ltd, Eco-Efficiency in the Transport Sector: Applying the Concept to Public Policy and Individual Travel, Report for the OECD Programme on Sustainable Consumption and Production (Environmental Resources Management Ltd., July 1996).

Factor 10 Club, *The Carnoules Declaration* (Wuppertal Institute, 1994).

OECD (1995), *OECD/MIT Experts Seminar on Sustainable Consumption and Production Patterns* (OECD, ENV/EPOC/RD(95)6).

OECD (1996*a*), *Meeting of OECD Environment Policy Committee at Ministerial Level: Communiqué* (SG/COM/NEWS(96)15).

OECD (1996*b*), *Implementation Strategies for Environmental Taxes.*

OECD (1996*c*), *Workshop on Individual Travel Behaviour: "Values, Welfare, and Quality of Life"* (OECD/GD(96)199).

OECD (1997*a*), *Workshop on Individual Travel Behaviour: "Culture, Choice and Technology"* (OECD/GD(97)1).

OECD (1997*b*), *Environmental Taxes and Green Tax Reform.*

OECD (1997*c*), *Improving the Environmental Performance of Government* (General Distribution document).

OECD (1997*d*), *Literature Review on Individual Travel Behaviour* (General Distribution document).

OECD (1997*e*), *Workshop on Sustainable Consumption and Production: Clarifying the Concepts.*

OECD (1997*f*), *Economic Globalisation and the Environment.*

OECD (1997*g*), *Report of the OECD Expert Workshop on Sustainable Water Consumption,* (General Distribution document).

OECD (1997*h*), *Report of the OECD Meeting on Sustainable Consumption and Individual Travel Behaviour* (General Distribution document).

OECD (1997*i*), *Rethinking Paper Consumption: Report of the Oslo Workshop* (General Distribution document).

UNEP, *Global Environment Outlook* (1997).

Norwegian Ministry of Environment, *Report of the Symposium on Sustainable Consumption* (Norwegian Ministry of Environment, 1994).

Robins, N. and Roberts, S., "*Linkages II and Sustainable Consumption Patterns*" (IIED, Draft of September 1996).

Robins, N. and Roberts, S., *Rethinking Paper Consumption, Discussion Paper* (IIED, September 1996).

World Resources Institute, *World Resources: 1996-1997* (World Resources Institute, 1996).

Chapter 5

AID AGENCIES: CHANGING TO MEET THE REQUIREMENTS OF RIO

by

Bettina Söderbaum

OECD aid agencies, in the years since 1992 and the UN Conference on Environment and Development (UNCED), have risen strongly to the challenge of Agenda 21. Sustainable development has been incorporated as a guiding principle, and environment firmly established as an integral part of overall agency priorities. Much of this has been achieved through the use of innovative measures. Many agencies have also turned their energies outwards and contributed significantly to the international debate on environment and development in the wake of UNCED. Coupled with this has been a steady commitment to funding for the environment. These and other trends have recently been confirmed in a study entitled *Survey of DAC Members' Activities in Support of Environmental Goals*, undertaken during 1995 and 1996 by the OECD Development Assistance Committee (DAC) through its Working Party on Development Assistance and Environment.

OECD WORK ON DEVELOPMENT AND ENVIRONMENT SINCE RIO

Work on development and environment in the DAC had begun in earnest as far back as 1989. In the wake of the call for common action from the Brundtland Commission, the DAC established a Working Party to look at environmental issues from the particular perspective of development co-operation. In the lead-up to Rio, the Working Party was already helping to shape the policies that were ultimately spelt out in the messages of Agenda 21. The group then launched into the challenges of the post-Rio period with a mandate to ensure that aid policies and programmes engaged sound environmental management as a key contribution to sustainable development.

The period since has seen a common effort on the part of DAC Members to support each other in addressing the many and complex challenges of sustainable development. The major bilateral aid donors, using the DAC as a forum, have met regularly over the past five years to discuss the linkages between aid and environment. Drawing on the strength of collective action, they have addressed many of the frontier issues raised by Agenda 21, and in many cases broken entirely new ground in turning concept into practice. Pioneering work, for example, has been undertaken on environmental assessment, technology co-operation, trade, environment and development co-operation, and capacity development in environment. The debate has also been expanded to include multilateral organisations, international NGOs, and most importantly, developing countries themselves, providing a powerful conduit for interchange of ideas, good practices, and coherence of approaches.

A process of consensus-building has emerged that has in turn produced many practical and authoritative tools on aid and environment, aimed at both policy-makers and practitioners. An example of this is the series of nine *DAC Guidelines on Aid and Environment*, released between 1992 and 1996, which address the practical as well as policy aspects of a variety of environment/development topics, in a format designed for the non-specialist.

DAC Members' demonstrated willingness to collectively address internationally agreed goals has become even more significant in the light of new strategic targets adopted by DAC Development Ministers during 1996 in *Shaping the 21st Century: The Contribution of Development Co-operation* (see Chapter 2). Based on a model of development that is people-centred, participatory and locally owned, the *21st Century* document sets targets for environmental sustainability that call for national strategies for sustainable development to be in place by 2005, so as to ensure that current trends in the loss of environmental resources – forests, fisheries, fresh water, climate, soils, biodiversity, strato-spheric ozone, the accumulation of hazardous substances and other major indicators – are effectively reversed at both global and national levels by 2015.

Much of the work already done, and much that is slated for the future, for example on national plans for sustainable development, on indicators, on cleaner production technologies, and on the building of local capacities in environment, will directly contribute to maintaining the momentum of such internationally endorsed strategies as Agenda 21 and the *21st Century* vision. In addition, DAC Members are constantly vigilant to see that newly emerging politically crucial issues are identified at an early stage. An example of this can be seen in discussions launched in autumn 1996 on environmental security and displacement – an issue which has only recently begun to be recognised as a serious development problem at the dawn of the new century.

SUSTAINABLE DEVELOPMENT: FROM CONCEPT TO PRACTICE

The *Survey of DAC Members' Activities in Support of Environmental Goals* was a stocktaking exercise by the DAC, as part of its mandated commitment to monitor progress in the wake of UNCED. This snapshot in time of the 22 DAC Members showed them all to have vigorously engaged the guiding principles of UNCED, with the great majority of the aid agencies surveyed having integrated environment as part of their overall priorities.

The DAC study revealed that a number of factors were instrumental in this increased priority for environment. Chief among these was a strong commitment by policymakers, which outshines every-thing else in promoting effective integration of environmental goals. Other factors include increased public pressure; the influence of UNCED and its aftermath; a growing sense of urgency in developing countries about the need to address environmental considerations; and increasing scientific evidence concerning the seriousness of global environmental problems.

The report also identified a number of major trends which point to increased attention to environ-ment in OECD aid agencies: growing agency-wide environmental awareness; steady commitment to funding for environmental issues; growing institutionalisation of environmental expertise; and efforts to develop new instruments and procedures and to improve existing ones. Most agencies are also giving greater attention to the evaluation of defined environmental goals.

A clear relationship exists between the size of aid programmes and agencies and the extent of integration of environment in their development assistance programmes. In general, countries with large and medium-sized aid programmes have made the most progress. Countries with medium-sized aid programmes have contributed most to the development of innovative instruments and have also significantly shaped the debate on sustainable development and the integration of environment and development. Scarcity of resources, coupled with a weak capacity for policy formulation, has made it more difficult in general for countries with smaller programmes to develop a comprehensive approach to the integration of environment and development. However, in some countries with smaller programmes, political commitment has proven instrumental in overcoming these limitations. Two examples of this are Ireland and New Zealand which have been able to show substantial and innovative efforts in the integration of environmental goals.

An important evolution in DAC aid agencies has been the adoption of sustainable development as a guiding principle. This has worked well at policy level, but putting the concept into operation has frequently proven difficult. One of the main constraints is that the linkages between the environment and other dimensions of sustainable development are not sufficiently understood in the context of agency operations. Another is a lack of appropriate development programming instruments, especially at policy and programme level. Sectoral thinking in both developed and developing countries does not help either.

Interestingly, greater success in internalising sustainable development principles is evident at the country and project level. The sectoral approach has not disappeared altogether, but the way in which sectors are defined has changed and there are more cross-sectoral and multidisciplinary approaches. Examples include integrated water management and integrated land use programmes and projects. New themes, such as urban and industrial environment, and coastal zone management, have also emerged.

As a consequence of UNCED, OECD Members have given high priority to drawing up their own national strategies for sustainable development. Development co-operation issues have also been addressed in these strategies, albeit for the most part rather marginally. Australia, Denmark, Canada, Sweden and Switzerland are exceptions, and have formulated separate response strategies for their development assistance programmes. Many agencies have also assessed their programmes for compatibility with the principles of Agenda 21, although this has not entailed any critical review of the programmes themselves.

Almost all OECD countries have signed and ratified the three global environmental conventions on biodiversity, climate change and desertification. However, in bilateral development programming, levels of integration of global environmental issues are varied. Australia, Germany, Japan and the United States, for example, have all made major advances in integrating global environmental issues into their mainstream programming. Denmark, France and Switzerland have also commenced pilot programmes with similar objectives. Generally speaking, though, there is a need to develop additional implementation mechanisms for bilateral aid. For example, global issues are only integrated to a limited extent in environmental impact assessment (EIA) guidelines. On the other hand, a substantial number of aid agencies have reviewed programmes and developed strategies in response to the Biodiversity Convention, and there are mechanisms in place to ensure that the recently-ratified Desertification Convention will be well integrated into regular programmes. Most agencies have also established approaches in response to the Rio Forestry Principles.

INTEGRATING ENVIRONMENT IN AID PROGRAMMES

All aid agencies have an environmental unit or some form of resident environmental expertise, usually situated in a central advisory unit of the agency. The mandates of these units are wide ranging and include policy and instrument development, provision of environmental advice for both bilateral and multilateral programmes and projects, and participation in, or co-ordination of, aid agency input in global environmental issues. After several growth years, the number of staff with specific environmental expertise appears to have levelled out. The number of activities, however, continues to expand. Environmental units facing capacity problems tend to concentrate more and more on day-to-day issues, leaving less scope to invest in the development of policies or tools, or to review the environmental objectives of the agency. Capacity limitations also make it difficult to set up environment-oriented training. Judicious strategic planning and priority setting will be required in future to ensure that resources are allocated in such a way that environmental units can continue to contribute effectively to the overall policy objective of sustainable development.

Many agencies have introduced dedicated funding for environmental purposes, administered by their environmental units. Austria, Australia, Denmark, France, Germany, Norway, the Netherlands, Sweden, Switzerland, the United Kingdom and the European Commission have all established special environmental allocations, which have been vital in supporting new instruments and approaches for integrating environmental considerations. Initial results indicate that these special funds have been successful, although for the most part they have not yet been comprehensively evaluated.

One area which merits closer attention by agencies is the extent to which environmental expertise still remains concentrated in central environmental units. The majority of donor agencies need to give greater importance to strengthening environmental expertise agency-wide, in order to boost commitment to environmental goals in other parts of the agency besides the environment unit. This will encourage increased participation in the formulation of environmental strategies, and make for consistency in their implementation. The application of environmental tools and instruments will be smoother, and better attention to environmental monitoring and evaluation will follow.

Training programmes can play a large part in improving commitment to environmental goals in geographic branches, advisory units, and among management and field staff. Canada, Switzerland and the United States are good examples of countries at the forefront of setting up comprehensive environmental training programmes, and are consequently ahead in strengthening the environmental dimension throughout their development assistance programmes. Decentralisation of staff with environmental expertise to geographic programmes and to the field level is also something which more agencies could consider.

Agencies are increasingly recognising the importance of monitoring and evaluation of environmental goals at the agency, country, and project level. Four aid agencies, in Australia, Canada, the United Kingdom and the United States, regularly review progress towards achieving environmental goals, and have set high standards in this area. Seven more, in Denmark, the European Commission, France, Germany, the Netherlands, Norway and Sweden, have undertaken *ad hoc* reviews, or are in the process of doing so. Three important lessons can be drawn from these countries' experiences with environmental policy reviews and evaluations: *i)* there must be a recurrent character to the review; *ii)* it is important that clear operational recommendations are formulated; and *iii)* established feed-back mechanisms need to be in place.

Progress has been made in developing Management Information Systems (MISs) in which environment is one of the issues included. The majority of agencies, however, have had problems in assembling conclusive information on specific levels of funding allocated to environment-related programmes and projects. As a result, it is difficult to establish trends in shifts in the composition of environmental programme and project portfolios in most aid agencies. The difficulty is often related to conceptual confusion on what constitutes an environmental project, compounded by the different statistical categories.

During the past five years, most aid agencies have devoted considerable energy to the development or refinement of procedures, instruments, and guidelines to support the integration of environmental issues in development programming. However, planning instruments and procedures are still biased in favour of an essentially project-oriented approach to development programming. This is reflected, among other things, by the relatively large emphasis placed by aid agencies on the further development of EIA, which primarily focuses on the prevention of negative impacts of development projects. This trend may diminish, however, with the new generation of environmental assessment, which is increasingly geared towards an integrated perspective.

A number of aid agencies have started developing and experimenting with new instruments, offering good prospects for shifting the emphasis from project approaches to programme and more pronounced cross-sectoral approaches. Examples include work carried out on strategic environmental assessment at the policy and programme level, tools for programming for capacity development in the environment, environmental analysis, as well as initiatives related to economic environmental analysis and sustainability indicators. In addition, some aid agencies are in the process of modifying existing instruments, such as country-level planning tools, to ensure that these will increasingly reflect the agency's sustainable development objectives.

Further evidence of the maturing of environment as a priority policy area can be seen in the growing inter-agency co-ordination in most DAC countries. Co-ordination between aid agencies and ministries of environment has improved significantly in most OECD countries. This co-operation is largely centred around policy co-ordination related to Agenda 21 follow-up, and implementation of the Global Conventions. In a number of cases it also involves follow-up participation in the development of instruments (*e.g.* EIA) and the planning and implementation of training courses. In a few countries the environment ministry is also involved at the implementation level, especially in capacity development programmes and projects.

ENVIRONMENT AS A BILATERAL CONCERN IN MULTILATERAL AND NON-GOVERNMENTAL DEVELOPMENT CO-OPERATION

Bilateral aid agencies consider multilateral channels to be an important means of implementing environmental policies. DAC Member countries have made a sustained effort to advocate greater integration of environmental considerations in the programming of multilateral institutions, through their representation at those organisations and through targeted funding mechanisms. Aid agencies view experiences gained in their own bilateral programmes as pertinent to multilateral institutions as well. At the same time, the progress made by many multilateral agencies in integrating environmental considerations, and in the development of environmental tools and instruments, has resulted in the increasing use by bilateral agencies of multilateral studies and publications on environment-related topics.

In recent years, co-ordination has intensified between aid agencies and non-governmental organisations (NGOs) involved in environment. An important contributing factor has been the acknowledgement of the potential role of environmental NGOs in the wake of UNCED and the Global Conventions, both domestically, and in developing countries. Aid agencies, while still concerned about the limited implementation capacity of NGOs in general, are nevertheless giving significant support to a number of key international NGOs active in environment and development issues. These NGOs are especially valued for their contribution to the further operationalisation of sustainable development and for their activities in networking and information sharing. However, the overall impact of NGO involvement in policy discussions, policy evaluations and the development of consolidated country positions is limited, due to their lack of familiarity with operational procedures in donor agencies, their limited organisational capacity, and in certain cases a lack of specific environmental expertise.

The increased importance accorded to the role of the private sector in development co-operation and environment has emerged as a relatively new trend in a number of DAC countries. In addition to its now firmly-established role as an implementing organisation, private sector involvement is also extending to policy discussions on issues related to environment and development co-operation. Furthermore, the growing number of technology co-operation programmes, including co-operation in environmental technology, illustrate the importance given by aid agencies to the potential role of the private sector in building up an indigenous environmental management capacity in developing countries.

Many aid agencies are making greater use of research organisations as a source of knowledge and expertise in environment and development issues. Their contribution is being sought both in the process of operationalisation of sustainable development, and in the development of innovative programme and project approaches. In most aid agencies there is, however, scope to further involve research organisations in the development of alternatives to traditional approaches to development assistance and environmental management.

BACK TO RIO

The results of the DAC study are timely, not only for aid agencies, but also for the international community, as it assesses during 1997 global progress towards achieving the goals and targets set by UNCED. Many of the findings of the Working Party's assessment exercise are relevant in this context, in looking at strengths and weaknesses in the system. The Working Party, led by a group of members committed to translating the conclusions into practical action, is currently carrying out an analysis of the study's recommendations. Outcomes could include a heightened process of *reflexion* in and among aid agencies on better operationalising the relationship between the environmental, economic, political and social dimensions of sustainable development. This process should also lead to renewed efforts by agencies to maintain vital political commitment, by keeping awareness high, at all levels, of the integral links between environment and development.

BIBLIOGRAPHY

OECD (1997), *Capacity Development in Environment: Principles in Practice.*

OECD (1996), *Capacity Development in Environment: Proceedings of a Workshop held in Rome, Italy, 4-6 December 1996.*

OECD (1996), *Reconciling Trade, Environment and Development Policies: The Role of Development Co-operation.*

OECD (1996), *Coherence in Environmental Assessment.*

OECD (1995), *Promoting Cleaner Production in Developing Countries: The Role of Development Co-operation.*

OECD (1995), *Planning for Sustainable Development: Country Experiences.*

OECD (1995), *Guidelines for Donor Assistance to Capacity Development in Environment.*

OECD (1995), *Developing Environmental Capacity: A Framework for Donor Involvement*

OECD (1993), *Economic Instruments for Environmental Management in Developing Countries.*

The *DAC Working Party on Development Assistance and Environment.* (Information Brochure)

DAC *Guidelines on Aid and Environment*:

No. 1. *Good Practices for Environmental Impact Assessment of Development Projects.*

No. 2. *Good Practices for Country Environmental Surveys and Strategies.*

No. 3. *Guidelines for Aid Agencies on Involuntary Displacement and Resettlement in Development Projects.*

No. 4. *Guidelines for Aid Agencies on Global Environmental Problems.*

No. 5. *Guidelines for Aid Agencies on Chemicals Management.*

No. 6. *Guidelines for Aid Agencies on Pest and Pesticide Management.*

No. 7. *Guidelines for Aid Agencies on Disaster Mitigation.*

No. 8. *Guidelines for Aid Agencies on Global and Regional Aspects of the Development and Protection of the Marine and Coastal Environment.*

No. 9. *Guidelines for Aid Agencies for Improved Conservation and Sustainable Use of Tropical and Sub-Tropical Wetlands*

Chapter 6

TRADE AND ENVIRONMENT IN THE OECD

by

Robert Youngman and Dale Andrew

In its work on trade and environment, the OECD has sought to contribute to the achievement of sustainable development by promoting the integration, compatibility and mutual reinforcement of trade and environment policies. Co-operative efforts involve the OECD, the United Nations Conference on Trade and Development (UNCTAD), the United Nations Environment Programme (UNEP) and the World Trade Organisation (WTO). The OECD's contributions are defined and advanced by its Joint Session of Trade and Environment Experts, which was set up in 1991.

EARLY ACCOMPLISHMENTS

History

In 1991, a General Agreement on Tariffs and Trade (GATT) panel ruled that a US law imposing a trade ban on tuna caught using methods not meeting US dolphin safety standards violated the GATT. Following the ''tuna-dolphin'' finding, trade and environment received significant public exposure, spurring an intense flurry of activity on this topic virtually overnight. This reaction was a function of public concern over the environment, which had grown in intensity throughout the 1970s and 80s, and was reflected in the strengthening of national environmental policies. Trade and environment was not, however, a new topic. As early as 1971,[1] the OECD was engaged in discussions and policy making on trade and environment.[2] At that time, some of the basic problems that would later receive much attention were explored, and important environmental principles such as the Polluter Pays Principle – the fundamental principle for the non-subsidisation of polluters – were adopted. But it was not until 1988 that the current trade and environment debate was launched.

That same year, the Swedish Delegation to the OECD proposed that the OECD Trade Committee undertake a systematic review of environment and trade policy links. The Committee began its preliminary examination of a range of trade and environment topics, culminating in a paper for the January 1991 Environment Ministers meeting. Of particular concern from the trade perspective were the effects of differing national environmental standards on trade – trade practitioners feared that differing standards could act as non-tariff barriers to trade, potentially reversing the gains already made in reducing such barriers. Other topics included trade measures to support environmental policies and to penalise ''free riders'', and trade measures involving processes and production methods. Concurrently, the OECD Environment Policy Committee began exploring the implications of trade, especially trade liberalisation, for environmental quality and policy-making. It quickly became clear to OECD trade and environmental officials that a collaborative effort within OECD on trade and environment was needed to reflect on ways of achieving an appropriate balance between securing environmental objectives and preserving the open multilateral trading system.

These initial steps generated the impetus to develop a co-operative, interdisciplinary approach to trade and environment analysis and policy formulation within the OECD. Environment Ministers called on OECD to "identify and analyse key trade-environment issues, particularly in relation to GATT principles, and to report to the OECD Ministerial Council in June 1992 with initial views on how the goals of protection of the environment and a dynamic international trading system can concurrently be achieved". Subsequently, the Environment and Trade Committees held a joint meeting where a report laying out the issues was reviewed and approved for submission to the 1991 OECD Council Ministers' meeting. With the Ministerial Council's endorsement of the report, the Joint Session of Trade and Environment Experts was born.

The Joint Session provides equal footing to each of the two policy communities. Its collaborative effort has enabled OECD to leverage the benefits of interdisciplinary expertise in both trade and environment. Moreover, the act of bringing together governmental experts on environment and those on trade has helped bridge the communication gap that often exists between different groups of government officials at the national level. The Joint Session's work has produced important results, particularly the procedural guidelines on trade and environment (1993), the methodologies for environmental and trade reviews (1994) and the report to OECD Ministers (1995).

Preliminary Results

The 1991 Joint Report on Trade and Environment identified a range of issues to be analysed by the Joint Session. Key issues included the following:

1. the effects of environmental policies on trade (focusing on identifying and analysing those environmental policies with the strongest trade effects);
2. the effects of trade policies, trade flows and trade agreements on the environment (based on sectoral case studies, again with the goal of prioritising those policies causing the most significant effects);
3. the conditions for greater compatibility or convergence (often referred to as "harmonization") of international environmental policies and standards;
4. the applicability of GATT rules and the OECD "Guiding Principles concerning the International Economic Aspects of Environmental Policies" to environment and trade concerns; and
5. developing country concerns, including the market access implications of differences between nations' environmental standards; the imposition of environmental measures through trade instruments; and international trade in clean technology.

The 1991 report also established the goal of developing guidelines on ways to protect the environment and preserve the open multilateral trading system.

In 1992, the Joint Session continued its work towards developing trade and environment guidelines, and completed studies on the environmental impact of trade in the agriculture, forestry, fisheries, endangered species, energy and transport sectors. As noted in the 1992 progress report to OECD Council Ministers, the studies suggested that the direct impact of international trade on the environment is generally small in relation to that of domestic economic activity, although the impact may be significant in cases such as certain endangered species. In the synthesis of the sectoral analyses, it was found that only a small share of environmentally-sensitive goods enters into trade; that trade is but one of many factors affecting the environment; and that trade is generally not the root cause of environmental problems, which are due to failures of the market or of government to internalise environmental costs in product prices. In the presence of such market or government failures, trade and trade liberalisation can generate negative environmental impacts in terms of product, scale, structural or regulatory effects. [See *The Environmental Effects of Trade (1994).*]

In 1992, the Joint Session also undertook an analysis of the competitiveness and investment impacts of environmental policy, and decided to address developing country issues in all areas of analysis rather than as a discrete category. A first informal meeting with environmental non-governmental organisations (NGOs) was held, and the Joint Session's meetings were also enhanced by the presence of Secretariat members from GATT, UNEP and UNCTAD.

Drawing on the considerable analysis already done, the Joint Session decided that in view of the complexity of the issues, the goal was to forge tools, rather than rules. Accordingly, the Joint Session drafted a series of "procedural" guidelines to help governments improve the mutual compatibility of trade and environmental policies and policy making.

These procedural guidelines, as endorsed by Ministers in 1993, covered the following four topics:

1. **transparency and consultation** in the development and implementation of trade policies with significant effects on the environment, and *vice-versa*;
2. **trade and environmental examinations, reviews and follow-up:** the report called on governments to assess the trade implications of environmental policies and agreements, and *vice-versa*, early in their development;
3. **international environmental co-operation**, particularly through the negotiation and implementation of environmental agreements; and
4. **dispute settlement:** the report called on parties to trade disputes with environmental dimensions, and *vice-versa*, to take into account all relevant expertise and to work to achieve transparency in the dispute settlement process.

These guidelines were accompanied by succinct checklists for policy-makers undertaking reviews of the trade effects of environmental policies and agreements, and vice-versa. As a follow-up, a questionnaire was sent to OECD Members regarding their implementation of the guidelines. The responses of 22 countries, which reflected some early successes as well as problems, were published in 1996.

In 1993, there was a shift in focus. Several new areas for analysis were identified. These included methodologies for conducting reviews of trade and environmental policies and agreements; processes and production methods (PPMs); life-cycle management and trade; trade and environmental principles and concepts; economic instruments, environmental subsidies and trade; and dispute settlement.

The Joint Session's activities in 1993 reflected this broadening perspective on trade and environment issues. In January, the Environment Directorate and the US Environmental Protection Agency co-sponsored a workshop on environmental policies and industrial competitiveness. In June, the Joint Session held its first joint consultation with representatives from both industry and environmental NGOs. In July, the Environment Directorate sponsored a workshop on life-cycle management and trade. Each of these events provided an opportunity for members of the growing trade and environment community to share views and to contribute to the OECD's thinking on the most complex and divisive topics.

In 1994, the Joint Session published an important report, *Methodologies for Environmental and Trade Reviews*. Building on the 1993 procedural guidelines on reviews, the methodologies report broke new ground on the relatively new topic of environmental and trade reviews, which have since become widely used. The report describes a step-by-step process for both environmental reviews of trade policies and agreements, and *vice-versa*: **selecting** which policies/agreements to review; determining the review's **scope**, **timing** and **participants**; choosing the appropriate **methodologies** for the review; **monitoring** implementation of the review's recommendations; and **follow-up**. The report also provides a framework for categorising both environmental and trade effects, and a checklist to aid governments in the review process.

In 1994, activities intensified, with trade and environment events covering a wide range of perspectives and issues. Two informal meetings were held with industry and environmental NGO representatives; a workshop on PPMs issues was held in Helsinki, and another on eco-labelling and international trade in London; an expert group met on environmental subsidies; and an informal workshop held by the Trade Directorate with economically dynamic non-member countries discussed trade and environment concerns. Developing country issues were also high on the agenda, with the OECD Development Co-operation Directorate's workshop on trade, environment and development co-operation. The DAC/DCD Working Party on Environment and Development Assistance analyses the linkages at the trade, environment and development interface, and draws conclusions for donor support in this area. Current efforts explore how private sector and trade-oriented tools and instruments can integrate environmental aspects, and support the shift from a defensive to a proactive approach towards environmental issues in developing countries.

Pioneer Analyses

In its work on trade and environment, the OECD has focused on laying the analytic foundations for trade and environment decision-making at the international and national levels. Clear analytical frameworks can facilitate productive debate and help generate balanced, well-considered solutions. The OECD has produced a number of pioneer analyses which have helped shape and inform the trade and environment debate, including analyses on the environmental effects of trade and trade liberalisation, processes and production methods, and life-cycle management.

The Joint Session's conceptual framework for the **environmental effects of trade and trade liberalisation** divides these effects (both positive and negative) into five main categories. **Product effects** are associated with changes in levels of trade in specific products which can enhance or harm the environment. **Technology effects** occur in connection with changes in production technology due to trade-related technology diffusion. When increased trade generates higher levels of economic growth, **scale effects** may be positive or negative depending on whether appropriate environmental policies are present to address increased pollution and draw-down of resources. **Structural effects** of trade measures or agreements may be positive when they promote efficient resource allocation and production and consumption patterns, or negative if policies to internalise environmental costs and benefits in the prices of goods are absent when economic activity patterns change. **Regulatory effects** are associated with the impact of a trade measure or agreement on the ability of governments to enact and implement appropriate environmental regulations.

Environmental measures relating to **processes and production methods (PPMs)** have emerged as a cross-cutting area striking at the heart of issues of ensuring consistency with the rules of the multilateral trading system. In its analysis of PPMs, the OECD first categorises PPMs according to whether their environmental impact is transmitted by the product itself (*e.g.,* where processes leave dangerous traces of chemicals in foods). Non-product-related PPMs, which are more common, are then grouped according to whether they have spill-over effects (*i.e.* whether they have transboundary or global effects, and not simply local effects). The OECD's PPM classification system, and its approach in considering the different motivations for using PPMs, factors impacting their feasibility, environmental effectiveness and efficiency, and available alternatives, should be useful in aiding understanding and minimising conflict [See *Trade and Environment: Processes and Production Methods.*]

Another current issue, **life-cycle management** (sometimes known as the "cradle-to-grave" approach), is increasingly used by environmental policy-makers to address products' overall environmental impacts. OECD's workshop and publication on life-cycle management (1994) focused on the potential trade effects and trends in the fast-growing areas of eco-labelling, eco-packaging and recycling, and on the advantages and disadvantages of alternative policies with smaller trade impacts.

Dialogue

Transparency, a topic embracing notions of openness and broad participation in the decision-making process, has been given high priority. The OECD has taken major strides in increasing the transparency of its work on trade and environment to interested parties outside of government.[3] As noted above, dialogues have been held annually with representatives of industry and with environmental non-governmental organisations (NGOs). The Joint Session has also engaged industry and environmental NGOs in joint meetings, which have acted as a testing ground for efforts to establish a business-environmental dialogue on divisive issues. At a minimum, they have served to increase awareness of the different perspectives, priorities and concerns of each side; they may also have served as a useful opportunity to remind participants where they may find greater common cause in the future. At a 1994 meeting, for example, business and environmental representatives agreed that developing countries needed to be brought into the debate; that trade measures can be necessary to make international environmental agreements effective under certain circumstances; that special considerations were needed to prevent the use of PPM measures for protectionist aims; and that a clear link was necessary between the use of PPM-based trade measures and financial and technical assistance to help developing countries meet developed country requirements.

Dialogue with developing countries and countries in transition has also been actively pursued. Through its Development Co-operation Directorate (DCD), the OECD has sought to integrate non-OECD country perspectives in its trade and environment analyses. The DAC's Working Party on Development Assistance and Environment, for example, has urged Member countries to dedicate more aid toward helping developing countries benefit from the "greening" of consumer preferences, and adapt to the widening range of increasingly complex and stringent environmental regulations in external markets. The Trade Committee has also held workshops at which trade and environment issues were discussed with a number of economically dynamic non-member countries, who have shown a keen interest in these issues. At the September 1994 workshop, many participants noted the danger of not addressing gaps in trade rules regarding the use of trade measures in environmental agreements. A majority also asserted that a uniform approach to harmonizing environmental policies needs to be treated with caution, because it cannot fully take account of differences in environmental quality preferences, national capacities to assimilate pollution, and benefits accruing to different groups from pollution abatement and control.

Conclusions

The Joint Sessions's 1995 *Report on Trade and Environment to the OECD Council at Ministerial Level* [OCDE/GD(95)63] was the culmination of over four years of work. This report reached conclusions on a number of contentious trade and environment topics. First among these topics was the unilateral use of trade measures for environmental purposes, and unilateral import restrictions based on PPM-related requirements. Broadly speaking, a minority position differed from that of most OECD Members who were strongly opposed to endorsing any unilateral use of trade measures or PPM-related import restrictions. Lying at the heart of the debate was the appropriateness of the following actions: *a)* imposing unilateral trade measures not expressly sanctioned by existing multilateral environmental agreements (MEAs); *b)* instituting environmental policies incorporating non-product-related PPM requirements applicable to products from abroad; or *c)* instituting life-cycle policies incorporating such non-product-related PPM requirements.

OECD Governments confirmed their commitment to UN Conference on Environment and Development (UNCED) Agenda 21 and Principle 12 of the Rio Declaration, that unilateral actions to deal with environmental challenges outside the jurisdiction of the importing country should be avoided. The report states that environmental measures to address transboundary and global problems should as far as possible be based on an international consensus, and that these principles also extend to unilateral import restrictions based on PPM-related requirements. Noting the use of trade measures in some MEAs, including those against non-Parties or non-complying parties, the report identifies the need to develop further internationally-agreed principles to guide the use of trade measures in MEAs while avoiding protectionism and disruptions of the trading system.

Similarly, declaring that environmental concerns related to PPMs with transboundary or global environmental effects are best addressed through international co-operation, the report recommends that the appropriate and effective role of PPM-based trade restrictions in MEAs be further explored. With regard to life-cycle approaches, the report notes that they are a central feature of product-related environmental policies, providing valuable tools for governments, industry, and consumers to understand the complex environmental effects of products from ''cradle to grave''. They can be used for making environmentally-informed production and purchasing decisions. In order to avoid unnecessary trade impacts from life-cycle programmes, OECD Governments are advised to – and encourage private programmes (such as eco-label programmes) to – take steps to:

– ensure transparency and consultation with, and time for adaptation by, trading partners;
– take into account foreign suppliers' different conditions and make provisions for developing countries and economies in transition;
– ensure that life-cycle programmes do not effectively discriminate against foreign producers;
– ensure that criteria are environmentally justified and based on scientific/technical information, taking into account relevant environmental principles; and
– pursue harmonisation, convergence, equivalency and mutual recognition approaches.

A number of firm conclusions were reached in the 1995 report:
– Trade liberalisation will have a positive impact on the environment provided effective environmental policies are implemented.
– Demands for the use of protectionist measures such as ''green countervailing duties'' to compensate for real or perceived negative competitive effects of environmental policies should be firmly rejected.
– It would be inappropriate to encourage investment or to promote exports by relaxing domestic health, safety or environmental requirements or their enforcement.
– The feasibility and appropriateness of border adjustment for domestic process taxes[4] needs further exploration. However, OECD Governments should consult with trading partners during the design and implementation of economic instruments with significant expected trade impacts.
– OECD Governments expressed confidence that new WTO[5] provisions provide panels handling trade disputes with environmental aspects with the means to call upon relevant environmental and scientific expertise. It is understood that WTO panels do not have the mandate to question the merits of environmental objectives reflected in national programmes or international agreements.

CURRENT ACTIVITIES

Effects of Trade Liberalisation on the Environment

Tariff escalation: A recently completed study provides background to the discussion on tariff escalation in relation to environmental considerations. The heart of the study documents the practices of tariff escalation in OECD countries, based on the trade-weighted incidence of tariffs on the commodity processing chains for products of export interest to developing countries.

Transport sector study: International freight is an essential service in international trade, and the demand for freight is derived from economic activity, including international trade. In view of the growing pressure on the environment caused by various modes of transport, the Joint Session undertook an empirical study, in three phases: first, looking at the relationship between international trade and international transport, and focusing on the effects of trade liberalisation and liberalisation of the transport sector itself; second, by surveying the major effects on the environment of international freight movements; and, finally, by combining the first two phases, attempting to assess the effects on the environment of growth in international freight movements, attributable to trade liberalisation and deregulation. Case studies on the liberalisation of freight markets in North America and in Europe are underway.

Life-cycle Approaches and Trade: Actual Effects of Eco-labelling Programmes

Considerable work has been conducted on the *potential* trade implications of eco-labelling programmes. The relatively recent trend for eco-labelling programmes to be based on more extensive life-cycle criteria, specifically production-related criteria, is a source of trade concerns with respect to eco-labelling schemes. On the other hand, little empirical work had been undertaken to date. The OECD therefore launched a study examining the actual effects of eco-labelling programmes based on a selection of such programmes operating in OECD countries. The study focuses on the market impact of the schemes and their trade effects, but also looks at consultation processes and their transparency, and the schemes' environmental effectiveness. The schemes contained in the study include the EU Eco-label Award Scheme; Nordic Swan; Swedish Environmental Choice; Environmental Choice Programme (Canada); Blue Angel (Germany); *NF Environnement* (France), Eco-mark (Japan) and Green Seal (United States).

Use of Trade Measures for Environmental Purposes

The Joint Session has also discussed experience with the use of trade provisions in the Montreal Protocol (on substances that deplete the ozone layer). In this context, it was decided to continue its examination of actual experience with trade measures in two other multilateral environmental agreements with more or less global membership: the Convention on International Trade in Endangered Species of Wild Fauna and Flora (CITES) and the Basel Convention on the Transboundary Movements of Hazardous Wastes and their Disposal. These studies will analyse the purposes and the effectiveness of the trade provisions in the Conventions, how problems of non-compliance and illegal trade are addressed by the Conventions and how developing country interests have been addressed (*e.g.* through technology transfer, capacity building, and promotion of economic incentives). The relationship of each Convention's trade provisions to the multilateral trading system is also being addressed.

CHALLENGES AHEAD

Amongst the numerous areas where trade and environment policies interact, a few warrant deeper and broader analysis to assist in promoting the mutual reinforcement of trade and environment policies.

The OECD International Economic Guiding Principles, Particularly the Polluter Pays Principle

Adopted in 1972, the Guiding Principles were intended to promote the efficient implementation of national environmental policies and to mitigate any potential trade-distorting effects of such policies at the international level. All four principles (polluter pays; harmonization; national treatment and non-discrimination; and compensating import levies and export rebates) have some relevance to current trade and environment discussions, but the Polluter Pays Principle (PPP) is central. The PPP states that polluters should bear the costs of pollution control and prevention, and that the cost of pollution control and prevention measures should be reflected in the cost of goods and services which cause pollution in production and/or consumption. The PPP therefore covers two important policy aspects of environmental economics: environmental cost internalisation and the principle that polluters should not be subsidised to reduce pollution.

The trade and environment debate has been referred to as *"GATT + PPP"*. In other words, how can the objectives of multilateral trade liberalisation and environmental cost internalisation be simultaneously pursued, particularly when conflicts arise? In 1995, the Joint Session advocated greater use of economic instruments in environmental policy, noting that if they are well-designed, economic instruments lead to trade, production, and consumption patterns which more fully reflect all costs, including environmental costs. Greater use of economic instruments (such as environmental taxes and charges, tradeable permits and deposit refund systems) raises questions on how multilateral trade rules currently relate to such instruments, and how they can best accommodate the environmental cost internalisation principle. In the particular case of border tax adjustment, WTO rules have not been interpreted as allowing for taxes on the basis of domestic process taxes. In 1995, the OECD noted, however, that there would still be scope for examining the feasibility, benefits and potential risks associated with border tax adjustment for domestic process taxes.

New Trade Policy Areas

Services

Growth of trade in services and the adoption of the General Agreement on Trade in Services (GATS)[6] during the Uruguay Round of trade negotiations raises new trade and environment questions. For example, does the relationship between the environment and trade in services differ from that between the environment and trade in goods? Are moves to liberalise services sectors with international activities (both in the GATS and in additional upcoming negotiations on services) adequately taking account of environmental concerns? As explained above, these questions as they apply to international freight transport, a services sector with real environmental effects, are already being investigated. The tourism sector – including hotels and restaurants, tour and marina operators, and tourism transport services – may also warrant some examination in light of its environmental impacts and variety of applicable environmental regulations. In addition, a review of the OECD guidelines for the environmental review of trade agreements may be appropriate in the post-GATS world to ensure that the environmental effects of trade in services are adequately covered.

Use of Trade Measures for Environmental Purposes

As seen in the historical discussion above, the goal of agreeing on prescriptive guidelines on the use of trade measures in environmental policy-making proved elusive between 1991 and 1995. Nevertheless, the 1995 report specifically pin-pointed a few areas where the need exists for additional policy guidance tools. One of these, internationally-agreed principles to guide the use of trade measures within the context of MEAs, may well still elude agreement for some time into the future. However, work done already on the Montreal Protocol, CITES and the Basel Convention, underscores the need for further monitoring – particularly for the recent MEAs – and a deepening of the analysis of actual experience where success has not always been unambiguous.

It may also prove useful to extend work on PPM-based trade measures. Trade restrictions imposed on products *made with* controlled substances, or on those not based on environmentally preferable processes, are by definition process and production method (PPM)-based measures. As noted in the 1995 report, the appropriate role of PPM-based trade restrictions in MEAs needs to be further examined, as well as the effective role of PPMs in helping to achieve the environmental objectives of MEAs. A related area for future analysis would involve valuing the costs of PPM-based measures compared with the costs of other policy options considered to be feasible and equally effective.

The Joint Session will continue to support the activities of other international organisations as well as to maintain its consultations with industry, environment NGOs and non-OECD countries on environment and trade-related matters.

NOTES

1. In 1972, the GATT established its Working Party on Environmental Measures and International Trade, which was not convened until 1991.

2. Only shortly after the creation of the OECD Environment Committee in November 1970, the OECD Council adopted in 1971 a resolution establishing a notification and consultation procedure for the adoption of environmental measures covering certain chemical products. One of the intentions of the procedure was to minimise possible undesirable effects on other countries' economies and trade.

3. In response to calls for greater transparency, the OECD has published much of its wide-ranging work on trade and environment (see listing of publications).

4. The application to imported products of domestic taxes on the processes, or process inputs, with which like (*i.e.* legally identical) products are made, and the remission of domestic taxes on exports of like products.

5. With the conclusion of the Uruguay Round of multilateral trade negotiations in 1994, the former GATT was replaced by the World Trade Organisation.

6. The GATS covers eleven service sectors: 1) business services, including professional services; 2) communication services, including telecommunication and audio-visual services; 3) construction and related engineering services; 4) distribution services; 5) educational services; 6) environmental services; 7) financial services, including insurance and banking services; 8) health related and social services; 9) tourism and travel related services; 10) recreational, cultural and sporting services; and 11) transport services, including maritime, waterways, air and road transport services.

BIBLIOGRAPHY

1997

Processes and Production Methods: Conceptual Framework and Considerations on the use of PPM-based Trade Measures, (forthcoming)

Trade and Market effects of Eco-labelling schemes, OCDE/GD(97), (forthcoming).

1996

Tariff Escalation and Environment, OCDE/GD(96)171.

Implementation of the OECD Procedural Guidelines on Trade and Environment, OCDE/GD(96)98.

1995

Trade Principles and Concepts, OCDE/GD(95)141.

Dispute Settlement in the WTO, OCDE/GD(95)140.

Dispute Settlement in Environmental Conventions and Other Legal Instruments, OCDE/GD(95)138.

Environmental Principles and Concepts, OCDE/GD(95)124.

Report on Trade and Environment to the OECD Council at Ministerial Level, OCDE/GD(95)63.

1994

Methodologies for Environmental and Trade Reviews, OCDE/GD(94)103.

Life-Cycle Management and Trade, OECD Documents Series.

Trade and Environment: Processes and Production Methods, OECD Documents Series.

The environmental effects of trade, OECD Publication.

1993

Increasing the compatibility of environmental policies, OCDE/GD(93)136.

Trade and Environment (June 1993), OCDE/GD(93)99.

Environmental Policies and Industrial Competitiveness, OECD Documents Series.

1992

Trade and Environment: A Progress Report (May 1992), OCDE/GD(92)97.

1991

Joint Report on Trade and Environment (June 1991), OCDE/GD(92)25.

[All documents in the series ''OCDE/GD'' are available through website at: http://www.oecd.org/ech/act/envi.htm].

Part II

SECTORAL ISSUES

Chapter 7

ENERGY CHALLENGES AND OPPORTUNITIES FOR ACTION

by

Lee Solsbery

INTRODUCTION

As a critical factor in the engine of economic growth, energy will always be a commodity of central importance to nations. It contributes directly to meeting both basic and more sophisticated human needs. Energy is also a fundamental part of the globalisation process. Energy markets have become more diversified and increasingly transparent. Energy is treated more and more as a service best delivered through competitive markets. At the same time that the efficiency of global energy markets is improving, pressures have arisen to address the continued growth projected to occur in global energy demand and the patterns of energy production and consumption which underlie that growth.

Experience in OECD countries shows that the amount of energy required to produce economic output (*i.e.,* energy intensity) tends to decrease over time. However, robust growth in global energy demand, driven especially by the rapid rate of expansion in many key developing countries and increased consumer demand for services as personal incomes rise, presents a significant challenge to policy makers and to the energy community.

Even if energy intensity does continue to decline over time due to technological advances, those gains stand to be dwarfed by the absolute rise in global energy demand and the near-term reliance on existing energy sources resulting from the inertia in energy systems and the rigidities in energy infrastructure. Non-OECD countries have become more important in the world energy balance and their importance will continue to grow. Under these conditions, energy policies related to global environment issues can succeed only if they give due weight to the non-OECD dimension.

The International Energy Agency (IEA), an autonomous body affiliated with the OECD, has long sought to improve the functioning of global energy markets through increased transparency and efficiency, communication among all market participants and sharing the experiences of its Member countries to establish the framework conditions most conducive to effective market performance. Provision of adequate and secure energy supplies on an environmentally sound basis is still the basic point of departure for the IEA.

REGIONAL LINKAGES

The Challenge Posed by the Increasing Demand for Energy

Almost every aspect of OECD energy markets and every facet of energy policy is subject to strong influence from developments in non-OECD regions. While the importance of the Middle East as a source of oil has long been recognised, the broader energy significance of developing countries for the OECD had not been recognised until relatively recently. The main reason for this is that energy markets have been and, to a large extent, are still dominated by OECD countries. Canada, for example, still accounts for a larger share in global commercial energy consumption than India. Yet, the threat of global climate change from energy-related CO_2 emissions has been a very strong reminder of the growing interdependence between OECD and non-OECD countries.

These developments have made apparent the direct energy-related linkages between OECD and non-OECD countries. There are many examples of this: the switch of China in the early 1990s from an exporter to an importer of oil and the possibility that Indonesia, a significant exporter of oil and a key member of OPEC, might also import oil during the next decade, have highlighted the possibility that OECD oil imports might face new competitors in the future. Since Europe depends for its rising gas imports on Russia and Algeria (and Japan on Indonesia and Malaysia), developments in these countries' energy markets are of common concern. The reduction of coal subsidies in Europe has provided a welcome boost to coal exports from countries like Venezuela, South Africa and Colombia. It is not very surprising that the most vociferous opponents to the possibility of carbon taxes have been fossil fuel exporters, given the implications for their foreign exchange inflows.

There are also many indirect linkages between apparently unrelated energy markets that operate through interfuel competition. For example, potential large-scale imports of Siberian gas into China, even if they originate from new basins and do not compete directly with European gas imports, could reduce pressure on global oil markets which in turn could impact on European gas prices. Similarly, the accident at Chernobyl has set back nuclear expansion programmes in most countries and provided a boost to gas exporting countries.

IEA's projections up to 2010 and beyond include the following key features:
- world energy demand is likely to increase by some 60 per cent between 1994 and 2010;
- fossil based fuels will account for more than 90 per cent of primary energy demand in 2010 and probably at least 80 per cent in 2020;
- the bulk of growth in demand will originate in the five largest non-OECD countries (Russia, China, India, Brazil and Indonesia) and in other developing countries;
- CO_2 emissions will rise rapidly; more than a third of the increase will be in India and China;
- international and intra-regional trade in energy will become more widespread;
- OECD oil and gas import dependence will increase sharply;
- very large investment requirements will need to be satisfied in non-OECD countries;
- greater energy efficiency could have a dramatic impact on energy developments in the final demand for heat, mainly in the non-OECD world.

These projections raise some important conclusions and political implications, such as:
- technology-led improvements, especially in the power generation sector, are extremely important for the long-term level of energy use and CO_2 emissions;
- huge uncertainties surround the future energy consumption of China and India, the oil and gas production of the Middle East and production potential of Russia;
- while long-term energy supplies are perceived to be sufficient, their geographical distribution is highly uneven and there is substantial scope for instability;
- energy policy is a key determinant of energy market developments but needs to take into account the slow turnover of capital stock;
- the objectives of sustainable economic growth, energy security and environmental protection may lead to conflicting policy undertakings;
- there should be commonality of interest between OECD and non-OECD countries in pursuing jointly the objectives of energy security and of environmental protection.

Energy Intensity

It is important to note that in OECD countries, as well as other countries, improvements in energy intensity have been triggered by the two oil shocks, *i.e.,* in 1973-1975 and in the second and double oil shock of 1979 and 1980. While global energy intensity has been declining over the past 20 years, there is a sharp contrast between developments in OECD and in developing countries. In the OECD, concerted efforts at energy conservation followed the primary energy price increases of the 1970s. As a result, growth in energy demand was strongly decoupled from GDP growth in 1974-75 and in 1980-82. Commercial energy intensity in most developing countries, on the other hand, has been rising. While the recent sharp increase in the intensity of Russia is quite exceptional and only due to the strong recession affecting that country, in India, Indonesia and Brazil commercial energy intensity increased by more than 1 per cent per annum since 1971.[1]

The different patterns in energy intensity are due, to some extent, to the different stages in the process of development. As countries industrialise and their standard of living increases rapidly, their commercial energy intensity tends to rise. In more mature countries, it is the service sector and high technology industries that tend to grow faster. However, the divergence in intensities between OECD and non-OECD regions could also be due to the relocation of energy intensive industries from OECD countries. Over the past 20 years, industrial energy demand declined in OECD countries while it grew by more than 5 per cent per annum in rapidly industrialising countries. While overall industrial production grew very rapidly over the same period in OECD countries, most of this growth took place in light and high technology industries. Many energy intensive industries, such as steel, actually declined as countries like Brazil and Korea changed from being importers of steel into significant exporters. It is interesting to note that the relocation of industry to non-OECD countries may actually involve an increase in global energy demand as many of these countries benefit from significantly lower energy costs and adopt more energy intensive technologies.[2]

Rising energy intensity in developing countries is not expected to continue because the move from non-commercial to commercial energy has slowed. The fastest growing regions are already showing some decline.

Changing Regional Patterns

The distribution of CO_2 emissions tends to reflect reasonably closely that of energy. The main differences arise out of the use of greater or smaller proportions of carbon intensive fuels. Thus the OECD's share in emissions is lower than that of energy because of the use of nuclear power while the reverse is the case for China and India whose energy systems are dominated by coal. The absence of any increase in the share of Brazil in world CO_2 emissions reflects the very large proportion of hydro use in this country. Brazil has the cleanest energy system among all major countries. There is a gradually shifting balance of energy-related emissions away from OECD countries, which now account for around half of global emissions.

The rapid growth in energy demand in developing countries over the past 25 years has not alleviated two aspects of global energy consumption, namely, persistent inequities across countries and energy shortages in developing countries. While North Americans consume around 1 500 kilogramme of oil equivalent (kgoe) per year just for their transportation needs, total per capita energy consumption in India is less than 25 kgoe per year. Similarly, the average OECD person in 1994 consumed 30 times the electricity that the average Indonesian consumed, despite the fact that Indonesian electricity consumption increased by more than 20 times since 1971! It is also not clear that energy supply is rising rapidly enough to meet anticipated demand in many developing countries. There are many reports that energy shortages are becoming a hindrance to growth in both India and China.

Urbanisation and Non-commercial Energy

Urbanisation is extremely important for energy consumption patterns. The commercial energy intensity of urban areas is much higher than that of rural areas where a large amount of biomass is consumed. Also, the type of fuels and their quality differs greatly from rural to urban areas with cities being much more transportation and electricity intensive than villages. The likely extent of urbanisation is highly uncertain especially for the most populous countries. For example, it is very hard to conceive of the prospect of nearly three-quarters of a billion of Chinese peasants attempting to move to cities.

Non-commercial fuels play a significant role in the energy markets of developing countries, although these are not included in the figures presented here. The use of these traditional fuels is estimated to account for about one third of total energy consumption today. However, the increase in demand is likely to be met increasingly by commercial energy.

Despite the fast growth rates expected for the energy demand of developing countries and the deceleration in the growth of population, the world by 2010 will continue to be characterised by extreme inequality. Three major observations can be made: First, the differences in per capita energy consumption are significantly smaller than those in per capita GDP unless one uses a PPP (Purchasing Power Parity) basis. Second, the differences both in terms of GDP and energy per capita tend to diminish with the highest differences by 2020 being 30 and 14 times respectively (both comparisons refer to North America and India). Third, while rich regions tend to grow more slowly than poor ones, they continue to grow. Saturation seems extremely unlikely, at least by 2010.

Two major implications follow from this persistence of inequality. First, the scope for further growth of energy demand beyond 2010 is very large indeed as the bulk of the world's population at that time will be still consuming a fraction of energy of even the 1990 level of developed countries. Second, in the context of "burden sharing" for dealing with the greenhouse gas emissions, this explains the position of most non-OECD countries that current concentrations are exclusively due to rich countries and that developing countries should not bear any of the costs.

THE IEA COMMITMENT TO ACTION

Since the Rio Declaration, IEA Member and non-member countries alike have embraced the concept of sustainable development and have sought to create a policy context which promotes the clean use of energy through, *inter alia*, access to cleaner fuels, improvements in energy efficiency and accelerated development and deployment of less-polluting technologies.

In 1993 IEA Ministers adopted a new set of "Shared Goals" which summarise IEA Members' overall approach to energy policy (see Annex I to this chapter). The Agency's Shared Goals expressly refer to sustainable development; indeed, six of the nine stated goals deal directly with the environment, efficiency and clean technology dimension of energy.

In 1994 and 1995, IEA Ministers reaffirmed the aim stated in 1993 to create a policy framework consistent with the IEA Shared Goals and the balance reflected in those Goals between energy security, sustainable economic development and environmental protection and enhancement.

Energy and Climate Change: A Top IEA Priority

The UN Framework Convention on Climate Change (FCCC) has profound implications for energy markets and for energy policy. In particular the Climate Convention and the Berlin Mandate to fix post-2000 greenhouse gas emissions reductions under that Convention call for effective actions to be taken to reduce both the energy and the carbon intensity of our economies. Clearly, energy must be a major part of the solution to the climate problem.

IEA Ministers support the political commitment made under the Climate Convention in Rio and the aims expressed in the Berlin Mandate regarding future commitments. They seek to address those commitments in an effective manner which encompasses all the energy policy objectives of the IEA and offers a viable, long-term, cost-effective approach to the problem.

At its second special Ministerial-level meeting, IEA Ministers focused exclusively on energy and climate issues (Aarhus, Denmark, June 1996), and reaffirmed their commitments made under the FCCC in Rio and Berlin, emphasizing the need for the energy sector to play a positive role in meeting those commitments. In the run-up to the Second Meeting of the Conference of the Parties (COP-2) to the FCCC held in July 1996, the IEA participated as a ''partner organisation'' in the Climate Convention process.

Results of IEA analysis on Activities Implemented Jointly (AIJ) under the FCCC, made available at COP-2, suggested that there is a significant potential to reduce energy-related greenhouse gas emissions in the energy sector in developing countries through AIJ. The IEA is leading the development of a principal corpus of analysis on this topic.

The Agency's *Energy Environment Update* reports IEA findings on AIJ and the policy aspects of renewable energy in IEA Member countries. *Climate Change Policy Initiatives, Volume II, Selected Non-IEA Countries, 1995/96 Update* summarises the climate programmes and key statistics on energy-related CO_2 emissions in 20 major non-IEA countries. IEA, in collaboration with OECD, has produced studies on *Policies and Measures for Common Action* for the Annex I Expert Group. They were made available to Parties to the FCCC to assist their deliberations. The IEA led analysis and produced studies regarding the potential to mitigate greenhouse gas emissions through:

- removing market barriers and improving market access;
- implementing full cost pricing, and
- taxation (*i.e.* carbon/energy).

Modelling economic and energy markets impacts

The IEA held a first international ''Modelling Seminar'' in May 1996 to obtain insights from modellers on the economic and energy market impacts of quantified emission limitation and reduction objectives under the UNFCCC for an audience of policy-makers. Its main conclusions were:

- modellers should better contribute to policy-makers' intuitions on what are the key components of this question, rather than provide overly simplistic, ''pre-digested'' results;
- the degree of rigidity in energy systems and other infrastructures is an essential factor in the economic cost of climate change energy responses, and further analysis is required in that regard beyond what is available in existing global economic models.

A second international ''Modelling Seminar'' was organised in November 1996, in collaboration with the Intergovernmental Panel on Climate Change (IPCC), to address the question of ''no-regrets'' policy options in different energy-related services (electricity generation and end-use, transportation, and stationary use of fossil fuels): how to best use existing market and capital stock dynamics to implement most cost-effective greenhouse gas mitigation options. The seminar participants stressed the importance of distinguishing between the technical, economic, and commercial potentials for greenhouse gas reductions. Participants also recognised the role of political will to mobilise government resources to be able to implement cost-effective measures, where market barriers are present and hamper rational economic choices. It was also stressed that policy-makers cannot act beyond what is acceptable to their electors and that, therefore, political feasibility also affected what could be realistic ''no regrets'' options.

Role of Renewables

Most IEA countries increasingly promote renewable energy as part of their response to climate change, though renewables policy may be motivated by other factors such as energy diversification and security, local pollution abatement and agricultural/regional aid. As a result, the use of some renewables has increased since the early 1990s. Most of this increase was in hydropower, though the role of non-hydro renewables, especially wind-based power generation, is growing: non-hydro renewables contributed some 155 million tonne oil equivalent (Mtoe) or 3.6 per cent to the IEA's total primary energy supply in 1994, and generated 141 terawatt-hours (TWh) or 1.8 per cent of electricity in the same year.

According to a new IEA analysis,[3] the biggest barrier to increased non-hydro renewable energy use is its cost, and much of the current effort undertaken by governments is aimed at making investment in renewable energy sources more favourable, for example the German Electricity Feed Law, the regime of financial incentives in Japan, Denmark and Sweden, the District Heating Promotion Act in Austria, and competitive bidding procedures for renewables-based electricity in the United Kingdom. These policies have shown that potential investors will invest in renewable energy sources if it is in their economic interest to do so.

The policy mix used to achieve this aim varies widely among countries, as do the targeted end-uses (*e.g.* electricity and heating) and the type of renewables (*e.g.* some countries explicitly encourage certain renewables and not others). The most widespread measures used are financial incentives, but voluntary agreements, ''green pricing'' and targets are also used. Emphasis is being given to renewables-based electricity production in numerous countries, with many guaranteeing a market for all or part of such production.

Governments are making use of financial incentives for renewables, such as grants and tax exemptions for the construction of electricity generating plant, solar water heater installation and production of biofuels. Overall subsidies for renewables production are increasing, even though many such programmes have not been fully evaluated on energy, economic or environmental terms.

While the costs associated with increased use of renewables (*e.g.* expenditure on subsidies or on R&D) are often borne by public budgets, the benefits of such a policy may be hidden, qualitative or unquantified. Evaluation of renewable energy policies is also complicated by the fact that several policy objectives may be mixed. For example, raising farmers' income via subsidies for biofuels may help to maintain a country's food production capability, increase regional development, maintain rural employment levels and reduce emissions of CO_2 as well as increase use of renewables.

Other renewables programmes may develop technology export capabilities. All of these may be perceived as desirable objectives for political, environmental or other non-energy and/or non-cost reasons. The increased energy security and flexibility that arises from greater use of renewables may also have a strategic value for governments. Governments may therefore be willing to pay a premium over a certain time period in order to maintain or expand options in this area.

Two IEA technology Implementing Agreements, GREENTIE (Greenhouse Gas Technology Information Exchange) and CADDET-Renewables (Centre for the Analysis and Diffusion of Demonstrated Renewable Energy Technologies) are designed to disseminate information about successful new renewables and environmentally benign technology which can reduce greenhouse gas and other emissions.

Role of Technology

In the long term, the development of energy technology will be a decisive factor in how easily and cheaply countries are able to meet collective climate change objectives. Technology can also help governments meet other policy objectives, including energy security and local environmental protection. IEA governments support the development and deployment of technology in a number of ways, including direct public spending on R&D programmes and information dissemination or support for private sector R&D, through grants, subsidies and tax incentives.

Government R&D efforts have been declining since the mid-80s in response to lower real energy prices, budget austerity and changing attitudes to the role of government in the economy. In 1994 expenditure by IEA governments on energy R&D totalled over US$ 8.7 billion, around three-quarters of which was accounted for by Japan and the United States. In addition the European Commission undertakes a substantial programme that cost about US$ 356 million in 1993. The focus of publicly funded R&D varies considerably among countries. In 1994 over 56 per cent of such R&D expenditure was devoted to nuclear energy including nuclear breeders and fusion, followed by fossil fuels (11 per cent), energy efficiency and conservation (11 per cent) and renewables (8 per cent).

Many IEA countries are now, however, changing the balance of their R&D programmes by reducing or freezing expenditures on nuclear energy. In many cases, at least some of the resources so released are being switched to work on renewable energy sources and energy efficiency (*e.g.* in Italy, Sweden, Switzerland, the United Kingdom and the United States), though overall spending on these areas is thought to be declining. Government R&D programmes may also need to respond to the effects of deregulation of the electricity and gas industries, which may lead to reduced utility spending on long-term R&D projects and increased emphasis on technology that is closer to deployment.

IEA Energy Technology Collaboration facilitates international co-operation to increase benefits and reduce costs of energy technology research, development and dissemination concerning fossil fuels, renewable energy sources, efficient end-use, and nuclear fusion technology. The success of the programme has meant that the number of participating organisations has increased by 45 per cent since 1990, from 275 to over 400 in 1996. The programme involves governments, utilities, industry and universities. Current projects are described in a 1996 IEA report.[4]

PRIORITY AREAS FOR MITIGATING ENERGY-RELATED EMISSIONS

Dynamic implementation of the best available technology has a vital role to play in mitigation of the climate impact of the energy chain. A stable, transparent and level playing-field is essential to create clear market signals and to allow new climate-friendly technologies to be selected through normal commercial decision-making.

Energy pricing which better reflects costs is potentially a win-win strategy. In practice, the situation is more complex because it is impossible to identify the ''true'' cost of all externalities, and an increase in price to reflect these externalities may not be painless in the short term. Nonetheless, moving towards elimination of subsidies and incorporation of identifiable externalities into prices will in general be a key component of climate change responses.

Policy also has a role to play in technological development. The major challenge is to combine a favourable context for research, development and deployment with market-based evaluation and implementation mechanisms. The IEA/OECD Climate Technology Initiative (CTI) is one aspect of Member countries' response to this challenge.

In a complex world, no single response option is uniquely viable. Because of widely varying effects of given policy instruments in different national circumstances, it is difficult to define in general terms a mix of policies and measures which would be universally applicable. This suggests that policies should be part of a learning process, whereby the implementation of responses provides information about their effectiveness and enables improved development of a flexible and adaptable policy framework over time.

The Climate Technology Initiative

To support the implementation of the Climate Change Convention, 23 IEA Member countries and the European Commission announced the setting up of the Climate Technology Initiative (CTI) at COP-1. The CTI aims to assist all interested countries in meeting both the shorter-term and longer-term objectives of the Climate Change Convention, by enhancing markets for and reducing barriers to available new and improved technology that has the potential to reduce greenhouse gas emissions. It also aims to stimulate research, development and diffusion of medium-term to longer-term technology that can contribute to more far-reaching reductions that will eventually be required to meet the goals of the Convention. Preliminary work by the IEA/OECD in detailing the fundamental role that current and future technology is expected to play in reducing greenhouse gas emissions played an important part in developing the Climate Technology Initiative.[5]

The CTI is a linked set of practical national and international measures that aim to:

• Promote awareness of technology-related activities already under way to assist with responses to climate change concerns.

• Identify and share expertise and experience among countries already working on particular topics, as well as with countries having limited expertise in particular areas.

• Identify gaps in national and multilateral programmes that could be addressed in order to strengthen climate response strategies.

• Strengthen and undertake practical collaboration activities between countries to make technology responses to climate change concerns more effective.

The IEA/OECD released an extensive inventory of CTI-related activities outlining technology-related programmes in IEA/OECD Member countries, and bilateral and multilateral programmes that contribute to various parts of the CTI (July 1996). Task forces have also been established to develop additional action plans for strengthening activities under the CTI.

Longer-term research, development and demonstration (RD&D) is needed to develop and demonstrate cleaner and more efficient technologies for energy production and end-use. Ongoing technological progress requires commitments to long-term investments in RD&D, particularly to achieve further de-carbonisation of the fuel mix, to promote CO_2 capture and storage, to improve end-use energy efficiency.

Efficiency standards have demonstrated their potential effectiveness. By accelerating the introduction of more efficient equipment, efficiency standards have had positive effects on end-users' welfare.

International or national emissions trading offers a potentially efficient means of reducing the marginal and overall cost of controlling greenhouse gas emissions, while providing an incentive for early action by those participants for which it is cost-effective to do so. Joint implementation of activities and projects between Annex I and non-Annex I countries could complement an emissions trading scheme subject to addressing issues such as baselines, performance monitoring and crediting of avoided emissions. Furthermore, these options offer helpful opportunities for co-operation with developing countries wishing to participate through projects consistent with their domestic energy needs.

IEA "Statement on the Energy Dimension of Climate Change"

The IEA "Statement on the Energy Dimension of Climate Change," has become part of the official documentation under the FCCC's debate of a possible protocol or other legal instrument to strengthen the Convention. It describes the principal driving forces and key underlying factors relevant to the energy aspects of the global greenhouse gas problem. In particular, it points out that:

• National circumstances vary widely among IEA countries and explain, in turn, why energy systems (*i.e.* the fuel mix and energy prices) are so different.

- Different dynamics of the main energy services (mobility, electricity use and heat) involve different infrastructures, different technologies and capital stocks, and different behaviour among end-users, as well as different trends in relation to GDP growth over time.
- The extent and age of existing energy infrastructures constrain the rate at which cost-effective reductions in energy-related emissions can be achieved in the near-term.
- Enhanced use of best available technologies could help reduce energy requirements and associated emissions within the possibilities of current infrastructure, but barriers to the adoption of currently available and cost-effective technologies will have to be overcome.
- Every time energy-using capital stock and infrastructure is installed anywhere in the world, there is a unique opportunity to adopt climate-friendly technologies.
- Early involvement of all actors concerned will help foster innovation and change in long-term trends and infrastructure and achieve emissions reductions at minimum cost.

The promotion of sustainable economic development requires providing and expanding energy services while simultaneously reducing their energy and CO_2 content. Market dynamics, the rigidity of infrastructures and attitudes, and the rate of capital stock turnover define the basic parameters of viable response options, pointing to both limitations and significant opportunities.

NOTES

1. It should be noted that the historical increase in energy intensity in developing countries is likely to be overestimated to some extent due to the decreasing role of non-commercial fuels which are not included in these calculations.

2. The impact of relocation has been examined for the case of the iron and steel industry in IEA. It was found that as a result of the relocation of the industry, global energy demand increased by some 5 per cent between 1980 and 1990.

3. IEA, *Renewable Energy Policy in IEA Countries* (to be published in two volumes in 1997).

4. IEA, *International Technology Collaboration: Benefits and Achievements* (OECD: Paris, 1996).

5. IEA/OECD, *Scoping Study on Energy and Environmental Technologies to Respond to Global Climate Concerns* (OECD: Paris, 1995).

BIBLIOGRAPHY

IEA (1997), *Renewable Energy Policy in IEA Countries* (forthcoming).

IEA (1997), *Voluntary Actions for Energy-related CO$_2$ Abatement.*

IEA (1996), *Climate Change Policy Initiatives – 1995/96 Update (Selected Non-IEA Countries) – Volume II.*

IEA (1996), *Climate Technology Initiative – Inventory of Activities.*

IEA (1996), *Comparing Energy Technologies.*

IEA (1996), *Factors affecting the Take-up of Clean Coal Technologies – Overview Report* (CIAB).

IEA (1996), *International Energy Technology Collaboration: Benefits and Achievements.*

IEA (1996), *The Role of IEA Governments in Energy.*

IEA (1996), *World Energy Outlook – 1996 Edition.*

IEA (1996), *Energy Policies of IEA Countries – 1996 Review (Compendium).*

IEA (1995), *New Electricity 21: Designing a Sustainable Electric System for the Twenty-First Century (Paris).*

IEA (1994), *Energy Technologies to Reduce CO$_2$ Emissions in Europe: Prospects, Competition, Synergy (Petten).*

IEA (1994), *Reconciling Transportation, Energy and Environmental Issues: The Role of Public Transport (Budapest).*

IEA (1994), *Development and Deployment of Technologies to Respond to Global Climate Change Concerns (Paris).*

IEA (1994), *Climate Change Policy Initiatives – 1994 Update (OECD Countries) – Volume I.*

Annex I

INTERNATIONAL ENERGY AGENCY "SHARED GOALS"

The 23 Member countries* of the International Energy Agency (IEA) seek to create the conditions in which the energy sectors of their economies can make the fullest possible contribution to sustainable economic development and the well-being of their people and of the environment. In formulating energy policies, the establishment of free and open markets is a fundamental point of departure, though energy security and environmental protection need to be given particular emphasis by governments. IEA countries recognise the significance of increasing global interdependence in energy. They therefore seek to promote the effective operation of international energy markets and encourage dialogue with all participants. In order to secure their objectives they therefore aim to create a policy framework consistent with the following goals:

1. **Diversity, efficiency and flexibility within the energy sector** are basic conditions for longer-term energy security: the fuels used within and across sectors and the sources of those fuels should be as diverse as practicable. Non-fossil fuels, particularly nuclear and hydro power, make a substantial contribution to the energy supply diversity of IEA countries as a group.

2. **Energy systems should have the ability to respond promptly and flexibly to energy emergencies.** In some cases this requires collective mechanisms and action: IEA countries co-operate through the Agency in responding jointly to oil supply emergencies.

3. **The environmentally sustainable provision and use of energy** is central to the achievement of these shared goals. Decision-makers should seek to minimise the adverse environmental impacts of energy activities, just as environmental decisions should take account of the energy consequences. Government interventions should where practicable have regard to the Polluter Pays Principle.

4. **More environmentally acceptable energy sources** need to be encouraged and developed. Clean and efficient use of fossil fuels is essential. The development of economic non-fossil sources is also a priority. A number of IEA Members wish to retain and improve the nuclear option for the future, at the highest available safety standards, because nuclear energy does not emit carbon dioxide. Renewable sources will also have an increasingly important contribution to make.

5. **Improved energy efficiency** can promote both environmental protection and energy security in a cost-effective manner. There are significant opportunities for greater energy efficiency at all stages of the energy cycle from production to consumption. Strong efforts by Governments and all energy users are needed to realise these opportunities.

6. **Continued research, development and market deployment of new and improved energy technologies** make a critical contribution to achieving the objectives outlined above. Energy technology policies should complement broader energy policies. International co-operation in the development and dissemination of energy technologies, including industry participation and co-operation with non-member countries, should be encouraged.

7. **Undistorted energy prices enable markets** to work efficiently. Energy prices should not be held artificially below the costs of supply to promote social or industrial goals. To the extent necessary and practicable, the environmental costs of energy production and use should be reflected in prices.

8. **Free and open trade** and a secure framework for investment contribute to efficient energy markets and energy security. Distortions to energy trade and investment should be avoided.

9. **Co-operation among all energy market participants** helps to improve information and understanding, and encourage the development of efficient, environmentally acceptable and flexible energy systems and markets world-wide. These are needed to help promote the investment, trade and confidence necessary to achieve global energy security and environmental objectives.

The "Shared Goals" were adopted by IEA Ministers at their 4 June 1993 meeting in Paris.

---

* Australia, Austria, Belgium, Canada, Denmark, Finland, France, Germany, Greece, Ireland, Italy, Japan, Luxembourg, Netherlands, New Zealand, Norway, Portugal, Spain, Sweden, Switzerland, Turkey, United Kingdom, United States.

Chapter 8

TRANSPORT, ECONOMIC DEVELOPMENT
AND SOCIAL WELFARE

by

Stephen Perkins, Barrie Stevens and Régis Confavreux[1]

INTRODUCTION

Access to other people, places, goods and services is fundamental to social and economic welfare, thus transport has a crucial role in sustainable development. Transport industries are an integral part of the global economy, both influencing and being influenced by the pattern of economic development. Their direct contribution to GDP is substantial, they create valuable employment opportunities and the indirect benefits associated with transport in terms of regional development and globalisation are large. Transport is a major driving force behind trade and the globalisation of production and service sector industries. Transport is also, however, a source of considerable cost to welfare, notably in terms of accidents, pollution and degradation of ecosystems and landscapes.

There is increasing awareness that the root causes of most of the problems are deficiencies in, or barriers to, the efficient operation of markets. Environmental costs and other externalities are systematically neglected or underestimated in transport prices. This distortion leads to inefficiencies, waste of natural and economic resources and reduced social welfare. All the costs and benefits covered by the concept of sustainable mobility need to be brought to bear in the decisions made at the margin by economic actors that determine whether and how passenger or freight movements should happen. The key is establishing incentives that alter behaviour to reduce external costs. Policies to ensure that such an "internalisation" of costs is achieved aim at integrating the external effects into the market and into the decision making of individual actors. The objective is to improve the economic efficiency of markets and decision-making, be it by adjusting market prices directly or through indirect regulatory instruments.

Striking the right balance between the benefits and costs of transport is very much at the heart of policy-making in OECD countries. As the following sections illustrate, OECD governments have on the whole pursued a set of policies which have aimed to bring market forces to bear more strongly on transport sectors, particularly by promoting liberalisation and strengthening competition policy, while at the same time seeking ways to address more effectively environmental and safety issues. The OECD takes a broad, multi-disciplinary approach to transport. Work in several directorates spans technology, industry, environment, energy, territorial and urban development. The OECD is closely linked to the European Conference of Ministers of Transport (ECMT) with representation from virtually all European countries and observers from many non-European OECD countries.[2] Trends and policies are followed not only in OECD Member, but increasingly in non-member countries and in co-operation with institutions of the European Union and United Nations.

◆ Figure 1. **Passenger and freight transport trends, 1970-1995**

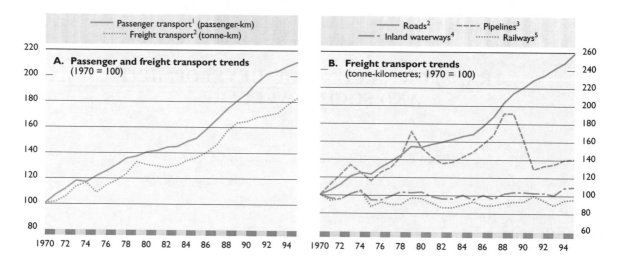

1. 16 countries: A, B, CH, D, DK, E, F, FIN, GR, I, N, NL, P, S, TR, UKR.
2. 16 countries: A, B, CH, D, DK, E, F, FIN, GR, I, L, N, NL, S, TR, UKR.
3. 12 countries: A, B, CH, D, DK, E, F, I, N, NL, TR, UKR.
4. 10 countries: A, B, CH, D, F, FIN, I, L, NL, UKR.
5. 18 countries: A, B, CH, D, DK, E, F, FIN, GR, I, IRL, L, N, NL, P, S, TR, UKR.

Note: A = Austria; B = Belgium; CH = Switzerland; D = Germany; DK = Denmark; E = Spain; F = France; FIN = Finland; GR = Greece; I = Italy; IRL = Ireland; L = Luxembourg; N = Norway; NL = Netherlands; P = Portugal; S = Sweden; TR = Turkey; UKR = Ukraine; CZ = Czechoslovakia; EST = Estonia; H = Hungary; LT = Latvia; LV = Lithuania; PL = Poland; RO = Romania; SK = Slovakia; SLO = Slovenia.

Data for the former Czechoslovakia have been taken into account up to 1992 to ensure a degree of continuity in the series over a lengthy period of time; from 1993 onwards the data provided by the Czech and Slovak Republics have been used. Furthermore, German reunification led to a break in the series as a result of the incorporation, from 1991 onwards, of data relating to the new *Länder*, which resulted in a corresponding increase in the results for the ECMT as a whole.

Source: Trends in the Transport Sector, 1970-1995, ECMT 1996.

INLAND TRANSPORT

Trends

Inland traffic has doubled in OECD countries in the last 25 years (see Figure 1) as a result of growth in disposable incomes combined with liberalisation of trade, liberalisation of transport sector industries and change in industrial management and organisation patterns. Most national forecasts anticipate significant further growth in the next 25 years. Car ownership has increased and vehicle occupancy rates declined whilst public transport has seen relatively little growth. Steep increases in road traffic in the late 1980s have focused attention in regard to sustainable development on roads. The 1990s are witnessing continued growth in road transport both in OECD and many other countries. The environmental impacts of this growing road traffic are, with accidents and economic efficiency, the key issues for sustainable development.

Inland transport costs in terms of accidents and environmental impact may represent around 5 per cent of GDP (measured in terms of willingness to pay) according to recent literature.[3] Accidents probably account for half of this figure. Road accidents kill 500 000 people and injure 15 million every year, world-wide. In ECMT countries alone the figures were 51 700 killed and 1.9 million injured in 1994. Even though the number of fatalities has fallen sharply over the last two decades in western Europe, it is difficult to believe that current casualty rates could be considered an acceptable trade-off under any definition of sustainability. The number of accidents has increased substantially in both eastern and western Europe since the historical low point of 1985. These trends mask wide variations in accident, death and injury rates between individual countries, implying that much can be done to reduce accident costs in many countries even without going beyond conventional safety policies.

Environmental impacts are concentrated in urban areas and in sensitive areas such as mountain valleys or where infrastructure crosses fragile ecosystems or landscapes. Recent evidence suggests that the impact on health of small particulate emissions from diesel motors, tyres and road surfaces is severe in urban areas, photochemical smog is a persistent problem due to difficulties in reducing Nox and volatile organic compounds (VOC) emissions from internal combustion engines and noise is a major nuisance. At a regional level Nox emissions from transport also contribute significantly to acidification and, together with VOCs, to the large-scale formation of tropospheric ozone. At the OECD level, road transport has become the largest and most intractable anthropogenic source of CO_2 emissions.

Extrapolations of recent historical trends are not necessarily a reliable guide to future developments in demand for particular transport services. Though increased traffic has been correlated with economic growth in the recent past, over the longer term the relationship is dynamic as patterns of production and consumption change. Growth in transport activities and economic output may become uncoupled in the future. The relationship between traffic growth and environmental impact is also dynamic.

Environmental impacts have been affected by a number of factors. In response to progressively tighter regulations for passenger cars, better engine design and fuel quality, together with catalytic converters, have improved emissions control. Figure 2 illustrates recent and projected trends in motor vehicle emissions for some major air pollutants. Noise from individual vehicles has also been reduced in response to standards and market pressures. Specific fuel consumption and CO_2 emissions decreased in the early 1980s in the wake of the second oil price shock and ensuing recession. More recently, fuel consumption has tended to increase with gains in vehicle weight, resulting from improvements in safety, comfort and equipment levels which have been the focus of innovation in markets where real incomes have been rising. Steep declines in real oil prices in the mid-1980s reduced incentives for saving fuel. For the future, changes in technology, in oil markets and in taxation policy all have the potential to counter-balance recent trends in vehicle weight and fuel efficiency.

In freight markets maximum truck sizes have grown, increasing the impact of individual vehicles though possibly slowing fleet growth somewhat. Meanwhile growth in service industries has led to a rise in light duty goods vehicle traffic. Deregulation has contributed to the increase in traffic whilst regulatory barriers, imbalances in trade flows, increasing vehicle specialisation and inadequate information systems result in frequent empty runs. Vehicle capacity utilisation has improved but empty runs still account for around 30 per cent of total vehicle kilometres driven. There may be scope to reduce empty runs in the future, particularly through deregulation of cabotage and improved logistics. Earlier developments in logistics, such as just-in-time management, generated additional environmental burdens whereas today's advanced logistics should have the opposite effect. In urban areas such systems can make an important contribution to reducing congestion through joint deliveries, advanced dispatching systems, multi-functional logistics centres and applying advanced electronic information and communications systems.

Efficiency and Sustainability

Inland transport markets are frequently inefficient. Government allocation has substituted for markets, with infrastructure funded mainly from tax revenues and charges for its use applied only indirectly (through vehicle and fuel taxes for roads and through administrative allocation in the

◆   Figure 2.   **Trends and projections: motor vehicle emissions of selected air pollutants in OECD countries**
(In million tonnes)

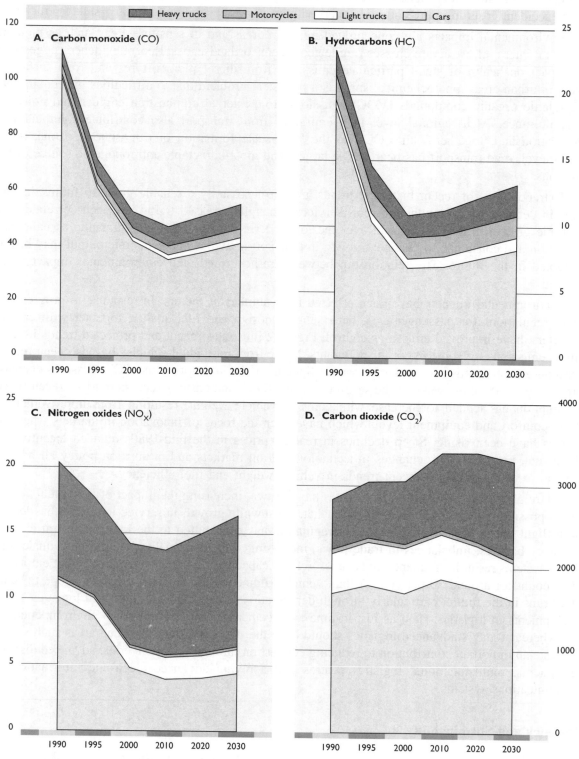

Note: See original publication for projections methodology.
Source: *Motor Vehicle Pollution Strategies to 2010*, OECD, 1995.

accounts of integrated rail enterprises). This results in only weak pricing signals at the key points of decision. Taking roads for example, on the supply side large sums have been invested in expanding infrastructure capacity but, in the absence of direct feedback through prices, demand often rapidly outstrips new capacity. The result is rationing in parts of the system, usually in the form of excessive congestion. Symptoms of these market inefficiencies have become apparent. Following 10-20 per cent increases in road and rail investments in the second half of the 1980s, in many ECMT countries investment in roads and rail is being scaled back in the mid-1990s, and in some, maintenance programmes have suffered.

Effective financial management of infrastructure investments is a key element of sustainable mobility. For railways, uncovered infrastructure costs amount to some ECU 8 billion per year (0.1 per cent of GDP) in 15 countries of western Europe.[4] Chronic debt accumulation has been a feature of most ECMT railway systems. Efforts to improve financial control have begun with the separation of infrastructure from operations, at least at the accounting level. Over and above this, major gains in productivity will be required if railways are to regain competitiveness with road transport. In the USA, railway reform began much earlier, with the result that rail freight transport is now growing.

Public expenditure on roads is covered to a large degree by road-user taxes in ECMT Member countries, although heavy goods traffic is cross-subsidised by car users in many countries. Lower fuel taxes in North America result in a net government deficit, although the size of this deficit has diminished in recent years with traffic (and revenue) growth and reduced investment. Efforts to restrain government spending have led to cuts in investment in most OECD countries. Relating user charges more closely to long run marginal infrastructure costs would bring expenditure and demand into better balance where infrastructure is congested. Where inadequate infrastructure is a constraint on economic development, investment in building or upgrading roads and railways is an important priority for governments in view of the large economic and social benefits it can bring. The capital intensity of the infrastructure built has to be carefully matched to the potential demand. Over-provision of infrastructure, in terms of quality or quantity, can damage economic development through an accumulation of uncovered debt. Opportunities for cost recovery through user charges have to be pursued, but where this is not an option, (particularly in developing countries), subsidies should be made transparent and accorded as part of specific policy for the provision of public goods, in order to minimise the risk of financing disruptions over the long term.

Policy Responses

Progressive deregulation characterises most OECD inland transport markets, with the main aim of reducing transport costs whilst improving services. Internalisation offers a framework for developing sustainable inland transport policies that is highly compatible with deregulation. It can only be effective in markets that are reasonably efficient, so expanding the role of market discipline is an essential step in improving sustainability.

Effective policies will be based on a mix of regulatory and pricing instruments. The primary strategy for internalisation is not to increase prices (road transport in particular is already highly taxed) but to structure them more efficiently, particularly by readjusting the balance between variable and fixed charges, so that prices can provide incentives for efficient behaviour. At the same time, subsidies need to be made transparent to reduce distortions if incentives created by internalisation are to be effective. For the long term, pricing the use of roads by distance travelled (per passenger or per ton of freight) and vehicle characteristics and setting prices closer to long run marginal costs (including externalities) would probably have a more direct effect on behaviour than fuel or vehicle taxes. This implies varying charges depending on the time of day (higher charges at peak times) and depending on the type of vehicle according to specific pollution characteristics. Road pricing is a promising instrument for internalisation but experience with marginal cost pricing is limited and technical advances in charging systems will be required to bring the costs down for wider deployment.

Local and Regional Air Quality

Regulatory standards have been successfully employed to control air pollution and tighter future standards will have a significant role in reducing air emissions, noise and some other impacts. In the long term, emissions regulations for new vehicles will have a major effect, eventually reducing emissions at least of ozone precursors close to levels currently judged sustainable in most areas. For the short and medium term, however, strict enforcement of existing regulations beyond the factory gate through maintenance and widespread spot checks could reduce emissions significantly as could removal from the fleet of the most polluting vehicles through more stringent application of existing road worthiness tests. Recent research, particularly in Switzerland, France, Germany and the United Kingdom, is beginning to reveal the full magnitude of the impact on health of small particulate emissions, emitted largely from diesel engines. This together with the relatively high specific NO_x emissions from diesel engines, outweighs the fuel efficiency benefits associated with diesel and suggests the tax incentives diesel widely enjoys should be phased out.

Climate Change

Regulatory approaches have also proved effective in influencing fuel efficiency where applied, but are perceived to have had undesirable secondary effects in distorting car market segmentation. Attention is therefore turning to economic instruments. One example is product labelling combined with higher taxes for high specific CO_2 emissions characteristics. The uncertainties in estimating both the impact of greenhouse gas emissions and the costs of energy-efficient technology have led governments to pursue voluntary agreements with industry. This approach aims to encourage industries to develop technological responses and find cost-effective approaches to enhancing sustainability, avoiding the need for direct intervention by government.

Land Use Planning and Urban Transport Policy

Improving the integration of land use and development planning with transport policy is an essential part of enhancing the sustainability of urban development. The location of green-field sites and redevelopment projects has major impacts on traffic patterns and growth, and vice versa. Land-use planning can limit the need to travel in a number of ways, notably by reducing the distances between places of residence, employment and commercial activities. This is particularly pertinent given that traffic growth in OECD countries over the last 50 years can be attributed more to longer trip distances than to the growing number of trips made. Parking controls and encouragement/provision of alternative means of transport are also essential parts of the package for managing urban traffic.

Strategic environmental assessments at the level of policies and programmes can be a useful tool to promote sustainability if undertaken well ahead of the authorisation of individual projects. In the transport sector strategic assessments are particularly suited to addressing inter-modal questions. They are also appropriate for major international infrastructure projects where they can be used to overcome purely national perspectives in determining routes and interconnections. Strategic environmental assessment is a relatively new procedure and its development will rely on both exchange of information and training on successful methodologies.

Road Safety

Many decisions concerning land use, infrastructure investment and road planning have implications for safety but the biggest improvements in road safety have been achieved through regulations on

◆ Figure 3. **Road safety trends, 1970-1995**

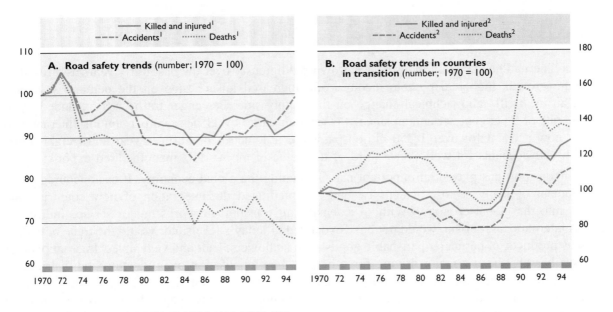

1. 18 countries: A, B, CH, D, DK, E, F, FIN, GR, I, IRL, L, N, NL, P, S, TR, UKR.
2. 9 countries: CZ, EST, H, LT, LV, PL, RO, SK, SLO.
Note: A = Austria; B = Belgium; CH = Switzerland; D = Germany; DK = Denmark; E = Spain; F = France; FIN = Finland; GR = Greece; I = Italy; IRL = Ireland;
L = Luxembourg; N = Norway; NL = Netherlands; P = Portugal; S = Sweden; TR = Turkey; UKR = Ukraine; CZ = Czechoslovakia; EST = Estonia;
H = Hungary; LT = Latvia; LV = Lithuania; PL = Poland; RO = Romania; SK = Slovakia; SLO = Slovenia.
Data for the former Czechoslovakia have been taken into account up to 1992 to ensure a degree of continuity in the series over a lengthy period of time;
from 1993 onwards the data provided by the Czech and Slovak Republics have been used. Furthermore, German reunification led to a break in the series
as a result of the incorporation, from 1991 onwards, of data relating to the new *Länder*, which resulted in a corresponding increase in the results for the
ECMT as a whole.

Source: Trends in the Transport Sector, 1970-1995, ECMT 1996.

drink-driving and the wearing of seat belts. Safety has also been improved through better vehicle design and technological advance in braking systems and passive safety features. There is always a danger that improved safety for vehicle users increases risks for pedestrians and other classes of road user, as drivers respond to improved perceived security with higher speeds and more aggressive driving styles. Recent policy initiatives have focused on reducing speeds, especially in urban areas, through speed limits and/or road layout and design. Enforcement of speed limits and traffic regulations requires determined political support which is nevertheless being facilitated by automation, with the deployment of video surveillance and related techniques. A number of OECD countries have achieved significant improvements in road safety over the past decade, suggesting other countries could follow suit and, even in those where safety levels are high, ambitious targets have been set for further improvement. Long-term programmes with specific intermediate targets are proving particularly successful (see Figure 3).

Transport of Hazardous Goods

Enforcement of existing international codes of practice, such as the OECD Guiding Principles on Chemical Accident Prevention, Preparedness and Response and the UN ECE's Agreement on Carriage of Dangerous Goods by Road, can help reduce risks in the transport of hazardous goods, and in accident and clean-up costs, mainly through the insurance market or, failing this, through industry providential funds.

AIR TRANSPORT AND SUSTAINABLE DEVELOPMENT

Trends

The international aviation industry has grown prodigiously over the past thirty years as a result of economic growth, higher disposable incomes and increased leisure time on the demand side, and falling airline tariffs and technical change on the supply side. Passenger traffic has expanded at an average rate of 9 per cent per annum since 1960 and air cargo by 11 per cent per annum. International airlines now account for over 1 350 billion passenger kilometres of traffic a year and freight transported by air accounts for well over a third of the value of the world's manufactured exports.

Air transport has played an important part in shaping the global economy. It has encouraged the development of many sectors of activity, and has facilitated the integration of new countries and regions into the global economy. Without extensive air transport networks, major service industries, such as international tourism, would not have expanded to today's levels, nor would the trade of certain overseas products, in particular perishable goods such as flowers, fruit and vegetables. International air transport has also been a major driving force behind the globalisation of production and distribution systems, providing the means to synchronise and co-ordinate geographically dispersed activities. In return, globalisation has reinforced air transport's comparative advantage. It is expected that the expanding engagement of internationally operating corporations in the joint development and production of high-technology components will boost the share of high-value low-bulk products in international trade. In addition, the proliferation of just-in-time concepts and lean production methods will substantially shorten production cycles and increase the pressure for rapid and reliable delivery.

These trends in the globalisation of production will have important effects not only on air cargo, but also on passenger transport. Changes in management strategies, such as the adoption of global sourcing, coupled with improved information and communications systems, are increasing the demand for international personal mobility. The rising importance of service-sector activities in industrialised countries, which are more travel-intensive than manufacturing, is also enhancing demand for air services. In particular, tourism, which already accounts for a large share of overall air travel, is expected to continue its development towards a global industry, with growth rates well above those for general world output. Most forecasts project growth during the years 1996-2010 to be in the range of 5 per cent per year for air passenger traffic, and 6.5 per cent per year for air freight. The most dynamic flows are expected to be intra-Asia, between Europe and Asia, and trans-Pacific, with traffic growth rates well in excess of the average.

Efficiency and the Role of Markets and Government

The international aviation sector is confronted by a wide variety of challenges resulting from new economic and social trends, new technologies and breaks with old trends. New markets are emerging and the requirements of established ones are changing. Systemic risks in passenger and cargo markets, together with uncertainties, such as the possibility of international trade conflicts, the speed and path of technological development or increasing global environmental pressures, could substantially alter the course of developments. For international aviation, this would have important implications for the size and pattern of both passenger and cargo markets which may prove difficult to foresee. It is also a time of fresh ideas in regulatory policy and, partly related to this, the structure of the airline industry is itself undergoing important change. If international air transport is to continue to contribute fully to the sound evolution of the world economy in the coming decades, it will need to be in a position to respond efficiently and rapidly to change and uncertainty.

Ultimately, the key to coping with uncertainty is through more flexibility in the way the industry operates. There are indications that this type of response is already occurring in some parts of the international aviation industry. Examples include the widespread uptake of leasing of aircraft, the contracting out of some airport services and maintenance, and the increase in alliances, franchising arrangements, and cross-share holdings. There has also been change on the policy front in international air transport. Over the past fifteen years, the focus of aviation policy has begun to shift from protection of existing airlines to enhancing efficiency and responding to consumer interests. Still, a complex range of problems remains, related in large part to restrictive institutional arrangements which could inhibit the restructuring process, thus preventing the sector from adjusting to ongoing dynamic changes in the economic, social and technological environment. The problems can be divided into five broad groups: 1) the operation of markets, 2) government support to carriers, 3) ownership, 4) infrastructure, and 5) environment.

Government regulation of competition in international aviation has traditionally involved major restrictions on market entry and exit and also on other freedoms such as those affecting capacity and fares. At the global level, the institutional setting for international aviation consists predominantly of bilateral air service agreements. These have the considerable merit of flexibility and can be tailored to meet the requirements of specific markets. Their underlying weakness, however, is that they cannot accommodate international network traffic flows which are multilateral in nature. Liberalisation has gradually been taking place within the existing bilateral agreements and in the framework of regional groupings, but given the challenges confronting international aviation, future development and extensions will be required. Within national markets, aviation is in many countries still considered a special case warranting specific competition policies, whereas in fact general competition policies should normally be adequate to handle any imperfection or grave distortions in the market. And at international level, governments often differ in their approach to and intervention in competition policy. As with other internationally operating sectors, such differences may impose high transaction costs on airlines and consumers, ultimately impairing efficiency in the international air transport sector.

Parts of the international airline market are characterised by high levels of direct and indirect subsidies. These can distort markets, and reduce managerial incentives. However, in practice, subsidies are often ill-defined and poorly targeted so that their economic objectives are not achieved. In addition, regulations and the ways money is spent are often not enforced, and the conditions governing state aid are not consistent across countries, sometimes giving rise to tensions between countries.

The nature of ownership often influences the efficiency of an airline and affects the operational and financial options open to it. State-owned carriers are often more prone to government interference in their day-to-day operations, a situation which can weaken the market stimulus to act commercially. In addition, state-ownership can make an airline's long-term planning the subject of political rather than economic and financial criteria. Reliance on national capital markets or on government sources for funding reduces the range of possible finance open to an airline. Restrictions on foreign ownership have been relaxed in some countries, but many still maintain limitations on foreign investment in and control of airlines. Such restrictions can impede the long-term restructuring of the sector, impair access to adequate financing and thereby adversely affect the efficiency of airline services.

Infrastructure bottlenecks lead to increasing congestion and pollution, and also pose one of the most serious impediments to the efficient functioning of the international aviation sector. Expanding overall infrastructure capacity is frequently a prerequisite for coping with increasing traffic volumes. Given past experience and the complexities of the planning processes, however, there are doubts as to whether currently proposed infrastructure investments in OECD countries and elsewhere will be fully realised. Even if they were realised it is clear that this would not mean surplus capacity and that air traffic congestion would continue to pose severe problems in many parts of the world. In addition to building more facilities, capacity can be enhanced and congestion reduced by increasing the efficiency in the operation of the existing infrastructure. Progress has been made at some airports, for example, by basing the allocation of runway capacity on economic criteria and by the removal of restrictions on access to ground handling. In general, however, current pricing of air transport infrastructure is rarely economically efficient, and suppliers of various airport-related services continue to be confronted with physical, regulatory and other impediments.

Aviation is a sector which poses a variety of environmental, safety and security challenges. At the local level, access to airports creates congestion and imposes a variety of atmospheric pollutants on adjacent residents. Take-offs and landings are noisy although increasingly less so with the development of engine technology. At the global level, commercial aviation has been estimated to contribute about 2 per cent of greenhouse gas emissions because of its production of some 500 million tons per annum of carbon dioxide. The rise in aviation-related CO_2 emissions has accelerated in recent years, and continuing rapid growth in air traffic is expected to put further upward pressure on emissions in the future. Nitrogen oxide emissions at cruising altitudes are thought to increase ozone concentrations with a global warming impact that could be of the same order of magnitude as that of aviation CO_2. At lower levels it can contribute to the acid rain problem. Aircraft are already subject to a number of international regulations limiting their environmental impact on take-off and landing, and some OECD countries are considering emission charges on air traffic. As in other sectors, there are good economic reasons for internalising the environmental and safety costs of aviation through either fiscal or regulatory policies. Environmental policy measures must be related directly to environmental costs and apply internationally, otherwise they can affect the basis of competition between airlines and between airports. Equally, there is a need to ensure that appropriate measures aimed at safety and security in international air transport are efficient, cost effective and continually reviewed.

Policy Responses

There has been broad recognition among governments in the recent past, in particular in the OECD countries, of the necessity to establish aviation markets which allow for more use of competitive processes. A more efficient international aviation industry, it is widely believed, will help to foster economic and social development, while at the same time permitting policy to be designed in such a way as to reduce harmful environment consequences. More specifically, the recently concluded OECD Project on International Air Transport[5] proposed a set of policy recommendations, including the following:

- International air transport should be treated within the general framework of competition policy. The sector should, wherever possible, be subjected to national or, where relevant, supranational competition laws controlling cartels and other anti-competitive agreements, as well as mergers and abuse of dominance. Moreover, the process of convergence of national competition policies and enforcement practices, which is already underway in the OECD area, needs to continue. Care should be taken that convergence is towards an adequate standard.
- State aid to facilitate structural adaptation of air carriers should be strictly limited; when ongoing subsidies are given for essential services they should be on a clearly defined basis.
- The movement to more private ownership of international airlines should be encouraged, and restrictions on foreign ownership and control of international airlines gradually reduced, with necessary steps taken to ensure that such changes do not facilitate the emergence of flags-of-convenience.
- Air transport infrastructure capacity should be managed efficiently. Appropriate economic pricing of infrastructure should be employed with the aim of signalling commercial needs and priorities to market participants. Access to international air transport infrastructure should be non-discriminatory. At airports, market entry by carriers should not be unduly hindered, and the

development of secondary slot trading and other market-based allocative mechanisms should be explored.

- International action must continue to ensure international aviation is safe, secure and not excessively environmentally intrusive. Effective policies should be developed to foster environmental protection to the extent that the benefits outweigh any adverse implications for airline operations. International harmonisation of environmental and safety standards for air transport should be further encouraged.
- Appropriate multilateral avenues of policy dialogue should be considered in order to foster co-operation in the future development of international air transport policy.

This wider embrace of market forces, not least the provision of appropriate incentive structures and flexibility, is reflected in the 1996 OECD Ministerial Communiqué, where ministers committed themselves to "further work for liberalising, in the interest of all, international air transport within bilateral and multilateral frameworks in order to ensure that the aviation sector contributes fully to economic development in OECD countries and in the world more generally".

MARITIME TRANSPORT

Maritime transport is generally associated with lower environmental impacts than aviation, road or rail transport. The main concerns, apart from accidental spillage of cargo, arise from failure of some operators to observe internationally agreed rules and standards concerning the safety of ships, and persons on board and the protection of the marine environment. Initiatives to ensure efficient implementation of such rules and standards are taken within certain international fora – in particular the International Maritime Organisation (IMO) has pre-eminent competence over these issues.

Trends

Globalisation of production and expanding trade are driving rapid growth in maritime shipping. World-wide freight earnings of the shipping industry in 1995 were US$160 billion (US$120 billion for general cargo and US$40 billion for dry/liquid bulk cargoes) from seaborne trade of 4.7 billion tons (including 1.8 billion tons of crude oil and oil products). Liner trade volume increased 34 per cent between 1985 and 1995 and containerised liner trade 137 per cent. Total fleet capacity in 1995 was 767 million dead-weight tons (DWT).

Forecasting bulk trades is always a difficult exercise because of the unpredictability of the demand, which is susceptible to volatile factors such as the seasonality of trade and its dependence on general economic circumstances. However, there will most probably be a slow but steady commodity-related increase in demand for bulk capacity over the next ten years, some of which will be absorbed by current over capacity (which is only marginal) but much of it will need new ships. Total liner trade is expected to grow at the same pace during the ten coming years, and the expected growth in container trade is around 8 per cent annually. As a result of the present developments on the market, the structure and organisation of the liner industry will change fundamentally. It will be more integrated (liner activity will be increasingly multimodal) and more concentrated (with the emergence of "strategic alliances" and global mega-carriers). Operators from Dynamic Non-Member Economies (DNMEs) and China will increase their market and fleet shares.

In terms of tonnage, the OECD flag fleet decreased by 29 per cent over the past two decades whereas the world fleet grew by 45 per cent, from 339 to 491 million gt.[6] Primarily due to problems related to the transition from a planned to a market economy, the share of national flag vessels from the Newly Independent States of the former Soviet Union and Central and Eastern European Countries declined slightly from 7.5 to 6 per cent. Flags from "rest of the world" more than doubled their share, from 9.5 per cent in 1975 to 23 per cent in 1995. This increase was principally due to the sharp rise in tonnage under flags of Dynamic Asian Economies (DAE) and China. The DAE flags share rose from 4.2 per cent in 1981 to 8.3 per cent fourteen years later whereas China almost doubled its share in world tonnage reaching 3.4 per cent of the total in 1995.

Table 1.   **Development of the share of regional groups in the world fleet**
(vessels above 1 000 gt)

	MID-75		MID-81		END 95	
	Million gt	%	Million gt	%	Million gt	%
OECD	195.5	56.0	214.7	51.0	139.5	28.4
Open Registers [1]	88.5	27.0	105.3	25.0	213.0	43.4
NIS/CEECs	25.4	7.5	30.3	7.2	28.8	5.9
Rest of the world	29.5	9.5	70.5	16.8	131.3	22.3
(of which DAEs)			(17.8)	(4.2)	(40.5)	(8.3)
(of which China)			(7.7)	(1.8)	(16.9)	(3.4)

1.   Antigua and Barbuda, Bahamas, Bemuda, Cayman Islands, Cyprus, Gibraltar, Honduras, Lebanon, Liberia, Malta, Mauritius, Oman, Panama, Saint-Vincent and Vanuatu.

Efficiency and the Regulatory Framework

The declining OECD flag trend has to be seen against the phenomenon of so-called "open registries", *i.e.* registries which are "open" to shipowners of any nationality and, contrary to traditional registers, do not require a genuine link between the flag and the vessel, in the form of some kind of nationality requirement for the crew, management of the company, etc. Such registries, which increased from 88.5 to 213 million gt during the period 1975/1995, were first established by countries such as Liberia and Panama and, at a later stage, by, *inter alia*, the Bahamas, Cyprus and Malta.

The declining trend in OECD flag share clearly demonstrates that during the past twenty years OECD flag shipping lost out significantly in terms of competition vis-à-vis open registries. Through registering vessels in open registries ("flagging out"), OECD shipowners were offered a number of commercial advantages over traditional OECD registers resulting in dramatic reductions in operating costs. The following are the most important advantages: flexible low-cost manning regulations (in traditional registers there is often an obligation to man vessels with nationals of the flag country and at the corresponding wage levels); no corporate tax on profits and on corporate equity, no taxation on extraordinary results from the sale of vessels, avoidance of tax liabilities on seafarers' earnings and often, but not always, less stringent environmental and safety regulations than in traditional maritime countries. Analysing open registry fleets from the viewpoint of beneficial ownership reveals a significantly less dramatic decline of the OECD shipping industry. In 1995, some 65 per cent of the world fleet was still owned by OECD interests.

Shipping (including inland waterways) remains the most economical mode of transport in terms of energy use per tonne/km. It also remains the least damaging mode of transport in terms of CO_2/NO_x emissions. Combustion of bunker fuel in 1990 was responsible for about 2 per cent of global fossil fuel related CO_2 emission; shipping emissions of CO_2 and NO_x (in grams/tonne-km) are lower than for other modes (except pipelines – and railways as far as NO_x is concerned). However, maritime transport imposes environmental costs in terms of routine discharges of oily bilge and ballast water; accidental spills of oil, toxic chemicals or other cargo; dumping of non-biodegradable solid waste; toxic effects of hull paints; and air emissions from the vessels' power supply. More indirectly, harbours generate intense land traffic in their hinterland with consequent impacts on land use, pollution and nuisance significant particularly where ports are adjacent to urban areas.

Deregulation of markets and increased competition can create safety and environmental risks, especially where lack of adequate policing allow some shipowners to operate sub-standard vessels. By doing so, these shipowners can also obtain competitive advantages which distort markets. The adoption of stricter safety rules and the initiatives taken in order to improve the implementation of existing rules by the Flag states – and where appropriate by port states authorities – are designed to minimise these environmental and safety risks. Attention needs to be given to prevent any player from evading its obligations.

Policy Responses

Faced with a steady increase in low cost competition from vessels sailing under open registry flags and, more recently, from Dynamic Asian Economies, OECD Governments have pursued three main policy approaches:

- *No Sector Specific Policy:* In its pure form such policy signifies for example no sector specific depreciation allowances, no special provisions for carry-forward or back of losses, no corporate tax exemptions for shipping companies, no exemptions from income tax or social security payments for seafarers, no nationality requirements for crews servicing on national flag vessels, no second registers, etc. A number of countries still adhere to this ''laissez faire'' policy (some countries in Asia for example), however, as a level playing-field for maritime shipping does not exist, this policy approach is gradually disappearing.
- *Provision of Subsidies to Protect and Support the Industry:* Traditional maritime countries have always criticised public support policies for the market distortions they engender but, contrary to this principle, they have traditionally adopted support measures primarily designed to improve the competitiveness of their fleets and sometimes even to maintain companies in business.
- *Provision of a Maritime Framework Policy.* Framework policy, coupled with subsidies, is now the most frequent approach employed by OECD governments to promote industry's chances of generating profits and preserve a viable national shipping industry. The main elements of such a framework focus on promoting liberalisation in the shipping industry.[7] Despite the subsidies, this approach has contributed to the promotion of free access of fleets to international traffic, free and fair competition in shipping markets, removal of discrimination in the provision of maritime and auxiliary services.

OECD Member countries account for two-thirds of world-wide imports and exports but the emergence of important maritime nations outside OECD has led to the necessity to establish a dialogue with the Dynamic non member economies and with the NIS/CEECs in order to secure the observance of the OECD shipping principles by more and more non-member maritime nations. Consultations with the NIS/CEECs led in 1993 to the ''Understanding on Common Shipping Principles''. Similar ''understandings'' are envisaged with other major Asian and Latin American players.

In addition to the above ''policy'' framework and as a reaction to cheap open registers a number of European countries (Denmark, France, Norway, Spain, Portugal, for example) have set up ''second registers'' in addition to the existing first registers. The advantages offered are, to a large extent, comparable to companies having registered their vessels under open registries. OECD Member governments' policies have been unable to stop OECD shipowners from flagging out to non-OECD registers.

Nevertheless, it is commonly agreed that the initiatives taken have contributed to avoiding an even more massive transfer of vessels to non-OECD registers.

The IMO is the unique body responsible for adopting and implementing international rules and standards for maritime safety and environmental protection. Several Conventions have been adopted among which the MARPOL Convention relates to the prevention of pollution from ships. It contains provisions on bulk carriage of oil (Annex I), bulk carriage of chemicals (Annex II), carriage of packaged chemicals (Annex III) and refuse disposal (Annex V). Annex IV on sewage is still awaiting ratification and an Annex VI on air pollution from ships should be adopted by Parties to the MARPOL Convention in September 1997. Annex VI contains provisions banning the emission of halons and CFCs, limiting the emissions of SO_x and NO_x, and introduces specifications for incinerators and reception facilities. Other Conventions concern, *inter alia*, the prevention of marine pollution by dumping of waste and other matters (1972), the civil liability for oil pollution damage (1969), and the establishment of an International Fund for Compensation of Oil Pollution (1972).

INTER-MODAL CONSIDERATIONS

A growing number of freight and passenger movements involve several stages, combining road, rail, air and shipping modes. Transport modes are thus increasingly interlinked and none can be considered in isolation. Thus airports and seaports generate heavy road traffic to provide access to them for passengers and freight. They also create demands for new or upgraded rail infrastructure. Improving inter-modal infrastructure links will be very important to ensuring that advances in transport logistics deliver their full potential in terms of increased efficiency and reduced environmental impacts.

Differences in the assignment of liability for cargoes, in terms of fraud, theft and accident, between the various modes of transport is also a key issue. The agent responsible for goods in transit varies as they pass from truck, to train to ship. This creates legal uncertainty. Multiplicity of paperwork linked to complex administrative procedures (customs, veterinary checks, restrictions for transport of hazardous goods and other safety standards) adds significantly to transportation costs and is not adapted for modern management of cargo flows. Additionally, it opens the door to criminal activities. Rationalising liability rules and administrative procedure at an international level would produce major benefits.

PRIORITIES FOR POLICY RESPONSES

Improving sustainability has implications for many aspects of transport policy – the list of issues addressed in this chapter is far from comprehensive – and packages of measures, including fiscal reform, will be required to address the issues effectively. The most far reaching measures are likely, however, to be the removal of distortions and barriers to free and fair competition in transport markets and the internalisation of accident and environmental costs in prices for transport services. Regulatory reform and organisational restructuring to promote efficiency is currently the key feature of inland, air and maritime transport markets, both within and beyond OECD countries. It is an essential condition for the development of sustainable transport systems.

Deregulation, however, creates new challenges for safety, environment and social policy. There are risks, particularly during periods of transition, that existing policy instruments are ill-adapted to emerging conditions. Prompt response in the application of instruments more suited to the new market conditions is essential. Providing the resources for effective enforcement is vital. Failure to act in the past has resulted in unacceptable working conditions in parts of the transport industry and avoidable environmental damage.

Internalisation, through the use of economic and regulatory instruments, is a response to managing accident, environmental, congestion and uncovered infrastructure costs eminently suited to sectors where the discipline of the market is replacing administrative controls. By incorporating these costs into market decision-making processes, it has the potential to achieve significant increases in social and economic welfare.

At the same time, development of new instruments should not detract from the enforcement of existing safety and environment legislation. Both in transport sectors where traditional administrative controls persist and in those that become more market oriented, traditional regulations will continue to provide an essential platform in regard to safety and environmental protection for the development of more sustainable transport.

NOTES

1. The text is the product of a multi-directorate drafting team. In addition to the three principal authors, input was also provided by Wolfgang Hübner, Reza Lahidji, Laurie Michaelis and Peter Wiederker.

2. Members: Austria, Belgium, Bosnia-Herzegovina, Bulgaria, Croatia, the Czech Republic, Denmark, Estonia, Finland, France, FYROM, Germany, Greece, Hungary, Ireland, Italy, Latvia, Lithuania, Luxembourg, Moldova, Netherlands, Norway, Poland, Portugal, Romania, the Slovak Republic, Slovenia, Spain, Sweden, Switzerland, Turkey, Ukraine and the United Kingdom. Associate Members: Australia, Canada, Japan, New Zealand, the Russian Federation and the United States. Observers: Albania, Armenia, Belarus, Georgia and Morocco.

3. Estimates of Externalities: Literature Review by the ECMT Task Force on the Social Costs of Transport.

4. Switzerland plus EU minus Sweden and Finland.

5. *The Future of International Air Transport Policy: Responding to Global Change*, OECD, 1997.

6. Gross tonnage = the total of all the enclosed commercial space within a ship, expressed in tons.

7. The most important elements of such a policy are contained Note 1 to the Annex A of the Code of Liberalisation of Current Invisible Operations and the ''Common Principles of shipping policy for Member countries'' [Recommendation of the Council C(87)11(Final), 13 February 1987], which has greatly contributed to the promotion of free access of fleets to international traffic, free and fair competition in shipping markets, removal of discrimination in the provision of maritime services and auxiliary services.

BIBLIOGRAPHY

ECMT (1997), *Strategic Environmental Assessment in the Transport Sector.*

ECMT (forthcoming in 1997), *Review of Policy Responses to Climate Change.*

ECMT (forthcoming), *The Social Costs of Transport.*

ECMT (1995), *Joint Declaration on Reducing CO$_2$ Emissions from Passenger Vehicles,* voluntary agreement negotiated with European automobile manufacturer's associations.

ECMT/OECD (1995), *Urban Travel and Sustainable Development.*

ECMT (1994), *Internalising the Social Costs of Transport.*

OECD (1997), *The Future of International Air Transport Policy: Responding to Global Change.*

OECD (1997), *Reforming Energy and Transport Subsidies.*

OECD (1997), *Towards Sustainable Transportation, Proceedings of Conference, Vancouver, March 1996.*

OECD (1996), *Competitive Advantages Obtained by some Shipowners as a result of Non-Observance of Applicable International Rules and Standards.*

OECD (1996), Communiqué from Meeting to Council at Ministerial Level.

OECD (1996), *Environmental Criteria for Sustainable Development.*

OECD (1996), *Integrated Advanced Logistics for Freight Transport.*

OECD (1996), *Maritime Transport.*

OECD (1995), *Motor Vehicle Pollution: Strategies Beyond 2010.*

OECD (1995), *Road Infrastructure Rehabilitation and Safety Strategies in Central and Eastern Europe.*

OECD (1995), *Roadside Noise Abatement.*

OECD (1994), *Congestion Control and Demand Management.*

OECD (1994), *Environmental Impact Assessment of Roads.*

OECD (1994), *Road Maintenance and Rehabilitation: Funding and allocation strategies.*

OECD (1994), *Targeted road safety programmes.*

OECD (1993), *Infrastructure Policies for the 1990s.*

OECD (1993), *International Air Transport: The Challenges Ahead.*

OECD (1992), *Advanced Logistics for Road Freight Transport.*

OECD (1992), *Strategies for Transporting Dangerous Goods by Road: Safety and Environmental Protection.*

OECD (1988), *Transporting Dangerous Goods by Road.*

Chapter 9

SUSTAINABLE AGRICULTURE

by

Ronald Steenblik, Leo Maier and Wilfrid Legg

Sustainable agriculture, by definition, is one that can indefinitely supply the goods and services demanded of it at socially acceptable economic and environmental costs. Demand for agricultural goods – namely, food and fibre – is certain to increase: current projections suggest that the world will have three billion more people to feed and clothe by the year 2025. Yet all these people will also need land to live on, and clean water to drink, putting pressure on the very same resources on which agriculture depends. Meanwhile, demand for the services to which agriculture contributes, such as attractive landscape and habitat for wildlife, will continue to increase as well.

OECD countries are acutely aware of the need to make their agricultural sectors sustainable. The experience of the past half-century, at least, provides reason for optimism. For the OECD as a whole, output has so far increased at a faster rate than population growth, with the result that many countries have become net exporters of food. What concerns Member countries is whether such progress can be continued without degrading biodiversity, water quality and the productivity of the land itself (Johnston, 1996).

AGRICULTURE NEEDS TO BECOME MORE SUSTAINABLE

The concept of sustainability in agriculture has two dimensions: ecological sustainability and economic sustainability. *Ecological sustainability* relates to agriculture's interactions with natural resources. It is clear that agriculture as practised in certain parts of the OECD is ecologically unsustainable. In some of the drier areas of the OECD, for instance, water for irrigation is being pumped from groundwater aquifers at rates that far exceed its natural replenishment. In other areas, surplus plant nutrients from animal wastes and fertilisers have led to eutrophication in surface waters, and pesticides have poisoned fish and fowl. And, until recently, expansion of cultivation into wetlands was responsible for destroying thousands of hectares of productive wildlife habitat across the OECD each year.

Agricultural land nonetheless forms an important part of the ecological mosaic. Numerous species of plants and animals are dependent to varying degrees on agricultural activities: not only the domesticated plants, but also many weeds of cultivation, some of which are incapable of surviving in the absence of a system of cultivation, harvesting and seed storage. Crops, especially the residue left after harvesting, often constitute an important source of food for migratory birds. Pastures offer habitat for ground-nesting fauna.

Economic sustainability relates to the degree to which agriculture is viable and can cover its costs in the long run. Currently, many farms in the OECD are unable to cover their costs of production and have become dependent on market protection – through tariffs on imports or other price supporting mechanisms – or subsidies to inputs, or both. Worse, the economic distortions created by such policies spill over into the environmental sphere, leading to inappropriate patterns of production and inefficient use of inputs, and discouraging the development and adoption of farming technologies that are less stressful on the environment.

In general, too few of the costs and benefits that spill over from agriculture to other sectors are reflected in farmers' accounts. Such ''market failures'' occur when agricultural chemicals leach into groundwater, thereby raising the costs of treating water for drinking. They occur too, when farmers refrain from taking actions that would add to the stock or flow of public goods – such as setting aside land that can serve as habitat for wildlife – because effective ways of making the beneficiaries compensate farmers for their costs are lacking. OECD countries are trying to correct these market failures. Doing so, in most cases, requires that they reform their agricultural support policies as well.

Reforming agricultural policies will help...

In fact, reform of agricultural policy has been a priority of OECD countries for more than a decade. In 1987 OECD Ministers committed themselves to reduce support levels, allow a greater role for market signals in farmers' decision-making, and better target measures to achieve those policy objectives for which markets might be inadequate (see Annex I in OECD, 1997a). *New Zealand* had already undertaken a comprehensive reform of its agricultural policies, starting in 1984, and *Australia* was eliminating most of its commodity-linked support. Subsequently, other countries, including *Canada*, the *EU, Mexico,* and the *United States*, began to shift support away from outputs and inputs, towards more direct means of income support, such as area-based payments, and in a few cases to reduce support to agriculture overall. Commitment to reform was further reinforced by the 1994 Uruguay Round Agreement on Agriculture, which obliged countries to replace all non-tariff barriers to trade with bound tariffs, increase access for imports, and reduce subsidies to exports, commodity production and farming inputs (Cahill, 1995; OECD, 1995d).

These changes to national agricultural policies are expected to improve the domestic and international allocation of resources, reduce incentives to over-use polluting chemical inputs and to farm environmentally sensitive land, and generally increase the market orientation of the farm sector – changes that generally should benefit the environment. The reform of agricultural policies is thus a necessary step in moving the sector closer to sustainability. But in many cases – where externalities are not internalised; where farmers lack adequate information; and, in general, where public goods are involved – it may not be sufficient. Other forms of policy intervention may still be needed.

... Especially when combined with more targeted environmental measures

Even before the Rio Summit, OECD governments recognised that there was an urgent need to improve the environmental and economic performance of agriculture (OECD, 1989). Over the past decade, most have introduced new programmes addressed to particular issues of sustainability, often as part of a wider package of agricultural policy reforms.

The measures that OECD countries are adopting share many common features. All countries, for example, have passed laws giving environmental or public-health authorities jurisdiction to deal with problems relating to pollution of air and water, and damage to ecologically or culturally sensitive areas. Activities that create high levels of pollution – such as dumping slurry or burning straw – are frequently proscribed via *direct regulations*. Direct regulations have also been used extensively to limit risks of serious damage to human health and the environment. Constraints on the use of new biotechnological products and on particularly toxic or persistent pesticides, for instance, are two areas where direct regulation is the norm (OECD, 1993b). Regulations are also used to set upper limits on animal stocking densities, to circumscribe periods during which the spreading of manure on land is permitted, and to forbid the collection of endangered plants and animals.

Dispersed environmental effects have generally been addressed via measures other than direct regulation. An approach that is becoming common is to set **minimum standards** for farm practices and to tie them to existing agricultural support programmes. Such ''cross-compliance'' measures have been used for several years in the *United States* and are becoming increasingly important in the *European Union* and other European countries. **Direct payments** are also being used extensively in several countries to encourage or maintain natural landscapes, to protect wildlife and to promote various environmental benefits specific to agriculture (OECD, 1997c). Often these payments are provided through fixed-term management agreements, though the rates of payment and the conditions attached to these agreements vary widely from country to country.

Virtually all OECD countries promote **research and development** (R&D) into technologies and farming methods that are less environmentally stressful (see Box), and on improving scientific understanding of the physical and biological links between agriculture and the environment. R&D is helping to reduce risks from pesticides, for example, through the development of: *i)* new strains of crops that are more naturally resistant to attack by pests (and less dependent on pesticides); *ii)* methods for growing crops that rely on safe yet effective biological processes or agents; and *iii)* chemical agents that are environmentally safe yet effective and affordable. Some of the funding for R&D is being channelled through joint agreements with industry.

Continuing technological innovation in the agricultural sector will be crucial to meeting the goals of sustainable agriculture. But as farming becomes more sustainable, it is certain to become more management-intensive, and in some cases more labour intensive, and focused on precision techniques. An OECD Workshop on Sustainable Agriculture (see OECD, 1992 and 1994c) concluded that this ''implies not only a redivision of producers' labour towards greater time spent on management and surveillance, but also an upgrading of farm-level skills necessary to master alternative farm planning and practices.''

Educated and informed farmers are more likely to be motivated to look after the productivity of their land, to be receptive to policies that constrain their activities in the interest of environmental protection, and to be able to implement any changes required of them. *Extension services* play an important role in this process. Improved information on the proper timing of fertiliser application, for example, has already helped reduce the loss of nutrients into water systems in several countries. Farmers are also more likely to adopt, adapt and further refine new practices when they are able to try them out first, at minimal financial risk to themselves, and when they can compare notes with other farmers. Technology is helping to facilitate such communication, both among farmers and between farmers and government agencies. Computers are being put to a wide range of uses, from training and education to integrating farm-level environmental plans across a rainfall catchment. And, as access to the Internet expands, more and more farmers are tapping into public databases in search of information on everything from reports of insect infestations to the daily weather forecast.

Finally, OECD countries are working to develop better tools for measuring trends in agriculture's impacts on the environment. Transforming disparate streams of data into ''agri-environmental indicators'' that are conceptually sound, measurable, and relevant for policy making, is one important aspect of this work. The OECD itself is actively involved in identifying a core set of agri-environmental indicators and in developing a common methodology for their specification (OECD, 1997d). Already, at this preliminary stage, some interesting trends are emerging. Despite the wide range of absolute levels in nutrient and pesticide use among OECD countries, for example, the general trend since the late 1980s appears to be downward, or at least stabilised.

Agricultural practices that have a high potential for sustainability

Sustainability in agriculture can often be improved by combining traditional practices with modern technologies. **Rotation** (*i.e.,* alternating two or more crops on the same piece of land) and **intercropping** (growing two or more crops simultaneously on the same piece of land) are examples of the former. Benefits from these practices arise because crops exploit different resources, or mutually interact with one another. If one crop is a legume it may provide nutrients for the others. The interactions between plants may also control pests and weeds.

One form of intercropping, **agroforestry,** involves the growing of annual crops along with perennial trees or shrubs (Bonnis, 1995; OECD, 1995*b* and 1996*b*). Deeper-rooted trees can often exploit water and nutrients not available to the annual crops. The trees also provide shade and mulch, while the ground cover reduces weeds and prevents erosion. **Silvipasture** – combining trees with grassland and other fodder species on which livestock graze – provides similar benefits for pastureland.

Conservation tillage combines an ancient technique with modern technology: placing seeds directly in the soil with little or no preparatory cultivation. Soil disturbance is reduced, thereby lessening runoff, soil erosion and nutrient losses.

Scientific management practices, which stress more detailed and frequent monitoring of actual conditions in the field, are also helping to make agriculture more sustainable. By using computers to map soil nutrient levels and crop nutrient uptake at a small scale, farmers can *administer fertilisers in precise doses,* thus reducing the amount of surplus nutrients released to the environment. By carefully monitoring pest levels and crop resistance, those practising *integrated pest management* can minimise the amount and frequency of chemical interventions. And by using *biological controls,* such as parasites or predators, they can in some cases forego chemical pesticides altogether.

National Approaches to Promoting Sustainable Agriculture Reflect Different Priorities

Because of differences in geography, climate, population density and level of economic development, the relative importance of particular environmental issues varies widely from one OECD country to another. Surplus manure production is much more of a problem in the wet and densely-populated areas of northern Europe than it is in semi-arid Australia. Australia, on the other hand, along with New Zealand, suffers from extensive damage caused by non-native rodents and other exotic pests. Soil erosion is a major concern in Canada and the United States, yet hardly at all in Ireland. It is not surprising, therefore, that different countries have taken different approaches to promoting sustainable agriculture.

Agri-environmental policy measures in OECD *Europe,* for example, seek not only to reduce agricultural pollution, but also to maintain the landscape, promote biological diversity and rural development, and improve animal welfare. Under *Norway's* ''acreage and cultural landscape scheme'' farmers receive area-based payments if they grow specified crops and refrain from making major changes to landscape features, such as streams, stone fences, pedestrian paths, and forest edges. In *Switzerland*, annual payments for various types of ''ecological services'' support integrated production methods, organic farming and improvement of animal welfare. The *European Commission* oversees a wide range of programmes under Council Regulation 2078/92, which was introduced as part of the package of measures accompanying the 1992 reforms of the Common Agricultural Policy. The main aim of this programme is to introduce or maintain production methods compatible with environment and landscape management. Various direct payments are given to reduce cattle stocking density, encourage new farming practices, maintain abandoned farmland, compensate farmers for providing public access to their land, and train farmers in all matters related to the above activities.

Measures adopted by EU member states under CR 2078/92 are co-financed with the EU, but are drawn-up by national governments and are tailored to their particular needs. *France's* ''whole-farm'' approach to sustainable development in agriculture, for example, is based around 10-year, farm-level sustainable development plans, which combine land consolidation with the encouragement of less-intensive animal production methods, and pilot projects in each major agro-ecological zone. The programmes offered in *Germany* similarly promote extensive production practices and special environmental measures tailored to regional circumstances. Their focus is on encouraging the adoption of less chemical-intensive farming techniques, reducing herd densities and setting aside ecologically sensitive lands, particularly wetlands. *Sweden* pays farmers to keep the landscape open in areas valued for their biological diversity and cultural heritage, while the *United Kingdom* supports the establishment of designated "Environmentally Sensitive Areas" on farms.

Because of its hilly terrain, heavy rainfall and intensive agriculture, *Japan's* approach to sustainable agriculture is oriented towards hydrological aspects: preventing flooding and water erosion, minimising nutrient leaching, and protecting forests. Its "Comprehensive Programme for the Promotion of Sustainable Agriculture", begun in 1994, seeks to promote "more environmentally friendly", low-input agriculture in ways that minimally affect the productivity of agriculture. Grants are given to local governments to help cover half the costs of demonstration projects, information activities and facilities for recycling waste. Japan also attaches high importance to R&D in support of sustainable agriculture.

The *United States* supports the adoption of more sustainable farming methods through numerous programmes. Its Conservation Reserve Programme (CRP) pays farmers on an annual basis for keeping environmentally sensitive land out of production in order to reduce erosion and sediment loading in streams, protect wildlife, minimise crop surpluses and boost farm income. Its Environmental Quality Incentives Program (EQIP) awards 5- to 10-year cost-share or incentive payment contracts to farmers who adopt approved land management practices or install structures for controlling animal waste. And its Integrated Farm Management (IFM) Systems and Integrated Crop Management (ICM) programmes encourage farmers to develop integrated strategies for managing their farm resources, while assisting them in meeting environmental quality standards. Privately-funded, non-governmental organisations are also actively involved in promoting their own vision of sustainable agriculture or land management.

Australia, *Canada* and *New Zealand* place great stress on community-based, self-reliant approaches to agricultural resource management. The aim of these approaches is to mobilise and motivate citizens to take on greater responsibility for the management of land, water and related vegetative resources in their local area. A recent OECD study (OECD, 1997 forthcoming; Steenblik, 1996) surveyed these programmes.

Australia's National Landcare Programme (NLP), which is the oldest and largest of its kind, channels much of its financial assistance through farmer-led community groups – known as "landcare" groups – which now number around 3 000, each typically with 30 to 40 members. Much stress is placed on improving information flows, upgrading skills and using peer pressure to attain results. The NLP provides grants to support group activities such as farm-level demonstrations and trials, resource monitoring, and property management plans. These plans encompass management of all physical and financial resources, and are being integrated into regional rainfall catchment area plans. *Canada's* programmes encompass not just agriculture but the entire agro-food industry and involve environmental groups, consumer groups, health-care professionals, producers, and governments at all levels. In *New Zealand*, various industry groups have become involved in promoting sustainable agriculture, by drawing up codes of good practice, and developing environmental strategies to address the entire life-cycle of the industry's products.

Several other countries are also discovering that improving environmental performance can be done much more effectively when the farmers themselves are encouraged to take a leadership role in the process. *The Netherlands*, for example, is conducting a special experiment with five farmer-led "eco-cooperatives" to see whether they can meet public policy objectives using their own innovative approaches. *Norway* supports groups of farmers working together in "experimental rings", which carry out field-level experiments and, based on their findings, provide advice to other farmers. In the *United States*, local governments and NGOs, as well as federal agencies, are working together with farmer groups to promote co-operative approaches to sustainability issues.

Some Examples of Specific Measures

To understand how policy measures in OECD countries are being formulated to address specific concerns, it is useful to look at a few examples in the areas of soil loss, nature conservation, nutrient imbalances and pesticide use.

Soil Loss

Most agri-environmental policies are ultimately concerned with influencing what farmers add to, subtract from or do not do with their *soil*. Soil loss is the main priority in *Australia*, *Canada*, *Japan*, *Mexico,* the *United States* and in countries bordering the Mediterranean Sea, while protection of soils from contamination, pollution and degradation are leading priorities in most northern European countries (OECD, 1994*b*). Initially, governments were motivated to stem soil losses because of concerns over the effects that erosion might have on crop yields. In recent years, however, they have come to realise that off-farm damage caused by the transport of soil particles – especially those related to the build-up of silt in rivers and dam reservoirs – often exceeds that which takes place on farms.

OECD countries are attempting to reduce soil loss in two ways: by discouraging the farming of highly erodible land, and by influencing grazing, cultivation and irrigation practices on land currently farmed. Reducing production-linked support has already helped accomplish the first goal in several OECD countries. After *New Zealand* eliminated support for livestock products in the mid-1980s, for example, stock numbers fell and, in general, pressure on the soils most susceptible to erosion was eased. In other countries, such as *Portugal*, reductions in price support for cereal crops, combined with grants to help convert previously tilled land to permanent pasture or forest, have helped to protect large areas of farmland from further erosion. Programmes in *Canada*, the *EU* and the *United States* that pay farmers to set aside arable land for extended periods, usually for ten years or more, also appear to reduce soil erosion (Maier, 1996; OECD, 1997*b*).

Programmes to reduce soil losses from farmland remaining in production have been in place for many years in several countries. Their aims are to reduce the forces of erosion through structural improvements to the land (*e.g.,* by planting wind breaks), and to encourage farmers to shift away from cultivation and cropping practices that cause erosion and towards tillage practices that are less eroding (*e.g.,* contour ploughing, low- and no-till farming). These policies, and the increasing tendency of governments to withhold support payments from farmers who plough up fragile lands, are among the principal reasons why rates of soil erosion are believed to be on the decline in the OECD area.

Conservation of Nature

Three decades ago OECD governments were concerned principally with protecting and maintaining populations of game species or species with some cultural or symbolic importance (such as the bald eagle in the United States). In the 1970s and 1980s emphasis began to shift towards conservation of wildlife habitats. More recently, maintaining biodiversity has become the main goal. Governments are trying to halt further encroachment of agricultural (and other) activities into ecologically sensitive areas, particularly wetlands. They are encouraging farmers to modify their farming methods so as to create less stress on plants, associated insects and animals. And, to maintain open landscapes, some are paying farmers to keep pastures from reverting to forests.

A common instrument for encouraging nature conservation on agricultural land is the management agreement, whereby a farmer receives a regular payment or other incentive in return for providing specified environmental services or refraining from certain activities. These payments are often related to farm size, the conditions that farmers are required to meet, and associated costs. The producers are provided with a schedule that sets out various measures, from which they select those to be implemented, depending on the areas that most urgently require attention from an environmental perspective. In almost all cases the agreements are voluntary. Most OECD countries now offer one or more types of management agreements to land owners and farmers.

In *North America,* private organisations with an interest in protecting migratory waterfowl have reached their own accords with farmers. One such programme is the 1986 North American Waterfowl Management Plan (NAWMP), a fifteen-year framework for international co-operation in conserving wetlands and restoring waterfowl populations. The NAWMP establishes joint-venture partnerships between the federal governments of Canada and the United States, various state, provincial, territorial and tribal governments, and private organisations in these countries. One of these projects, in Saskatchewan (*Canada*), combined the acquisition of conservation easements and marginal farmlands with outreach programmes aimed at encouraging farmers to adopt different farming practices. Another, in Arkansas (*United States*), demonstrated that, in flood plains, leaving plant residues and shallow water on harvested cropland during the winter would not only benefit migratory waterfowl but would also help the farmer control weeds and soil erosion.

In addition to trying to halt the destruction of wildlife habitat and conserving what habitat remains, some countries are now taking the further step of restoring farmland to something resembling its previous natural state and even to "creating" new natural areas. Under the *United States'* Wetlands Reserve Program, for example, farmers are being paid to stop cultivating former wetlands and to restore these areas to something approaching their former state. *The Netherlands* has embarked on a long-term programme to buy-up farmland in designated areas for the express purpose of creating new nature preserves. The *United Kingdom,* through its Habitat Scheme, is creating and improving a range of valuable wildlife habitats in areas taken out of agricultural production.

Nutrient Imbalances

In most OECD countries, problems concerning plant nutrients, particularly nitrogen and phosphorus, relate not so much to their overall availability, but to their maldistribution, in terms of timing and location. The increasing specialisation of agriculture, away from the traditional pattern of mixing crops and livestock on the same farm, has been a major contributing factor to the development of these imbalances. Two centuries ago farmers relied on animal manure collected on the farm, or from nearby farms, to fertilise their crops. Today, production of most commercial crops requires application of fertilisers produced from mineral sources. And most pigs and poultry are now raised intensively in concentrated areas, often using imported feed. Disposing of their manure in a manner that does not over-load the absorptive capacity of the soil has proved expensive. As a result, manure surpluses are still contributing to local pollution "hot spots" in many OECD countries.

Laws prohibiting the direct discharge of animal waste slurry to surface waters have existed in most OECD countries since the early 1970s. Policies to deal with the problems caused by spreading excessive amounts of animal wastes on agricultural land have often started with restrictions aimed at minimising nutrient losses due to leaching and run-off during periods when the potential for such losses is at its peak. Since the 1980s several European countries (including *Belgium, Denmark, The Netherlands* and *Sweden*) have banned the spreading of manure on arable lands during the autumn and winter months, generally between harvest and cultivation. Many more countries have encouraged the planting of "green fallow" – that is, cover crops – in order to retain nitrogen in the soil throughout the winter.

More common have been laws restricting activities of intensive livestock operations. *Austria, Denmark, Finland* and *Norway* require farmers to obtain environmental permits if they wish to keep more than a specified number of livestock units; permits for smaller installations are usually issued by local authorities. In other countries the expansion of intensive livestock facilities is often checked by local or regional planning procedures.

The Netherlands is pioneering a system of minerals accounting, first as a management tool, and eventually as a means for assessing a levy on surplus nutrient production (OECD, 1995*a*). Along with other EU countries, it must also meet the requirements of the *EU's* Nitrate Directive, which sets out maximum levels, to be attained by 1999, for manure applied to fields in zones that have been identified as being vulnerable to nitrate pollution.

Besides tackling nutrient problems attributable to the spreading of manure, many countries are also trying to reduce nutrient leaching from chemical fertilisers, particularly nitrates. The *United States,* for example, is conducting field trials on systems for precision application of fertilisers. The *United Kingdom,* under its voluntary Nitrate Sensitive Areas Scheme, pays participating farmers to follow practices that go beyond what the Government considers to be good agricultural practice, in order to reduce leaching in areas where nitrates seriously threaten the quality of groundwater. *Denmark* and *Sweden* both aim to reduce nitrate leaching by 50 per cent by, among other means, encouraging better timing of fertiliser and manure applications and the growing of winter crops.

Chemical Pesticides

Chemical pesticides have been a boon to agriculture, enabling much more food to be grown and preserved than was ever before possible. Their effects on human health and the environment, however, have not always been benign. These risks are influenced both by the physical and chemical properties of the chemicals themselves (*i.e.,* their toxicity, persistence and mobility through the soil) and by the conditions under which they are applied. Sustainability as it applies to pesticides implies balancing the various risks and benefits that they provide.

Pesticide registration is the primary means by which OECD countries have managed the types of chemical pesticides available on the market.[1] Nowadays new pesticides are approved for a limited time, typically five to ten years, and together with older products are subject to periodic reviews. As a result, pesticides are among the world's most thoroughly tested chemicals. These reviews are conducted to ensure that all products fulfill new – and generally stricter – testing requirements and that they continue to meet safety standards. Registration and re-registration programmes are based on the evaluation of test data showing the pesticides' possible risks to human health and the environment, as well as their efficacy in controlling agricultural pests and diseases. Nevertheless, even pesticides that are found to be highly toxic or persistent may sometimes be approved for use if they are judged to be the only effective means of controlling a pest, and if steps can be taken to protect the environment and any people who might potentially be exposed to them.

To supplement their registration programmes, OECD countries have implemented a wide range of other measures. Mandatory testing and certification of users of the most highly toxic pesticides is now required in many countries. This ensures that users know how to apply pesticides safely and efficiently. Equipment is also often required to be tested and certified. This helps to ensure that safety standards are met and enables governments to prevent the introduction of new spraying methods that are less efficient in administering pesticides than those already in use.

More direct regulations have been introduced in recent years, aimed both at reducing total volumes used and at limiting the build-up of residues. Since 1993, for example, growers in *The Netherlands* have been forbidden, except in exceptional circumstances, to treat their soil with fumigants more than once every four years. One expected effect of this regulation will be to force farmers to rely more on crop rotation. In other countries, such as *Denmark,* regulations now restrict the frequency of pesticide applications within a crop season.

Increasingly, farmers are being forbidden from using chemical agents near surface waters and ecologically sensitive areas. Such regulations are intended to reduce the environmental impact of pesticides, but they also reduce total volumes used. *Denmark* has banned the spraying of pesticides within two metres of open water. In *Switzerland,* farmers participating in the "integrated production" programme must maintain a fertiliser- and pesticide-free green strip of at least three metres between their fields and any water courses or forests on which they border.

Governments are also trying to encourage farmers, through voluntary programmes, to adopt more environmentally benign ways of controlling pests, or to stop using chemical pesticides altogether. Virtually all OECD Member countries now support adoption of so-called "integrated pest management" (IPM) – an approach to pest management that strives to maximise reliance on natural controls and minimise the amount and frequency of chemical interventions. To the extent that pesticides are needed, they are supposed to be used sparingly and selectively. Many governments also offer grants to help farmers convert their operations to "organic" farming.

CONCLUDING REMARKS

As both a major "user" of natural resources and a "supplier" of environmental services, agriculture is a key sector in the process of sustainable development. The all-encompassing nature of sustainability draws particular attention to the need for coherence among policy measures. Information, advice and training for farmers cannot be effective as long as agricultural and environmental policy measures are sending them contradictory signals. Greater coherence is beginning to be achieved as agricultural policies are reformed, and new agri-environmental programmes are introduced. As a result, farmers in the OECD are becoming increasingly aware of the rewards of adopting more environmentally sound agricultural practices and technologies.

As progress is made in understanding agricultural systems' sustainability, the trade-offs that may be required to achieve different objectives will become more evident. Sustainability began with the recognition that some gains in environmental quality were obtainable at little or no economic cost. Technological progress and better management of farm resources should continue to help keep these costs down, but the further pursuit of sustainability will in many locations require much higher levels of investment than made in the past. This conclusion reinforces the need to advance those agricultural policy reforms that lead to a more efficient and economical allocation of resources in agriculture.

Interest in sustainable agriculture is certain to grow. The OECD will continue to play an important role in informing public discussion of the issues. By examining different approaches it will help governments formulate better measures to address agricultural and environmental policy objectives. By engaging countries in peer reviews of each others' policies, and of the environmental performance of their agricultural sectors, it will help them assess their progress against common standards. And by co-ordinating the development of indicators it will provide them with the necessary tools to do this. Such work will benefit not just OECD countries, but other countries striving to achieve sustainable agriculture as well.

NOTE

1. The OECD itself is playing an important role in encouraging greater cross-country acceptance of re-registration reviews performed by different countries. The aim is to reduce duplication of effort and increase the efficiency of the review process.

BIBLIOGRAPHY

BONNIS, Gérard (1995), "Farmers, forestry and the environment", *The OECD Observer*, No. 196 (October/ November), pp. 38-40.

CAHILL, Carmel (1995), "OECD Agriculture after Uruguay", *The OECD Observer*, No. 196 (October/November), pp. 32-35.

JOHNSTON, Donald (1996), "Food security and sustainable agriculture", *The OECD Observer*, No. 203 (December), pp. 4-5.

MAIER, Leo (1996), "Letting the land rest", *The OECD Observer*, No. 203 (December), pp. 12-15.

MAIER, Leo and Ronald STEENBLIK (1995), "Towards sustainable agriculture", *The OECD Observer*, No. 196 (October/November), pp. 36-37.

OECD (1989), *Agricultural and Environmental Policies – Opportunities for Integration*.

OECD (1992), "Agents for Change–A report from the OECD Workshop on Sustainable Agriculture Technology and Practices", Paris, 11-13 February, 1992, General Distribution Document OCDE/GD(92)49.

OECD (1993a), *Agricultural and Environmental Policy Integration: Recent Progress and New Directions*.

OECD (1993b), *Safety Considerations for Biotechnology: Scale-Up of Crop Plants*.

OECD (1994a), "Agricultural policy reform: environmental externalities and public goods", in *Agricultural Policy Reform: New Approaches – The Role of Direct Income Payments*.

OECD (1994b), "Public policies for the protection of soil resources", Environment Monographs No. 89 (General Distribution Document OCDE/GD(94)18).

OECD (1994c), *Towards Sustainable Agricultural Production: Cleaner Technologies*.

OECD (1995a), *Environmental Performance Reviews – Netherlands*.

OECD (1995b), *Forestry, Agriculture and the Environment*.

OECD (1995c), *Sustainable Agriculture – Concepts, Issues and Policies in OECD Countries*.

OECD (1995d), *The Uruguay Round – A Preliminary Evaluation of the Impacts of the Agreement on Agriculture in the OECD Countries*.

OECD (1996a), "Activities to Reduce Pesticide Risks in OECD and Selected FAO Countries – Part I: Summary Report", General Distribution Document OCDE/GD(96)121.

OECD (1996b), "Workshop on Forestry, Agriculture and the Environment – Country Case Studies", General Distribution Document OCDE/GD(96)5.

OECD (1997a), *Agricultural Policies in OECD Countries: Measurement of Support and Background Infomation*.

OECD (1997b), *The Environmental Effects of Land Diversion Policies*.

OECD (1997c), *Environmental Benefits from Agriculture: Issues and Policies*.

OECD (1997d), *Environmental Indicators for Agriculture*.

OECD (1997), *Cooperative Approaches to Sustainable Agriculture*.

PARRIS, Kevin (1996), "Environmental indicators for agriculture", *The OECD Observer*, No. 203 (December), pp. 10-12.

STEENBLIK, Ronald (1996), "When farmers fend for the environment", *The OECD Observer*, No. 203 (December), pp. 16-18.

Chapter 10

SOUND MANAGEMENT OF TOXIC CHEMICALS

by

Dian Turnheim

OECD has a mandate to work in sectoral areas to improve co-operation and development in social as well as economic policy. Under the framework of the Organisation's efforts to improve environmental protection while ensuring economic growth, Member countries have devoted substantial resources for the past 20 years to the development of policies and instruments for the management of chemicals in the OECD area.

Our society's dependence on chemicals is a comparatively recent phenomenon. The chemicals industry today is a US$1.55 trillion global industry, nearly four times as big as it was just 30 years ago. World-wide, the industry employs some 12 million people. The chemical industry in OECD Member countries accounts for 76 per cent of world-wide production. Chemicals and related products represent 14 per cent of total imports and exports of manufactured goods for OECD nations, and they make up 12 per cent of Gross Domestic Product for some countries. The rapid expansion of the chemical industry, which includes pharmaceuticals, pesticides and industrial chemicals, has also played a central role in the evolution of OECD countries' environmental protection policies.

The fast-paced expansion of the chemical industry has brought with it the possibility of the escalation of risks, endangering both human health and the environment. Maximising safety and minimising risks are therefore important aims for sustainable development for both governments and the chemical industry world-wide. The OECD has taken the lead in assisting countries in the development and co-ordination of environmental health and safety activities on an international basis. The forum provided by OECD enables countries to work together to discuss policies, clarify issues and protect the well-being of man and the environment, while giving due consideration to economic and trade concerns in its search for solutions.

THE OECD CHEMICALS PROGRAMME

The Chemicals Programme, which was established in 1971 under the Organisation's Environment Programme, was substantially expanded in 1978 to make use of extra-budgetary resources provided by the great majority of Member countries in a Special Programme on the Control of Chemicals. The principal objectives of the Chemicals Programme are to:

- assist Member countries' efforts to protect human health and the environment through improving chemical safety;
- make chemical control policies more transparent and efficient; and
- prevent unnecessary distortions in the trade of chemicals and chemical products.

Over the years, the Programme has responded to the changing needs and priorities set by Member countries which have reflected the evolution of their philosophy of chemicals management. At the beginning, policies and instruments were developed in OECD for responding in a concerted way to concerns posed by specific, persistent and highly toxic chemicals, like mercury, CFCs and PCBs. This largely reactive mode of international action was replaced by the end of the 1970s by a more proactive, comprehensive one at a time when Member countries were beginning to develop legislative and administrative tools to prevent environmental health and safety problems arising from the manufacture, use and disposal of chemicals. OECD's role was to catalyse the development and implementation of harmonized policies and instruments for chemicals management in order to avoid erection of non-tariff trade barriers that might have been created by countries acting independently to establish, for example, notification systems for new chemicals, rules on confidentiality of chemical safety data or requirements for the generation of test data.

Once Member countries had established well-harmonized comprehensive systems for managing chemicals, they turned in the 1980s to taking a closer look at the risks that might be posed by chemicals which had long been on the market. In order to avoid duplication and save resources to both governments and the chemical industry in undertaking this formidable task, OECD began a burden-sharing programme to co-operatively test and assess chemicals produced in high volumes. More recently, in the face of globalisation of the market for chemicals and of the potential concerns they pose to human health and the environment, OECD acts as a forum for advancing sustainable development in this sector in Member countries as well as in non-member countries. It not only makes the fruits of its work in the past three decades available to non-members, but also involves the latter in its ongoing work, especially in the prevention and management of risks posed by chemicals. Since 1992, OECD's Chemicals Programme has been a major contributor to the international efforts to implement Chapter 19 of Agenda 21 on Sound Management of Toxic Chemicals and is one of the six international organisations (together with five UN organisations) which have banded together since UNCED to co-ordinate their programmes, avoid duplication and identify gaps under the Inter-Organization Programme on the Sound Management of Chemicals (IOMC).

CURRENT ACTIVITIES IN OECD RELATING TO UNCED OBJECTIVES

UNCED identified six programme areas where progress was to be made in the sound management of toxic chemicals. OECD, working with its Member countries, has contributed substantially to three of them – those related to assessment of chemical risks, harmonization of classification and labelling of chemicals, and risk reduction. It has also played an important role in reaching the goals set for two further areas, information exchange and capacity building. The details of OECD's contribution to date are set out briefly below.

Expanding and Accelerating International Assessment of Chemical Risks

The objectives as stated in Chapter 19 are ''to strengthen international risk assessment''. Several hundred priority chemicals or groups of chemicals, including major pollutants and contaminants of global significance, should be assessed by the year 2000, using current selection and assessment criteria'' and ''to produce guidelines for acceptable exposure to a greater number of toxic chemicals, based on peer review and scientific consensus distinguishing between health or environment-based on exposure limits and those relating to socio-economic factors''. In 1994, the Intergovernmental Forum on Chemical Safety (IFCS) – a mechanism for co-operation among governments for the promotion of sound management of chemicals – gave more specific guidance on priorities for action for meeting these objectives.

The OECD Chemicals Programme has already contributed half of the international risk assessments which are to be produced to meet the goals set by IFCS: 200 new international evaluations by 1997 and, if this goal is met, 500 by the end of the century. Member countries share the burden of systematically testing and assessing high production volume chemicals to identify those which are of potential concern to health and/or the environment. The chemical industry in OECD countries contributes resources to test chemicals to fill data gaps in the so-called Screening Information Data Set (SIDS) for characterisation and effects on and exposure to human health and the environment of specific chemicals selected by Member countries. The data is then assessed collectively in OECD by governments, and conclusions related to potential risk of the chemicals and recommendations on the need for further work are agreed. The data and the agreed assessments are then published and made available world-wide by UNEP Chemicals. From 1992 through 1996, approximately 100 chemicals were assessed in the OECD Existing Chemicals Programme, and over 200 more are in various stages of investigation.

This approach of "sharing the burden" of the investigation of high production volume chemicals – which in principle have a high potential for occupational, consumer and environmental exposure – government and industry resources are saved, duplication of effort is avoided and more evaluations are available for use in their decision-making processes by Member and non-member countries.

OECD has been a leader in developing a common basis for generation and interpretation of safety data on chemicals, another area where IFCS called for intensification of international efforts. The advantage of internationally agreed methods for hazard characterisation has been clear to Member countries for many years: not only can high quality test data be ensured, but immense resources can be saved by the chemical industry who are not required to repeat testing for regulatory purposes abroad. An integral part of the 1981 OECD Council Decision on the Mutual Acceptance of Data in the Assessment of Chemicals, the OECD Guidelines for the Testing of Chemicals continue to be updated in order to enhance the validity and international acceptability of safety data on the human health effects, effects on biotic systems, environmental chemical fate and physical chemical properties. Since UNCED, 26 new and updated Test Guidelines have been adopted, bringing the total number of guidelines available today to 88. The OECD Principles of Good Laboratory Practice, which ensure the quality and rigour of test data, are currently being revised and up-dated in view of increasing data reliability and removing potential non-tariff trade barriers caused by varying national standards.

The OECD Test Guidelines and Principles of Good Laboratory Practice are the *de facto* global standards for the generation of quality test data related to the safety of chemicals to man and the environment. In order to formalise this, efforts are currently underway to extend the OECD system of mutual acceptance of data to adherence by non-member countries. By using and accepting the same standards for the generation of safety data as those in OECD countries, non-member countries with a significant domestic or multinational chemical industry will be equal partners in the exchange of data for regulatory purposes and will have a chance to take part in the work in OECD regarding development and implementation of these standards.

The resources saved by the chemical industry through the application by national regulatory authorities of the OECD Council Decision on the Mutual Acceptance of Data are not only measured in such tangible ways as staff and laboratory resources for – often very costly – testing. The number of laboratory animals which are saved by not duplicating testing is also considerable. OECD has been very active in developing alternative test methods in toxicity testing which continue to reduce the number and suffering of vertebrate animals.

Progress has also been made in developing a common foundation for the interpretation of safety data for national decision-making related to risk management, as called for in the priorities for action set by IFCS. OECD has long been active in the work on assessment methodology. By sharing information and experience on the way chemicals are evaluated nationally, countries come closer to the long-term goal of the mutual acceptance of hazard assessments. Indeed, in the framework of the work on sharing the burden of the investigation of existing chemicals discussed above, agreed methodologies have been developed in OECD and are used in the OECD international assessment process. OECD continues to be a leader in the relatively new area of the development of methodologies for environmental effects and exposure assessment.

Harmonization of Classification and Labelling of Chemicals

Chapter 19 called for "a globally harmonized hazard classification and compatible labelling system, including material safety data sheets and easily understandable symbols, [to] be available, if feasible, by the year 2000." In order to attack this rather formidable task, a Co-ordinating Group for the Harmonization of Chemicals Classification Systems was established within the framework of IOMC. OECD, the International Labor Organization (ILO) and the UN Committee of Experts on Transport of Dangerous Goods (UNCETDG) are the key international bodies which are implementing the UNCED mandate. An internationally harmonized chemical classification and labelling system will: i) enhance the protection of man and the environment by providing an internationally comprehensible system for hazard communication; ii) provide a recognised framework for those countries without an existing system; iii) reduce the need for testing and evaluation of chemicals; and iv) facilitate international trade in chemicals whose hazards have been properly assessed and identified on an international basis.

OECD has taken the lead in the work on establishing harmonized classification criteria related to health and environmental hazards of chemicals. The work on harmonized classification criteria related to the various effects of chemicals on human health should be finalised by the end of 1997. Work on labelling and safety data sheets, being led by the other organisations, should be finished by 2000. Agreement among OECD countries – which are the major producers of chemicals – to implement the criteria would be a first step in the establishment of an international standard for implementing a globally harmonized system. Discussions are ongoing to resolve technical differences and to decide the form the international standard should take.

Information Exchange on Toxic Chemicals and Chemical Risks

The third area for work as stated in Chapter 19 was "to promote intensified exchange of information on chemicals safety, use and emissions among all involved parties" and "to achieve by the year 2000, as feasible, full participation in the implementation of the Prior Informed Consent (PIC) procedure, including possible mandatory applications through legally binding instruments contained in the Amended London Guidelines for the Exchange of Information on Chemicals in International Trade and in the FAO International Code of Conduct on the Distribution and Use of Pesticides, taking into account the experience gained with the PIC procedure."

OECD's work on information exchange related to banned and severely restricted chemicals in the 1980s was at the foundation of the current work on PIC and a legally binding instrument for its implementation. Member Countries adopted in 1984 a Council Recommendation on Information Exchange related to Export of Banned or Severely Restricted Chemicals, which called for provision of sufficient relevant information for importing countries to make informed decisions regarding chemicals which are restricted or banned in the exporting country. This was the basis for work in the UN which extended this concept globally through its Convention. It was considered that, once OECD Member countries – being the major producers – could agree to provide information to other countries to allow them to make appropriate decisions before importing specific banned or severely restricted chemicals, this concept could then be globalised through the UN system, in this case jointly through UNEP and FAO.

Information exchange, in general, continues to be the backbone of OECD's work on chemicals. The OECD has a comparative advantage over other international fora in this area due to the informal nature of much of its work. The various working groups, expert meetings and policy body meetings under the auspices of the Chemicals Programme are used as sounding boards where Member countries can share experience on new initiatives in the control of risks of chemicals, prevention policies, life cycle management of chemicals, etc.

In order to make use of the new possibilities for instantaneous global communication provided by Internet, the OECD Chemicals Programme maintains a home page (http://www.oecd.org/ehs/) allowing access to most of its publications and simple manipulation of several of its data bases.

Establishment of Risk Reduction Programmes

The objective, a stated in Chapter 19, is to "eliminate unacceptable or unreasonable risks and, as far as economically feasible, to reduce risks posed by toxic chemicals by employing a broad-based approach involving a wide range of risk reduction options and by taking precautionary measures derived from a broad-based life cycle analysis." Elimination, or at least reduction, of risk is, of course, the ultimate goal of all of the work described above. OECD provides a forum in which all concerned parties – governments, industry and non-governmental organisations – can analyse the risk posed by specific chemicals or groups of chemicals based on information about their effects on man and/or the environment as well as on the potential for exposure to the chemical and make recommendations about the most appropriate risk management options to be taken nationally and, under certain circumstances, internationally.

By working together in OECD's Risk Management Programme, Member countries share information and experience on a wide range of management options, from industry-led responsible care and product steward programmes, to labelling and hazard information sheets, through voluntary agreements between governments and industry to more coercive legislative arrangements. Although risk management requirements depend on the national situation (both related to exposure to the chemical and to economic considerations), in certain cases where there is significant trade or transboundary movement of chemicals proven to present a major risk, concerted international action is sometimes warranted. OECD has been a leader in reaching agreement on control measures for, *e.g.,* CFCs, mercury, PCBs and, more recently, lead. Voluntary agreements on the restriction of certain brominated flame retardants have been reached with the chemical industry.

OECD has developed a Guidance Manual for Governments on Pollutant Release and Transfer Registers (PRTR) in order for them to catalogue potentially harmful pollutant releases or transfer to the environment from a variety of sources. A PRTR can be an important tool in the total environment policy of a government, providing otherwise difficult to obtain information about the pollution burden, encouraging reporters to reduce pollution, and engendering broad public support for government environmental policies.

Strengthening of National Capabilities and Capacities for Management of Chemicals

UNCED expected that "by the year 2000, national systems for environmentally sound management of chemicals, including legislation, and provisions for implementation and enforcement, should be in place in all countries to the greatest extent possible". While this objective is somewhat outside of the mandate of OECD, increased outreach activities in recent years are contributing to meeting this ambitious goal. Besides provision of documentation on chemicals management relevant to non-Member countries on request, and in the framework of capacity building programmes in the UN systems, *e.g.*, UNITAR (an IOMC partner), the Chemicals Programme undertakes a specific activity in this area on its own related to promoting adherence of non-member countries to the OECD system of the mutual acceptance of data in the testing of chemicals, as described above. Experts from Member countries and the Secretariat give training courses and workshops on using the Test Guidelines and for Principles of Good Laboratory Practice and establishing national compliance monitoring programmes.

SPECIFIC ATTRIBUTES OF OECD

OECD has a special advantage in working with a relatively small number of countries with the same basic viewpoint which makes it possible to move quickly on issues which can then be taken up in larger global fora in the UN where necessary. The Montreal Protocol and the restriction of production of CFCs is another example of work which began in OECD and was expanded to a global level. The UNECE Convention on the Transboundary Effects of Industrial Accidents was another. The fact that the OECD countries represent by far the majority of the world's producers of chemicals, pesticides and pharmaceuticals (over 80 per cent) gives them a responsibility both domestically and abroad to ensure the safety of their products. It also means that a great deal of expertise is available in OECD countries, which naturally have a vested interest in contributing to global policy on chemicals management.

The cross-sectoral nature of OECD's work, which nevertheless remains primarily that of supporting improved economic policy, makes objectives such as avoidance of non-tariff trade barriers and promotion of trade a major consideration in its work related to the protection of man and the environment from the risks posed by chemicals. A great deal of work is done in OECD on policy integration between the sectors concerning health and safety and those dealing with, for example, agriculture, trade, development co-operation, science, industry and technology and public management. This is, of course, the very essence of sustainable development. By working with all the stakeholders – governments, industry and non-governmental organisations and consumer groups – to find the most cost-effective and least disruptive solutions to problems posed by chemicals, using informal methods to strive at consensus in technical groups, before moving an issue to the policy level, Member countries are able to reach timely results in OECD.

FUTURE TRENDS

Environment and development issues were high on the global agenda at the beginning of this decade, but have now been forced to a certain extent to make way for other issues which are currently considered more pertinent, such as employment. Sustainable development depends, however, to a great extent on a sustained effort to improve and maintain social stability and economic growth. A clean and healthy environment is a necessary ingredient of social stability, and can only be achieved through unrelenting efforts.

Given the fact that budgets are being cut across the board in most countries and less resources are therefore currently available nationally and internationally for chemicals management, more efficient ways of using those resources which remain must be found. Sharing the burden of testing and assessing chemicals, information exchange and outreach activities have proved to increase efficiency in this area. OECD can continue to contribute significantly to the establishment of agreed ways of undertaking the various steps in chemicals management, leading to confidence by Member countries in the outputs of others. By sharing results internationally, the burden on each government and industry is reduced while output is increased overall. Harmonization and confidence-building on further issues on a broader geographical basis will assure that progress continues to be made in chemicals management and that the goals set by UNCED will be met.

Experience has also shown that new, and more efficient, ways of managing specific risks can be found. Voluntary agreements between governments and industry are replacing regulation in many instances and serve as an example for the kind of partnerships which can replace more coercive government actions and get the same results.

More efficient ways of assessing and managing the risks posed by chemicals are being explored by dealing with groups of chemicals which are used in the same way, *e.g.* paint strippers or flame retardants, and considering safer alternatives in order to arrive at decisions which consider risk, cost-benefit and other socio-economic factors at the same time. International co-operation and sharing the burden to deal with such clusters of chemicals are attracting more and more attention in OECD.

Outreach to non-member countries has been high among the priorities of the Organisation for the past few years. Besides the country-specific capacity building activities touched on above, OECD, through its involvement with IFCS, has been able to make its policies and instruments on chemicals management more accessible to non-member countries, which may be able to profit from the experience of Member countries as they set up their own administrative frameworks. Through its work on co-ordination of bilateral capacity building projects undertaken by Member countries, OECD should be able to contribute to improved efficiency and information flow in this area as well.

Various projects, like that on classification and labelling of chemicals discussed above, are now being effectively co-ordinated through the IOMC, where the advantages and experiences of other international organisations can best be exploited to the maximum with the objective of managing chemicals throughout their life-cycle and throughout the world without unnecessary disruptions to trade and with the most advantages to human health and the environment.

BIBLIOGRAPHY

OECD (1996), *Pollution Release and Transfer Registers (PRTRs), A Tool for Environmental Policy and Sustainable Development, Guidance Manual for Governments.*

OECD (1995), *Guidance Document for Aquatic Effects Assessment, No. 3 in the OECD Series on Testing and Assessment.*

OECD (1992), *Guiding Principles for Chemical Accident Prevention, Preparedness and Response: Guidance for Public Authorities, Industry, Labour and Others for the Establishment of Programmes and Policies related to Prevention of, Preparedness and Response to Accidents involving Hazardous Substances.*

OECD (1992), *The OECD Principles of Good Laboratory Practice,* No. 45 in the OECD Series on GLP and Compliance Monitoring.

OECD (1989), OECD Council Decision-Recommendation on Compliance with Good Laboratory Practice, C(89)87 (Final)

OECD (1981), OECD Council Decision on the Mutual Acceptance of Data in the Testing of Chemicals, C(81)30 (Final).

OECD (1981), *OECD Guidelines for Testing of Chemicals.*

TURNHEIM, Dian, *"Evaluating Chemical Risks" OECD Observer,* 189, 1994.

UN-IPRTC (1995,1996), *Screening Information Data Sets for High Production Volume Chemicals, OECD Initial Assessments, Volumes 1-3.*

Chapter 11

CLIMATE CHANGE: POLICY OPTIONS FOR OECD COUNTRIES

by

Jan Corfee Morlot and Laurie Michaelis

TRENDS

Signatories to the United Nations Framework Convention on Climate Change (FCCC) have set themselves the goal of stabilizing greenhouse gas (GHG) concentrations in the atmosphere at a level that would prevent dangerous anthropogenic interference with the climate system (FCCC, Article 2). OECD and other industrialised countries have an international obligation under the UN FCCC to provide leadership in the international effort to achieve this objective. Industrialised countries made the commitment to adopt national policies and programmes which aim to stabilise GHG emissions at 1990 levels by the year 2000. OECD governments have made some progress in establishing policy frameworks for GHG reduction. However, recent indicators show that many OECD countries will not achieve their national targets for GHG reductions in 2000. Even more troubling is that actions taken to date appear inadequate to reverse longer-term trends of growth in overall GHG emissions.

Developed countries have had difficulty designing and implementing effective and comprehensive response strategies. Economic cycles, rather than more permanent changes in the policy or technology structure in economies, are the source of the GHG reductions achieved by some of the Annex I Parties. Economic, rather than environmental rationale, has been behind the implementation of most "climate change" policies and measures implemented thus far. Continuing to develop these "win-win" or "no regrets" options is an important step forward. However, action should not stop here, as a recent review of the progress made by Parties listed in Annex I to the FCCC states:

> *...for the majority of Annex I Parties additional measures would be needed to return CO_2 emissions to their 1990 level by 2000. (FCCC/CP/1996/12).*

The Intergovernmental Panel on Climate Change (IPCC) suggests that 10-30 per cent energy efficiency gains could be achieved relative to trends at little or no cost in many parts of the world through conservation measures and improved management practices over the next 2-3 decades. However, achieving such efficiency gains will require new policy intervention.

Since the first Conference of the Parties (COP) in 1995, attention has shifted away from progress on existing commitments to the negotiation of stronger commitments to achieve GHG emission reductions in the time-frames: 2005, 2010 and 2020. In response to the "Berlin Mandate", OECD Member countries are working together with other countries listed in Annex I to establish new, legally binding targets and to elaborate policies and measures to achieve GHG reductions within these new time-frames.

GHG MITIGATION RESPONSE STRATEGIES AND POLICIES

Economic Analyses and Modelling

Between 1992 and 1995, the OECD conducted extensive economic analysis and modelling of climate change response options (OECD, 1995a and 1992a). Much of the work was supported by the OECD's dynamic general-equilibrium model (GREEN). These analyses drew a number of conclusions about the economics of climate change policy:

- The costs of responding to climate change are controversial and uncertain. Differences in cost estimates from different models stem from differing views on the adaptive capacity of economic development and on the penetration of new (carbon-free) technologies.
- The costs associated with achieving global GHG reductions vary widely across regions. Extending the geographical coverage of political agreements to limit GHG will not only make stabilisation of atmospheric GHG concentrations possible, but should also increase the economic efficiency of policy responses by allowing low-cost emission reduction options to be developed first.
- A first step in responding to climate change is to fully develop the ''no regrets'' policy potential, *i.e.,* to encourage investment in cost-effective energy efficiency options. By definition these measures – which may include setting efficiency standards – do not cause any loss in economic output.
- Another type of policy response to climate change concerns policy to encourage research and development of new technologies to improve energy efficiency and to lower carbon emissions from energy use. Such policy begins to address the uncertainty of responding to climate change and could include both investment in basic science as well as technology R&D.
- An international carbon tax, or a system of tradeable emission permits could help to ensure cost-efficient abatement of GHG by equalising the marginal cost of emission reduction investment among participating countries.

The GREEN model results also showed that market distortions from existing energy taxes and energy subsidies influence the ability to design an effective strategy to curb emissions. For example, combining energy subsidy reform with a cost-effective global agreement could reduce the cost of emission reduction to OECD and non-OECD partners as a whole (OECD 1993a).

More recently, the results of OECD work indicate that:

- It is not possible to foresee where quantum leap solutions will come from to achieve global GHG reduction.
- Governments will need to provide the incentives for long-term change to effect a diverse set of actors (business, consumers and different levels of government) and economic activities.
- A mix of policy measures will be required and these may need to be carefully adapted to local and regional circumstances to maximise their effectiveness.
- A first step in this process is for policy makers to set clear targets for GHG reduction, in consultation with major stake-holders, thus providing a long-term vision of the future.

Once targets are established, a variety of policy instruments have been shown to be effective in achieving emission reductions over time. OECD work explores a range of policies and measures and different sectoral strategies:

- to remove market distortions and failures;
- to achieve ''no regrets'' emission reductions;
- to achieve further mitigation of GHG in a cost-effective manner.

OECD has quantified the effects of alternative response measures on GHG emission levels and on the economy over time; it has also evaluated barriers to implementation and explored the potential for international action.

Economic Instruments for Climate Change Policy

While the GREEN modelling results demonstrated the theoretical advantages of global economic instruments (*e.g.*, subsidy reform or international carbon tax or emission trading regimes), such modelling exercises do not address many practical questions about the design and use of economic instruments. Experience in OECD Member countries reveals that these instruments usually complement rather than replace existing regulatory structures. Practical experience with the use of economic instruments in OECD countries is increasingly well documented by the OECD and others in the wider literature (OECD, 1992*b* and *c*, 1993*b*, 1995*b*, and 1996*a*, *b* and *c*).

Subsidy Reform in the Energy and Transport Sectors

In 1992, the World Bank's World Development Report drew attention to an issue that had until then received little attention – the contribution of energy subsidies to environmental damage. Modelling studies at the OECD and the World Bank showed that removing energy subsidies could make a substantial contribution to the aim of returning industrialised countries' CO_2 emissions to 1990 levels in 2000. It seems to make sense that, before discussing carbon taxes and other measures to control pollution from energy use, subsidies for energy production should be removed.

Unfortunately, no easy formulae are available to policy makers wishing to reform energy subsidies. Supports to energy and transport form part of a complex web of policies woven for social, political, economic, and sometimes environmental reasons. While OECD studies have identified situations where reforming supports would have large environmental and economic benefits, they have also identified situations where the environment would suffer. National policy makers will need to make decisions based on their own, national situations, but some of the most promising areas to look for potential ''no-regrets'' outcomes are: removing coal producer grants and price supports; reforming subsidies to energy supply industry investment or protection from risk; and removing barriers to trade.

Subsidy reforms normally reduce costs, but they must be carefully designed to ensure that environmental and social objectives are met. Often, polluting activities are supported by several measures, all of which need to be reformed to reduce pollution. It is also important to consider what will replace existing policies.

The transport sector has different characteristics from the energy sector. Whereas international trade policy is one of the major reasons for subsidy reform in the energy sector, in the transport sector policy reforms tend to be driven much more by local concerns. Coal and electricity sector reforms might benefit from international co-ordination, although this is perhaps less important for the transport sector. Nevertheless, countries can learn a great deal from each others' experiences in the transport sector. Some of the most interesting transport policy reforms have been implemented at the local level, by metropolitan or regional governments (OECD, forthcoming in 1997).

Carbon/Energy Taxes

Any international carbon or energy taxation scheme must deal with the same implementation issues that have been experienced in the design of carbon/energy taxation at the national level (Baron

1996, OECD/IEA and Haughland, 1993). National carbon and energy taxation schemes observed to date have been characterised (and limited) by:

- tax rates set so low as to have little observable impact on carbon emissions;
- significant differences between tax rates imposed and the effective tax rates, due to exemptions associated with the tax schemes such as for energy-intensive industry;
- tax rates that are non-proportional with carbon content of taxed products, again largely due to exemptions;
- design associated with larger fiscal reform packages which aim to achieve fiscal neutrality, hence sometimes resulting in simultaneous reductions in related energy prices, that may lead to higher emission levels.

Another important set of design issues has to do with the distribution effects of carbon/energy taxes which are key to their public acceptance and political feasibility. Since different kinds of design options have varying effects on different economic sectors, income and special interest groups, sound assessment of alternative design options is necessary. Broad options for compensation exist and should be considered early in the design of the tax instrument: revenue recycling alternatives; retraining programmes and income-support programmes to address employment dislocations (OECD, 1996a).

An initial hurdle for the design of an international tax strategy is the existence of significant differences in national energy mixes, current pricing and taxation patterns. An international strategy might therefore include progressive implementation of carbon/energy taxes, along with fiscal reform, and a clear schedule for their evolution over time could help to minimise the costs of CO_2 reduction. While an international scheme might help to reduce opposition to a tax on competitiveness grounds, the issue is also complicated by differences in trading patterns among developed countries (Baron, 1996, OECD). In practice, national carbon/energy taxes are used as only one instrument in a much broader package of policies aimed at reducing GHG emissions. This must also be kept in mind when considering an international carbon tax instrument.

Tradeable Permits

While considerable experience exists in the United States with the use of tradeable permits to achieve various air and water pollution reduction objectives, it is otherwise limited in other Member countries to trading of fishing quotas. Evaluation of the performance of these programmes points to a number of important elements for their success. Markets for emissions trading have also best succeeded when: clear rules are established for the ownership rights and obligations; the time-scale is clearly set out; regulatory certainty is high and regulatory requirements are low. Factors affecting environmental performance of the systems include early agreement on performance targets (*e.g.*, emissions caps) and hence a clear understanding among participants of the environmental constraints of the system, as well as clear monitoring and reporting procedures producing verifiable performance data. Evidence points to significant cost savings for participating countries resulting from the use of tradable permit systems compared to traditional command and control approaches (OECD 1992b, 1993b, 1996b, and Mullins and Baron, 1997, OECD).

Geographic and temporal flexibility may enhance the cost-effectiveness of achieving new GHG reduction objectives. Experience in OECD countries indicates that GHG emission trading may be a means of ensuring an agreed environmental outcome while at the same time, allowing the market to minimise the costs of achieving this outcome.

Joint Implementation, Emission Trading and Transaction Costs

''Joint Implementation'' (JI) was originally conceived as a mechanism to offer cost-effectiveness advantages to two Parties which agree under the Convention to work together to implement policies to mitigate climate change. JI thus resembles other market instruments, and several design issues are similar to those encountered in assessing emission trading schemes.

Transaction costs could limit the success of trading schemes and JI-like projects. One of the most important factors in reducing costs may be acceptance of the policy innovation by regulators, thus allowing the system to operate without excessive regulatory intervention. A number of actions can assist in the development of a market for GHG reduction transactions: clear property rights of all participants; use of information exchange centres; agreed guidelines for the reporting on performance; and regular monitoring (OECD, 1996*b*).

> **Joint implementation and transaction costs**
>
> *As with any market or market-based regulatory system, a critical issue for the development of JI will be the functioning of the market. The market will function best (maximise net benefits) when transactions are costless and participants are competitive. If trades are prohibitively difficult to arrange, or if some players in the market exercise market power (e.g., a monopoly), the market will not operate optimally. Thus, the "macro" global gains expected from JI depend critically on the "micro" aspects of transactions and transaction costs.* (Dudek and Weiner in OECD 1996*b*, p. 4.)

Voluntary Agreements

Voluntary agreements (VAs) with industry to achieve energy efficiency or GHG emission reductions are a relatively new environmental policy instrument within OECD countries. Since the FCCC has come into force, and as countries attempt to find cost-effective policy responses to achieve GHG reductions, the number of VAs in OECD countries has grown considerably. Recent reviews of the use of VAs in the OECD have shown that the development of VAs in different countries has taken different forms. For example: some voluntary agreements have numerical targets; some are designed to meet specific performance goals; some aim to facilitate and accelerate research and development; and others aim more modestly to improve reporting on emission or energy efficiency performance. Given the variety of different forms that VAs might take, and limited empirical evidence on performance, it is difficult to generalise about their potential to achieve measurable GHG reductions in the short or longer term.

It is conceivable that VAs could be used to encourage firms to invest in ''no regrets'' or economical energy efficiency options. The IPCC estimates that the ''no regrets'' or cost-effective potential for energy efficiency in industry, in the 2010-2020 time-frame, could provide a 40-50 per cent reduction in CO_2 emissions compared to ''business as usual'' projections or approximately a 25 per cent reduction below 1990 emission levels from this sector (IPCC, 1996). These estimates are developed with the assumption that existing technology is replaced by best performing technologies already in use in the market. Voluntary agreements can be a mechanism to overcome market barriers that may otherwise hinder industry investments in energy efficiency and in this way, they could make an important contribution to GHG reduction in Annex I countries.

> **Voluntary Agreements**
> *(a basic definition)*
>
> *An agreement between government and industry to facilitate voluntary action with a desirable social outcome, which is encouraged by the government, to be undertaken by the participant based on the participant's self interest.* Storey, 1996, OECD.

The benefits of VAs may extend beyond their ability to achieve measurable emission reductions to positive ''soft effects''. Voluntary agreements may significantly influence the environmental culture of corporations by raising the profile of GHG performance or energy efficiency objectives. Thus they may assist in responding to climate change in the long term by shifting the behaviour of corporations towards greater awareness of the benefits of clean technology and practices (Storey, 1996, OECD).

Energy Efficiency Standards

Energy efficiency standards and labelling schemes for appliances and equipment play an important role in many OECD countries' energy and environmental strategies. The OECD has analysed the potential for efficiency standards to achieve cost-effective reductions in CO_2 emissions. This work indicates that 25 per cent reductions in CO_2 compared to ''business as usual'' levels by 2010 can be achieved in Annex I countries for household refrigerator/freezer units. Even greater savings could result from efficiency standards on major office equipment. These two product categories alone could provide close to 100 million tonnes of ''no-regrets'' CO_2 reductions within Annex I countries by 2010. If one considers the potential ''spill-over'' effects to non-Annex I regions of the world, the effects would be greater (Mullins, 1996, OECD).

Energy efficiency standards may be designed as regulations, technical specifications or industry norms. They may also be implemented through industry agreement to achieve specified performance levels over time for specific products. Often appliance standards are implemented in a package of complementary measures. These might include: labelling and other consumer information; incentives to consumers and to industry to invest in more energy efficient appliances; or government procurement programmes. Energy efficiency performance standards offer a way to achieve emission reductions with certainty within a specified time-frame. Comparisons of national performance standards would be facilitated through harmonised measurement procedures and testing protocols. Harmonising test procedures and protocols could be a first-step to harmonised energy efficiency standards, lowering trade barriers and creating global markets for energy efficient products.

Sustainable Transport Policy and Climate Change

The transport sector was the fastest-rising source of GHG emissions during the 1970s and 1980s, although this was counterbalanced to some extent by energy efficiency improvements. Since 1986, however, low fuel prices have led to a stagnation of energy efficiency in all transport modes, while traffic growth has accelerated. The first set of national communications under the FCCC indicates that the transport sector poses one of the greatest challenges for governments considering policies to reduce national GHG emissions. Climate change has been identified as one of the most intractable challenges to sustainable development of the sector (OECD, 1996d).

Alternative response strategies, being evaluated in a wide range of projects at OECD, International Energy Agency (IEA) and the European Council for Ministers of Transport (ECMT), include: removing subsidies and other market distortions; internalising environmental and other external costs; and introducing policies to accelerate the process of technological, behavioural and institutional innovation in the sector. A wide range of policies could play an important role: shifting taxes from fixed costs to variable costs; introducing user fees to reflect the full cost of road transport; additional measures to internalise external costs; and energy efficiency standards and tax incentives to bypass failures in the market for energy efficiency in new cars. These policies could achieve large reductions in GHG emissions from road transport relative to the underlying trend, but they would not achieve an absolute reduction in emissions from this sector (Michaelis, 1996, OECD).

Air and maritime transport pose a special challenge because of their international nature. Emissions from combustion of fuels in international transport are not currently allocated to any Party under the UN FCCC. Analysis of the potential for carbon taxes or charges to reduce GHG emissions from these sectors will be completed in 1997. Preliminary indications are that the rate of energy intensity reduction in the aviation sector has in the past been responsive to fuel prices. The price response in the maritime sector is much weaker. Meanwhile, any tax on marine bunker fuels would be almost impossible to enforce internationally unless it were part of a global tax on the carbon content of all fuels: offshore refuelling is already common and it would be a simple matter for ship operators to obtain untaxed fuel from any country not participating (Michaelis, 1997*a* and *b,* OECD).

Absolute reductions in road transport GHG emissions are possible, but would depend on significant changes in vehicle technology or mobility patterns. One indication of the strength of measures that might be needed to achieve substantial reduction in emissions comes from a joint ECMT/OECD study: *Urban Travel and Sustainable Development* (1995). This study outlined a sustainable development strategy for urban transport that included fuel price increases of 7 per cent per year in real terms over the next 20 years in order to achieve GHG emission reductions of about 50 per cent by 2015.

Innovations in technology, infrastructure and transport pricing have been introduced in many OECD countries at a local level. Ongoing work in the OECD is evaluating the potential for national government policies to encourage innovation in transport technology, behaviour and institutions. Such policies might encourage experimentation at a local level, in transport systems, policies and technologies. They could include: support and guidelines for R&D and demonstration projects; best practice programmes; information provision, methodological support and networking; and provision of a range of incentives and targets for GHG emission reductions by local governments, communities, and firms (Michaelis, 1997*c,* OECD).

OECD CONTRIBUTIONS TO THE FCCC PROCESS

The OECD and the IEA[1] Secretariats assist their Member countries, and more generally Annex I countries, to assess policy options to mitigate climate change and the feasibility of alternative GHG reduction strategies. Nine non-OECD countries having economies in transition, listed in Annex I of the Convention, along with OECD Member countries, participate in the *ad hoc* Annex I Expert Group on the FCCC.

The OECD programme provides analysis of climate policy issues, drawing on the latest scientific and economic research, and evaluates OECD experience through open discussion and peer review among governments. It helps to integrate climate change policy objectives into mainstream economic and development strategies of OECD governments.

The OECD and the IEA work with the:
- Intergovernmental Panel on Climate Change (IPCC)
- Annex I Expert Group on the FCCC
- UN FCCC and its subsidiary bodies

Legally binding targets, as called for in a Ministerial Declaration from the second Conference of the Parties (COP-2), will require new policy action in OECD countries in an initial step forward under the United Nations Framework Convention on Climate Change (FCCC) to achieve long-term emission reductions. In the lead up to the third Conference of Parties (COP-3) in Kyoto, a number of alternative policy options and strategies for action are being assessed by OECD and IEA for the Annex I Expert Group.

Developing Improved Methodologies

Improved guidelines and methodologies are essential for developing transparent, comparable and complete information on national policy performance under the Convention. OECD and IEA have worked with Annex I Parties to develop draft guidelines for their periodic "national communications" under the Convention. The communications include:

OECD and IEA products on reporting and review procedures under the Convention:
- IPCC Guidelines on National GHG Inventories;
- Recommendations on guidelines for Annex I national communications;
- Recommendations on the review process for Annex I national communications.

- national GHG emission inventories;
- estimation of the GHG effects of mitigation measures;
- GHG emission projection methods.

The OECD, in collaboration with the IEA, manages the IPCC/OECD/IEA National GHG Inventory Programme. A wide range of developing countries and countries with economies in transition participate in the programme which aims to test and refine methods and improve the availability of data needed to develop national GHG emission inventories.

Review of National Communications

In-depth reviews of Parties' national communications include: the review of national GHG inventories; policies and programmes; and projections of emission levels through 2000. These reviews involve site visits to the reporting country to discuss with government officials and other stake-holders, latest developments, challenges and opportunities in national policies and programmes to address climate change. The OECD and the IEA participated in roughly half of the visits in the first round of reviews of FCCC Annex I Parties' communications. Secretariat staff were also seconded to assist with the reports, which were released in conjunction with the first and second Conference of the Parties in 1995 and 1996.

OECD and IEA second staff to contribue to:
- UN FCCC In-Depth Reviews of National Communications
- UN FCCC Compilation and Synthesis Reports

ANNEX I EXPERT GROUP, TRANCHES I AND II POLICY STUDIES

Under the guidance of the Annex I Expert Group, the OECD and IEA Secretariats are conducting a series of studies on alternative policies and measures to mitigate climate change. The studies consider cost-effectiveness and environmental performance; administrative, institutional and political implementation design issues; and broader economic effects, including effects on other (non Annex I) countries.

Tranche I Studies:
- Reforming Coal and Electricity Subsidies
- Taxation *i.e.* Carbon/Energy
- Voluntary Agreements with Industries
- Energy Efficiency Standards for Traded Products
- Identification of Options for Net GHG Reduction
- Financing Energy Efficiency in EIT Countries
- Full Cost Pricing
- Sustainable Transport Policies: CO_2 Emissions from Road Vehicles

Tranche II studies:
- International Greenhouse Gas Emission Trading
- Competitiveness Issues Related to Carbon/Energy Taxation
- Marine Bunker Fuel Taxes
- Carbon Charges on Aviation Fuels
- Policies and Measures to Encourage Innovation in Transport Behaviour and Technology
- Financing Energy Efficiency in EIT Countries, Part II
- Electricity Sector

Results from the First Round of Studies

- *A range of "no regrets" policies and measures are currently available* to OECD and other countries to further advance GHG emission reductions and provide incentives for the adoption of cleaner technology. Cost-effective emission reductions have been documented in OECD countries through the use of: product efficiency standards, voluntary agreements with industry, fee-rebate systems for efficient vehicles, fuel efficiency standards and fuel taxes in the transport sector; full cost pricing for pollutants other than carbon; innovative financing to improve energy efficiency in industry and building sectors. While the potential "no regrets" options available in Annex I countries are only a fraction of what might be required in the longer term to reverse trends in global emission levels, OECD countries need to show progress at home to solicit co-operation from other global partners. Starting with "no-regrets" options is an initial and useful first step.
- *OECD/IEA national circumstances matter:* Policy options need to be carefully adapted to local or national circumstances and, in particular, designed to fit with other government policies. Therefore, each national government must decide for itself what is right for its own needs.
- *Policy packages are essential:* Policy packages are likely to be more effective than individual measures. Measures such as product standards can achieve higher levels of energy efficiency through faster development and uptake of economically viable, clean technology. They can achieve emission reductions by lowering the emission intensity of a particular activity. However these "emission gains" may be offset by an increase in the demand for energy using services or an increase in the volume of polluting activity. For this reason, policies that aim to improve technologies may need to be coupled with those that aim to limit or reduce the overall volume of polluting activity. For example, product labelling or standards might be coupled with full cost pricing to give consistent market signals to consumers. Policy packages also need to provide incentives for change and innovation, leading to more energy-efficient and environmentally friendly behaviour and technology. Long-term environmental targets may provide such incentives as can the use of market instruments to internalise external costs.
- *"Common action" by Annex I countries* might begin in the near term in a number of ways, for example:
  - through sharing information to build the basis for agreements in key areas (*e.g.*, energy or transport subsidy reform);
  - by agreeing on areas for common action, leaving flexibility on how to take action to participating governments (*e.g.*, setting targets to improve the market share of renewable energy technology);

– through co-ordination or harmonisation of specific measures and strategies to minimise economic consequences of action.

Given different national circumstances, harmonisation may only be relevant in special cases, such as for aviation or maritime transport policies, or for small coalitions of countries. Country coalitions for common action might be based on geographic regions, trading ties, common interests, industrial structures, or policies already in place.

OECD FORUM ON CLIMATE CHANGE

The OECD Forum, conducted in collaboration with the IEA, was initiated in 1995 to provide an opportunity for dialogue by stakeholders in Member countries on key policy issues. The Forum also helps to ensure coherence and strategic direction for work on climate change.

The 1996 OECD Forum on Climate Change addressed key issues in the lead up to Kyoto:

• Technology Transfer
• Joint Implementation
• Emissions Trading
• Compliance

NOTE

1. The IEA is an independent body of the OECD, see Chapter 7.

BIBLIOGRAPHY

BARON, R. (1996) Taxation (*i.e.,* Carbon/Energy) Policies and Measures for Common Action, OECD.

BARON, R. (forthcoming in 1997) Competitiveness Issues Related to Carbon/Energy Tax, Policies and Measures for Common Action, Tranche II Study, OECD.

ECMT (1995) Urban Travel and Sustainable Development.

HAUGHLAND, T. (1993), ''A Comparison of Carbon Taxes in Selected OECD Countries'', OECD Environment Monograph No. 78.

IPCC (1996), *Technologies, Policies and Measures for Mitigation of Climate Change, IPCC Technical Paper I.*

IPCC (1996), *Climate Change 1995: Impacts, Adaptations and Mitigation of Climate Change: Scientific-Technical Analyses, Contribution of Working Group II to the Second Assessment Report of the Intergovernmental Panel on Climate Change.*

KEPPLER, J. and T. Kram (1996), Full Cost Pricing, Policies and Measures for Common Action, OECD.

MICHAELIS, L. (1996), Sustainable Transport Policies: CO_2 Emissions from Road Vehicles, Policies and Measures for Common Action, OECD.

MICHAELIS, L. (1996*a*), Reforming Coal and Electricity Subsidies, Policies and Measures for Common Action, Tranche I.

MICHAELIS, L. (1997*a*), Marine Bunker Fuel Taxes, Policies and Measures for Common Action, OECD.

MICHAELIS, L. (1997*b*), Special Issues in Carbon/Energy Taxation: Carbon Charges on Aviation Fuels, Policies and Measures for Common Action, Tranche II Study, OECD.

MICHAELIS, L. (1997*c*), Policies and Measures to Encourage Innovation in Transport Behaviour and Technology, Policies and Measures for Common Action, Tranche II Study, OECD.

MULLINS, F. (1996), Energy Efficiency Standards for Traded Products, Policies and Measures for Common Action, OECD.

MULLINS, F. (1996*a*), Financing Energy Efficiency in EIT Countries, Policies and Measures for Common Action, Tranche I Study, OECD.

MULLINS, F. and R. Baron (1997), Emission Trading, Policies and Measures for Common Action, OECD.

OECD (forthcoming in 1997), *Environmental Implications of Energy and Transport Subsidies.*

OECD (1996*a*), *Climate Change, Economic Instruments and Income Distribution.*

OECD (1996*b*), ''Joint Implementation, Transaction Costs, and Climate Change'' ENV/GD(96)173.

OECD (1996*c*), *Implementation Strategies for Environmental Taxes.*

OECD (1996*d*), Environmental Criteria for SustainableTransport, Working Paper of the PPCG Task Force on Transport.

OECD (1995*a*), *Global Warming: Economic Dimensions and Policy Responses.*

OECD (1995*b*), *Environmental Taxes in OECD Countries.*

OECD (1993*a*), *The Costs of Cutting Carbon Emissions: Results from Global Models.*

OECD (1993*b*), *International Economic Instruments and Climate Change.*

OECD (1993*c*), *Taxation and the Environment: Complementary Policies.*

OECD (1992*a*), *Responding to Climate Change: Selected Economic Issues.*

OECD (1992*b*), *Climate Change: Designing a Tradeable Permit System.*

OECD (1992*c*), *Climate Change: Designing a Practical Tax System.*

OECD (1991), *Estimation of Greenhouse Gas Emissions and Sinks*.

STOREY, M. (1996), Voluntary Agreements with Industries, Policies and Measures for Common Action, OECD.

STOREY, M (1996a), Identification of Options for Net GHG Reduction, Policies and Measures for Common Action, OECD.

UNFCCC (1996), Review of the Implementation of the Convention and of Decisions of the First Session of the Conference of the Parties: Commitments in Article 4. FCCC/CP/1996/12.

UNFCCC (1996a), Policies and Measures for Possible Common Action: Progress Report to the fourth session of the *Ad Hoc* Group on the Berlin Mandate from the Annex I Expert Group on the UNFCCC. FCCC/AGBM/96/Misc.1.

Chapter 12

NUCLEAR ENERGY AND SUSTAINABILITY

by

Geoffrey Stevens

Nuclear reactors provided some 17 per cent of the world's electricity in 1995. This equates to about 7 per cent of total primary energy used in the commercially traded energy sector. Nuclear power reactors are operated in 32 countries, including 16 countries of the OECD where some 85 per cent of the world's reactor capacity can be found.

RESOURCES

The basic resource for nuclear energy is uranium for which there is no other significant use. Known world resources of exploitable uranium amount to 4.51 million tonnes, with geological modelling and other indications suggesting that a further 11 million tonnes would be available. At current rates of usage this resource would suffice for 220 years using currently exploited reactor technology. Using the central scenario of the World Energy Council for nuclear capacity growth [which envisages a capacity of 1150 GWe (gigawatt electrical) in 2050], the known uranium resource would last for 50 years. Using the already known but not yet commercially exploited technology of breeder reactors would multiply the energy content of the uranium resource base by a factor of 50 to 60. The total ultimate resource of uranium, including that widely distributed in the earth's crust and in sea water, is estimated at over 4 billion tonnes, thus providing a possibility of extremely long-term use of nuclear fission energy.

Another potential source that could be used as nuclear fuel in the longer term is thorium, which is also widely distributed on the planet. It too has no major uses, other than as a potential fuel. Its abundance is estimated to be higher than that of uranium, although not so much exploration has been done to identify its geological occurrences in readily exploitable deposits. The fuel cycle and reactor technology for using thorium has been demonstrated in experimental programmes.

As with other mining industries, the extraction of uranium ore has to be performed carefully in order to avoid long-term damage to the local and regional environment. This care was not particularly evident in the early stages of uranium mining, carried out under the exigencies of military programmes, but the operation and decommissioning of uranium mines in recent years has demonstrated that protection of the environment can be achieved.

NECESSARY CONDITIONS FOR SUSTAINABILITY

Thus there is a basic case for treating nuclear energy as a contributor to sustainable development. This case will be robust if there is satisfaction on five other points:
- control of radioactive emissions during operation of nuclear facilities;
- safe management of radioactive wastes;

◆   Figure 1.   *Cumulative uranium resources and requirements to 2050*

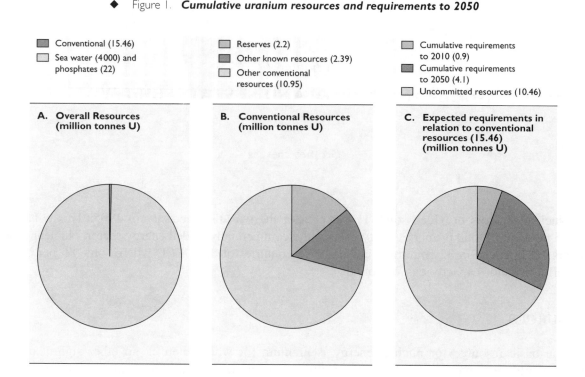

Conventional (15.46)	Reserves (2.2)	Cumulative requirements to 2010 (0.9)
Sea water (4000) and phosphates (22)	Other known resources (2.39)	Cumulative requirements to 2050 (4.1)
	Other conventional resources (10.95)	Uncommitted resources (10.46)

A. Overall Resources (million tonnes U)

B. Conventional Resources (million tonnes U)

C. Expected requirements in relation to conventional resources (15.46) (million tonnes U)

Source: NEA/IAEA Uranium 1995: Resources, Production and Demand.

- safety of plant operation;
- economic competitivity of nuclear energy,
- and avoidance of the spread of nuclear weapons.

The creation and preservation of these conditions is largely influenced by governments, with direct involvement required in four of theses areas, competitivity being in the first instance a concern of industry although within a frame established by governments.

The government role extends to providing a rich infrastructure of education, regulatory and research institutions and to ensuring public oversight of the nuclear industry. This necessitates a considerable investment in people qualified at a high technical level. Manufacturing and service industries capable of providing and maintaining high quality equipment are also needed to ensure continued good performance by the nuclear industry. In OECD countries these elements of infrastructure all developed out of government activities. The Nuclear Energy Agency (NEA) of the OECD studies the government role in preserving an adequate infrastructure. The work programme of the NEA also covers the first four points listed above, with the aim of assisting governments to create the conditions under which they and the public can have confidence in the continued use of nuclear energy.

Assistance in the development of infrastructures in non-OECD Member countries is one of the tasks of the International Atomic Energy Agency (IAEA). The IAEA, working with national governments, also has responsibility for preventing the diversion of nuclear materials and technology to the development and production of weapons, and these joint efforts have in recent years avoided the appearance of newly nuclear-armed states.

RADIATION PROTECTION

All operations in the nuclear fuel cycle are carried out within regulations that ensure that discharges of radioactivity or other pollutants to the environment are kept below levels where health risks might arise. The work of the NEA on radiation protection has helped governments to implement, in a practicable manner, scientific recommendations concerning the avoidance of emission levels that could lead to unacceptable risks to health. The Agency's work also enhances the dissemination of good practice in radiation protection both among regulators and within the nuclear industry.

WASTE MANAGEMENT

In the field of radioactive waste management the NEA has concentrated on the development of methods of analysing the expected performance of repositories and associated technology for the conditioning and disposal of highly radioactive and long-lived waste. The exchange of information and carrying out of joint studies between Member countries, including, for example, studies on natural analogues for deep geological repositories, has led to the publication of international consensus opinions such as that on the methods of evaluating the safety of such repositories. It is a feature of the consensus opinions that they are subscribed to by countries that have no nuclear power plants as well as by countries where nuclear power plants are operated.

Collective Opinions on Radioactive Waste Management

- "the liabilities of waste management should be considered when undertaking new projects;
- those who generate the wastes should take responsibility, and provide the resources, for the management of these materials in a way which will not impose undue burdens on future generations;
- wastes should be managed in a way that secures an acceptable level of protection for human health and the environment, and affords to future generations at least the level of safety which is acceptable today; there seems to be no ethical basis for discounting future health and environmental damage risks;
- a waste management strategy should not be based on a presumption of a stable societal structure for the indefinite future, nor of technological advance; rather it should aim at bequeathing a passively safe situation which places no reliance on active institutional controls."[1]

"Safety assessment methods are available today to evaluate adequately the potential long-term radiological impacts of a carefully designed radioactive waste disposal system on humans and the environment."[2]

NUCLEAR SAFETY

The study of the technical safety of nuclear installations is the subject of a very rich exchange within committees and working groups of the NEA. Technical information flows freely to enable all countries to benefit from the research and operational experience of other Member countries. Senior nuclear regulators from Member countries have their own committee and regularly discuss options for improving the effectiveness of nuclear regulation, as well as issuing consensus opinions about their approaches.

Consensus Views on Nuclear Safety

"Overall safety of a plant is assured by applying a *defence-in-depth* approach, with several levels of backup systems and several protective barriers. They act as safety nets and extend even to safety systems to prevent holes developing in the safety net."[3]

"Co-operation in the framework of the NEA brings the best minds to collaborate on safety issues, and provides for cost sharing, thus making each partner's research money go further. The effect of this work is to enhance the value of national efforts, extending their scope and amplifying their own results. It must be stressed, however, that international research projects cannot be a substitute for healthy national programmes; there is a level of effort below which national programmes become ineffective, even if they are invigorated by international collaboration."[4]

ECONOMICS OF NUCLEAR ENERGY

The economic studies of the NEA are designed to provide governments with expert consensus views on the costs of nuclear energy, and the resources (material and human) required for its use, as well as to exchange information on practices and policies that affect nuclear costs such as those on the funding of decommissioning. The future competitivity of nuclear energy in both developed and developing countries will depend in the medium term on the course of fossil fuel prices and the means adopted to reflect the external costs associated with their use. Studies over the last decade or so indicate that for many countries nuclear energy would be competitive, if it is not already, with only a moderate addition to fossil fuel prices. A major conclusion reached in the course of this work, is that there are no significant external costs associated with using nuclear energy, with back-end and decommissioning costs being funded by current revenues. This is a conclusion that has been supported in many other studies outside the OECD.

LOW ENVIRONMENTAL IMPACTS

The production of electricity from nuclear energy does not cause the release of gases or particles that produce environmental degradation such as acid rain, urban smog, or depletion of the ozone layer. As greenhouse gas emissions from the nuclear fuel cycle are of the order of 25 g/kWh compared with some 450 to 1 250 g/kWh (kilowatt-hours) when using fossil fuel, replacing the whole of the nuclear generation capacity by a mix close to that of the current non-nuclear sector would entail increasing the world's energy sector's carbon dioxide emissions by 8 per cent.

The emissions of greenhouse gases in the nuclear fuel cycle are among the lowest that have been identified for any of the means of producing electricity. Studies of the complete fuel cycle, including the indirect emissions of carbon dioxide and other relevant gases in the construction and dismantling of nuclear facilities, show that when operated in accordance with appropriate national regulations that accord with international norms, the whole of the nuclear fuel cycle is relatively benign in its effect on the environment.

BROADER CONSIDERATIONS

Nuclear electricity production is appropriate for relatively large distribution grids and so is not relevant in all countries. Its adoption can be successful only after the development of a high degree of technical competence in the associated industries and regulatory bodies. The rigour that is brought with

◆ Figure 2. **CO_2 emissions from electricity generation by different sources**
(grammes of CO_2 equivalent/kWh)

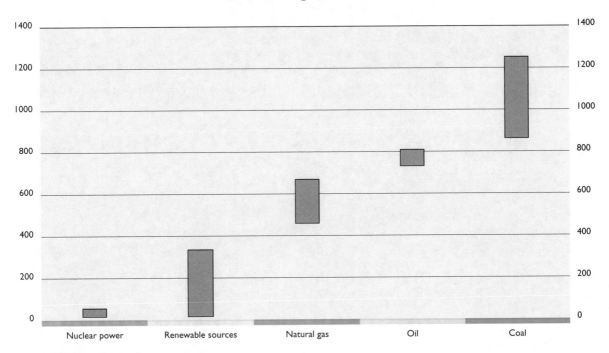

Note: The ranges correspond to differences in generation technology for the same primary source.
Source: IAEA-TEC DOC-892, July 1996.

nuclear technology in matters of quality assurance and safety regulation can in itself be of high value in the development of an industrial economy as has been seen in the evolution of nuclear energy in OECD countries. These spin-off benefits can be significant. They and the direct benefits of nuclear energy can be harnessed, however, only by a long-term commitment to using nuclear energy and that in turn requires that there is acceptance by public and political opinion that the advantages, including effects on long-term security of energy supply, outweigh the risks. The aim of NEA's work is that governments shall be fully informed on this balance.

NOTES

1. OECD Nuclear Energy Agency, The Environmental and Ethical Basis of Geological Disposal: A Collective Opinion of the NEA Radioactive Waste Management Committee, Paris, 1995.

2. OECD Nuclear Energy Agency, *Disposal of Radioactive Waste: Can Long-term Safety Be Evaluated? – An International Collective Opinion,* Paris, 1991.

3. OECD Nuclear Energy Agency, *Achieving Nuclear Safety: Improvements in Reactor Safety Design and Operation,* Paris, 1993, p. 12.

4. OECD Nuclear Energy Agency, *Nuclear Safety Research in OECD Countries: Areas of Agreement, Areas for Further Action, Increasing Need for Collaboration,* Paris, 1996.

Chapter 13

URBANISATION AND SUSTAINABILITY

by

Elina Berghäll and Josef Konvitz

INTRODUCTION

About three-quarters of OECD citizens live and work in urban areas. World-wide, the majority of the world's population is projected to reside in urban areas after the year 2005. Urbanisation is a central element of sustainable economic and environmental development. From the environmental point of view, cities reduce pressures on rural areas and pollution treatment costs, while expanding the opportunities for more efficient energy and natural resource consumption. In recent years, more initiatives have been taken to improve the quality of life and the urban environment in OECD Member countries. Simultaneously, however, many urban problems are intensifying. Problems include waste management, air, noise and water pollution, traffic congestion, the loss of open space and degraded land, the deterioration of buildings and infrastructure, and the degradation of the urban landscape. Environmental problems cannot be arrested or reversed without specific efforts aimed at the cities.[1]

Sustainable cities would generate social and environmental benefits that make people more productive and societies richer. Conversely, economic and social sustainability improve the possibilities for environmental improvements. Given that cities will change in the years to come, the challenge lies in attempting to channel the investments, innovations and developments that will be made so that cumulatively and incrementally, cities become more, rather than less, sustainable.

This can be done by promoting mixed land-use patterns, better co-ordination of transport modes, more transparent tax and price measures that reflect environmental costs, an entrepreneurial climate favouring new business activity, educational strategies for life-long learning, and building and planning codes that foster innovation. These strategies can enhance the adaptability of existing cities so that households and firms can better integrate environmental goals into their everyday routine. The pursuit of sustainability should promote technological innovation and better communications between government, the private sector and the public – both of which cities are uniquely able to promote. Thus, a national approach to environmental policy must have an urban dimension if it is to generate solutions to problems that for decades have accumulated in cities.

URBAN ENVIRONMENTAL PROBLEMS

Air Pollution

Local air pollution is estimated to cost about 0.4 per cent of GDP in OECD countries. Space heating, electricity generation, industrial activities (especially outmoded practices) and road traffic emit sulphur dioxide (SO_2), particular matter (TSP), nitrogen oxides (NO_x), carbon monoxide (CO), ozone (O_3), lead (Pb), other heavy metals and organic compounds. Pollution can be exacerbated by local meteorological and topographical conditions. Exhaust emissions contribute to smog, a range of health problems and degradation of buildings and monuments, made of vulnerable materials such as marble and calcareous sandstone.[2]

In West European cities, road traffic causes from 30 to 50 per cent of total NO_x and 90 per cent of CO emissions. Cities in Northern and Western Europe and some in Southern Europe have lowered their SO_2 concentrations by imposing strict emission standards. Nordic capitals (Helsinki, Stockholm, Copenhagen and Oslo) have been particularly successful, showing a decrease of 80 per cent in their SO_2 concentrations.[3] In Eastern Europe, exposure levels remain unacceptably high, and are poised to rise in the future, mainly due to rising urban traffic. In most European cities, lead concentrations appear to have been significantly reduced when there has been a shift to petrol with a lower lead content.[4]

Noise Pollution

Noise pollution levels vary greatly in OECD countries.[5] Noise pollution reduces property prices in affected areas and damages buildings through vibrations. The costs arising from lost productivity, rising health care expenditure, and reduced psychological well-being, are estimated at about 0.1 to 0.3 per cent of GDP.[6]

Noise pollution in urban areas is very difficult to combat. Very limited progress has been made in reducing the external noise of vehicles, which originates from surface contact of the tyre or the rail.[7] Dense city structures, prone to noise pollution, may be an important reason for persistent urban sprawl and flight from dense city centres.

Congestion

The cost of road congestion in OECD countries is estimated to be equivalent to about 2 per cent of their GDP. Road accident costs are estimated at 1.5 to 2 per cent of GDP in OECD countries.[8] Congestion is a major factor in air pollution and in lower-density land development.

"Brownfields"

Some "brownfields", formerly industrial or other commercial properties having contaminated soil, currently lie unutilised in spite of their redevelopment potential. Public and private entities seeking to do this find that in addition to the normal problems of redevelopment, contamination at these sites makes the business and financial community particularly reluctant to become involved. As a result, businesses may prefer to develop rural or suburban "greenfield" sites. A comprehensive strategy for urban land calls for efforts to clean up and rehabilitate brownfield sites.

Urban Travel and Land Use Patterns

In Europe, the amount of urban land per capita is now ten times greater than a hundred years ago. Current densities are mostly between 2 000 and 5 000 inhabitants per square kilometre, and falling.[9] Increased demand for urban land is a consequence of the trend towards urban sprawl and of the separation of urban land uses. Private cars have made lower density patterns possible, aggravating the rising demand for travel. Dispersed and "inefficient" city structures require relatively more investments in infrastructures per person, while dense settlement patterns are, together with mixed land use, generally more efficient in the use of natural resources.

Obstacles in the Way of Better Policies

Long-range vision and consistency in the pursuit of policy objectives are of vital importance if progress is to be made in governmental urban programmes. Electoral cycles, in particular, may severely shorten the time horizon of development projects. Other common obstacles in the way of better policies are:

- conceptual and institutional barriers such as specialisation and professionalisation in bureaucracies which perpetuate sectoral frameworks in policies;
- the long lag between the introduction of new policies and their effects in the presence of uncertainty and rapid urban change requiring immediate measures, and lack of feedback for follow-up;
- the need to reduce budget deficits and tax competition between municipalities, which reduces financing available for environmental investments;
- inadequate economic incentives to motivate people and firms to adopt more sustainable methods of production and operation;
- social barriers that isolate the public from policy making and that exclude different social groups from taking part in community development; and the difficulties posed in inducing changes in habits and life-styles.

THE SEARCH FOR SOLUTIONS

Trends in Urbanisation

In the next two decades, the number of urban agglomerations of all sizes is expected to rise in more developed regions. The highest growth will take place in cities with a population ranging from one to five million – from 22.7 per cent in 1990 to 24.2 per cent of the urban population in 2015. The share of urban population living in megacities (with a population of more than ten million) and in cities of less than half a million inhabitants is expected to decline slightly to 7.2 per cent and 54.5 per cent respectively by 2015.[10]

Policies to Reduce Urban Travel

Implementation of current best practices would only slightly improve the situation in the future than would otherwise be the case, but that situation would still be worse than at present. The various social, economic and political consequences of environmental problems on such a scale are difficult to predict, but it is clear that remedial solutions are likely to be more costly than preventive measures.

Significant improvements are possible with the available means. Better urban design and land-use planning can bring substantial reductions in energy and transport demand. To reduce the need to travel and dependence on the private car, governments have shifted to mutually reinforcing co-ordination of transport and land use planning. Transport policy should aim at reducing the demand for travel while increasing accessibility, by improving the internalisation of negative externalities in the cost of travel, including those related to spatial, air quality and noise pollution. While improved public transport has not, in general, attracted car users in sufficiently large numbers to affect congestion levels,[11] economic instruments can help. The temptation to allocate revenue from economic instruments as cross-subsidies to cover deficits in other sectors should, however, be resisted. Effective government policies include:

- strategies to reduce peri-urban development, and to promote the re-use of abandoned land in cities;

- incentives for land developers to promote mixed-use development, which minimises the need for car use;
- long-term building approaches to public and commercial property;
- relaxation of regulations that prevent work at home;
- improved security of public places, also for pedestrians and cyclists; and
- fiscal and monetary policies that foster stable property and land markets.

This discussion of policies to reduce the demand for urban travel shows how various urban environmental problems are linked, such that they cannot be treated each in isolation from the others. Integrative strategies and better co-ordination between different levels of government are necessary if progress is to be made.

Environmental Investments and Economic Sustainability

In most OECD countries, urban areas account for the majority of national GNP. Most dynamic new growing industries and commercial activities are located in urban areas. The urban agglomeration is often a nodal point serving a large surrounding area, whose economic performance may consequently be crucially dependent on the productivity found in the urban area. Urban policies can thus make a significant contribution to the economic performance of regions and nations. Unfortunately, in an economic system organised around macroeconomic policies that ignore spatial variations, the cost of better urban policies is often considered to represent a resource drain rather than an investment for the future.

For the city to be sustainable, it has to be able to organise the investments necessary for environmental improvements.[12] It is important for governments to anticipate urban environmental problems, in order to provide a stable and more predictable environment for the private sector to invest. The range of potential investors and funds should be broadened if possible to permit other organisations and institutions such as pension funds to invest in social and environmental sustainability of the community. In particular, measures aiming at economic and social sustainability need to ensure sufficient job creation in cities.

In addition to employment, poverty and livelihood aspects, crime, corruption and bribery affect sustainability. Urban areas tend to concentrate different activities and types of people in specific districts, with crime being more prevalent in poor neighbourhoods. Corrupt practices in government are likely to reduce trust and respect of codes of conduct. The credibility of improvement efforts can easily be compromised unless the roots of the problems are tackled. A widespread sense of responsibility and appreciation of common rules, regulations and assets must be created if public participation is to become an important factor promoting better urban environmental policies.

Awareness Raising and Social Participation in Cities, Households, Urban Lifestyles

Some forms of unsustainable development are concentrated in cities, and cities affect the quality of the environment over a larger area. As a result, people sometimes conclude that urbanisation is a major cause of unsustainable development. This view does not take account of the enormous progress that has already been made to improve the urban environment. To advance further, however, public participation must be enhanced. A passive attitude – waiting for a new technological solution or government action – is a reflection of the limited awareness of the scope of the challenge.

Increased individual and collective awareness, participation and civic engagement are prerequisites for the success of measures and policies aimed at improving the quality of the urban and its surrounding environment. Changes in attitudes, in turn, prepare the ground for political action. Indeed, "the actual test of the effectiveness of plans and policies is whether they are taken up in modified urban lifestyles".[13]

There are many liveability indexes, or studies which attempt to measure the quality of life in particular places on a comparative basis. The rankings show that cities which are not the largest or fastest growing are often at the top. Attitudes appear to favour medium-sized cities. Although it is not obvious what factors explain why a city rates high, or low, one survey found that controllable and humanly determined characteristics of urban life appeared to be chiefly responsible for this fact. This is another reason why social participation in urban development is of such central importance.

Local Tax Systems and Economic Sustainability

As far as public investment is concerned, competition amongst municipalities for investment and for tax-payers can lead to inefficient investment and deficiencies in environmental and planning measures. Tax rates may be kept unsustainably low, widening fiscal deficits. The consequent lack of public funds can be a hindrance to the introduction of policies more favourable to environmental and economic sustainability, such as higher water and electricity charges, for instance.

Under the pressure of competition between municipalities, how will the cost of environmental sustainability be met? Traditionally, local budgets have been covered mainly by property tax revenue. As cities become increasingly indebted, wealthy tax-payers may feel inclined to move out in the expectation of higher future tax rates. The present system of excessive reliance on property taxes has different impacts on growing and declining communities. Property tax systems provide a disincentive to the preservation of natural areas and agricultural lands, and generally affect land use policies towards preference for urban sprawl and less dense agglomerations. In order to achieve more sustainable trends in city structures, there needs to be a shift towards the use of other economic incentives and taxes.

More cities are finding that to become or remain competitive in the national or global economy, they must improve environmental conditions. Ultimately, market pressures may help cities take more responsible fiscal and investment measures.

Economic Instruments in the Internalisation of Negative Externalities

When the market does not internalise all externalities, economic instruments may help. Emission charges can reduce air pollution, noise exposure, indoor pollution and contribute to the availability of drinking water. Petrol and road pricing reduce congestion and pollution resulting from traffic. Energy pricing leads to more efficient use, while taxation of waste contributes to the adoption of recycling practices, and land pricing helps in preserving urban space. Economic instruments specific to the city may entail price discrimination (in tariff setting in order to influence demand and supply conditions relative to other areas and to internalise the negative externalities of agglomeration); higher parking charges in city centres relative to suburban areas are directed to reduce congestion and pollution in crowded centres.

Raising user charges to include negative externalities is easier said than done. Many of the costs of urban environmental problems cannot be traced to a small number of polluters who can be identified and then made to pay, but to virtually all households and firms. Consequently, as far as noise pollution is concerned, for instance, the "polluter pays" principle would require profound changes in taxing and pricing policies to be effective. Furthermore, internalising negative externalities to their full extent would affect people at different income levels to differing extents. Some people on low incomes may be pushed into an impossible situation, which would not contribute to sustainability, especially if shifts in prices reduce the supply of job opportunities or possibilities of taking advantage of them.

Innovation

Innovations in land-use planning, technology, and policy instruments are needed if urban environmental conditions are to improve, and if firms and households are to reduce the consumption of resources. Innovation can be present at all stages of policy development and implementation; it is critical to the process of priority setting, for evaluation, for the diffusion of information and knowledge, and for all kinds of policy whether it be proactive, mitigatory or adaptive. Cities already provide many of the factors that favour innovation (R&D, entrepreneurial climate to take up innovations, close interaction between government and the public, etc.), but they are not being directed forcefully enough to address urban problems. Innovation tends to emerge from the interrelations between initiatives for sustainability, partnerships between key local players within a network of cities, and/or from strategic, holistic approaches to urban development.[14] A shared approach is critical for problem solving between different tiers of government and between government, private sector and the community.[15]

Innovations may fail, but the costs and risks of innovation are relatively small compared to those of doing nothing. The most successful innovations combine environmental achievements and economic benefits while favouring social reconciliation and local democracy.[16] Improved information dissemination of successful innovations is also necessary to turn successful innovations into common knowledge.

WHY AN INTEGRATED APPROACH IS NECESSARY

Although the rate of economic, social and technological change is rapid, it is not uniform: some aspects of cities change rapidly and comprehensively, while others do not. Because the impact of cities on the environment is constantly changing, solutions are never permanent, but need to be sensitive and responsive to the latest developments. Moreover, as urban environmental problems today are highly inter-related, involving everyday routines of households and firms, they are too big and diffuse for governments to solve through sectoral regulation and legislation; sectoral policies may find a solution to one problem only to cause another. Consequently, integrative ecological policy-making requires cross-sectoral approaches: a combination of policy instruments, financial, regulatory, and strategic, directed at achieving multiple policy objectives. Such critical connections have been made in relation to transport and land use, housing and area regeneration, infrastructure provision, derelict and under-utilised land, waste and recycling, and greening programmes.

Integrative strategies promoted by the OECD are sensitive to local conditions and priorities, as they imply a high degree of decentralisation. Local governments are not only responsible for integrative policies, but also a means for implementing them. A major argument for a centralised authority is the cross-border nature of environmental problems. But local variations in the quality of information, the nature of environmental problems, and political circumstances make uniformity impractical. By making decisions at the level at which they apply, it is possible to reflect the uniqueness of local circumstances without compromising broader objectives. Changes in the workings of the public sector and in the relations between government, private enterprise and the public at large are inevitable when integrative policies are introduced. Of the approaches considered in the Ecological City project[17] those policies which were best able to educate, involve the community and reflect changing circumstances had the best record of success in practice.

There is still a vital role for national governments to play. In principle, local government and decision-making represent an instance which can bring competing objectives together to create tailor-made solutions to the area concerned. In practice, however, few cities have the administrative structure and capacity to ensure such integration. Consequently, governments should identify national policies which strengthen the ability of states and cities to develop and implement better environmental policies for cities, and enhance procedures for cross-ministerial co-ordination at the national level and for multi-sectoral, integrative administration at the state and municipal level. Clarity about measures taken at the national level is necessary for municipalities and states to be better able to adjust their policies accordingly. Central governments should give local governments latitude in setting priorities, and they should examine how municipalities and states can be given more flexibility to allocate resources and to introduce taxes or fees. Macroeconomic, structural and regional policies can have adverse environmental effects. In the field of sustainable regional development, public authorities are increasingly initiating new procedures specifically targeted at mitigating adverse effects on the environment. Furthermore, the urban area cannot be analysed in isolation from the region within which it is located. Even in a decentralised system, there is a role for national oversight in preventing "free-riding" situations, in which some communities are unwilling or lax about enforcing environmental regulations because of political priorities favouring the existing local production and employment structures and concerns over re-election.

Disaster management in cities should take account of current trends of outward growth, industrial development, waste generation and travel, and of changes that can be undertaken to reduce the vulnerability of cities to disaster and the harmful impact of urban activities on the environment. Governments should develop strategic plans and better mechanisms to monitor trends and set priorities with respect to building codes, spatial patterns and systems, as well as the costs and risks of disasters associated with environmental infrastructures and the built environment, in order to achieve a cost-effective strategy of risk reduction and post-disaster reconstruction.

THE NEED FOR BETTER INFORMATION AND DATA

Better measures and feedback mechanisms are needed to evaluate new policy strategies and their impact on cities, and to disseminate information on the quality of urban environmental policies, and on best practice. For cross-sectoral urban problems, good specific measures are: environmental budgeting, environmental impact assessment, partnerships and public participation, and economic instruments.[18] Noteworthy evaluation methods are environmental auditing, the ecological footprint, and environmental reporting. The potential of scenario building, vision making and simulation can be exploited by governments in the process of envisioning a more sustainable future direction for urban form. The ecosystems approach to land use is important in this area.[19] Eco-auditing is a new means with a lot of potential to impact the environmental performance of cities.[20]

Understanding about the functioning of cities, the environmental impacts of human activity and about how environmental conditions change, is still elementary, and difficult to incorporate into policy. Simultaneously, recent trends such as globalisation and structural economic change are changing the spatial structures of cities. Research is necessary to find out more about how cities function, the effectiveness of economic and regulatory instruments in altering travel demand and land use-patterns, new technologies which shape cities and resource needs, and the infrastructure costs of development on the urban periphery and of the redevelopment of already built-up areas.

CONCLUDING REMARKS

Present trends pose a serious threat for both economic and environmental sustainability, despite the considerable progress that has been made in terms of efficiency in resource use and equity in quality of life. There is increasing awareness of the problems and hence of the need to find solutions, but obstacles to finding lasting improvements persist.

Solutions to urban environmental problems are difficult to implement. This is the case, for instance, with urban travel: its growth is unsustainable, but combinations of the measures and policies available at present can bring about only a modest improvement in urban environmental conditions. Constant innovation is needed to discover more sustainable options for future development. Partnerships and civic engagement are crucial in stimulating innovation, as part of decentralisation, devolution, participation and empowerment. Strong local government is required to implement policy, and integrative strategies are required across local and central government to create linkages between key policy areas. In urban policy-making in general, environmental problems need a combination of policy instruments of financial, regulatory, and strategic nature, directed at achieving multiple policy objectives to be effective.

A major challenge facing policy-makers is to find ways to engage the private sector in the introduction of new priorities, criteria and guidelines for sustainability so that employment and economic growth can be enhanced. Economic and political conditions and trends may have as great an effect on urban environmental policy as any specific policy on the environment.

Progress on environmental problems on the world-wide scale cannot be made unless progress occurs at the urban level. Due to the world-wide nature of urban environmental problems, co-operation can bring high payoffs for all parties involved. Thus, the harmonization of policies, information sharing and dissemination about best practices, co-ordinated surveys, information on policy stances, standards, etc. create predictability on future policies and situations, and a more stable market for environmental goods and social organisation for improvements, as well as expanding trade in services. Governments should commit their countries to specific performance targets or outcomes, and to international co-operation as a means for achieving tangible results.

Because cities make an important contribution to economic productivity and competitiveness, it is important that their environmental costs be restricted as much as possible. Investments to improve urban environmental conditions will enhance competitiveness and strengthen the capacity of economies to respond to technological and economic change. If urban density and its expansion can be managed, cities may well be a more sustainable form of organisation on the world-wide level.

NOTES

1. EEA (1995), p. 289.

2. EEA (1995), p. 267 and 586.

3. Bernes (1993).

4. EA (1995) p. 267 and 586.

5. OECD/ECMT (1995), p. 63-66.

6. Quinet (1994) and OECD/ECMT (1995), p. 63-66.

7. OECD/ECMT (1995), p. 63-66.

8. OECD/ECMT (1995).

9. Hahn and Simonis (1991) in EEA (1995), p. 286.

10. With more developed regions it is refered to Northern America, Europe, Australia, New Zealand and Japan. Source: World Urbanization Prospects, The 1994 Revision, United Nations, Department of Economic and Social Information and Policy Analysis, Population Division, New York, 1995.

11. ECMT/OECD (1995).

12. EFILWC (1996), Part II.

13. EEA (1995), p. 289-291. In particular, economic and environmental sustainability could be greatly enhanced by a change of attitudes towards a preference for quality and durability of consumer goods, as well as from the better use of waste as a resource.

14. Mega (1995) and OECD (1996b), p. 98.

15. Gibbs (1994) and OECD (1996a), p. 39.

16. OECD (1996a), p. 36.

17. OECD (1996a), p. 98.

18. OECD (1996a), p. 100.

19. OECD (1996a), p. 62.

20. EFILWC (1995), Part I.

BIBLIOGRAPHY

Bernes, C. (ed.) (1993), *The Nordic Environment – Present state, trends and threats*. Nord 1993: 12, Nordic Council of Ministers, Copenhagen.

EEA, (1995), (European Environment Agency). Europe's Environment, The Dobrís Assessment. Edited by David Stanners and Philippe Bourdeau, Copenhagen.

EFILWC, (1995), European Foundation for the Improvement of Living and Working Conditions, The Sustainable City, A European Tetralogy, Part I: Urban Eco-Auditing and Local Authorities in Europe.

EFILWC, (1996), European Foundation for the Improvement of Living and Working Conditions, The Sustainable City, A European Tetralogy, Part II: The SMEs and the Revitalisation of the European Cities.

Gibbs, D., (1994), *Towards the Sustainable City, Greening the Local Economy*, Town Planning Review, Vol. 65, No. 1.

Hahn and Simonis, (1991), *Ecological urban restructuring*, Ekistics 58 (348/349), May/June-July/August.

Mega, V. (1995), *Well-being of Cities and Citizens*, in *Our Cities, Our Future*, proceedings of the International Healthy and Ecological Cities Congress, Madrid, 22-25 March.

OECD (1996*a*), *Innovative Policies for Sustainable Urban Development: The Ecological City*.

OECD (1996*b*), *Our Cities, Our Future: Policies and Action Plans for Health and Sustainble Development*, edited by Charles Price and Agis Tsouros, in cooperation with WHO Regional Office for Europe, Ayuntamiento de Madrid, and European Foundation for the Improvement of Living and Working Conditions.

OECD/ECMT (1995), *Urban Travel and Sustainable Development*.

OECD (1994), *Urban Policies for an Environmentally Sustainable World: The OECD-Sweden seminar on the Ecological City*, June 1994.

OECD (1993), *Environmental Data Compendium 1993*.

Quinet, E. (1994), *The Social Costs of Transport: Evaluation and Links with International Policies*. Published by the OECD as Internalising the Social Costs of Transport.

Chapter 14

BIOTECHNOLOGY AND SUSTAINABLE DEVELOPMENT

by

Carliene Brenner, Mark Cantley, Jean-Marie Debois, Peter Kearns,
Lisa Zannoni and Elettra Ronchi

INTRODUCTION

Over the past two decades, as a result of dramatic advances in basic biological research, man has acquired vast amounts of new knowledge about the structure and functioning of living organisms. Driven by both scientific curiosity and human needs, the new knowledge penetrates to the molecular level, to the universal genetic code of DNA – showing that at the core of all living organisms lies a self-reproducing data tape. The technological innovations that have followed have implications for all life sciences, and in particular for environmental protection, agriculture and the food system, and health care. These areas, and their management, are obviously of fundamental importance to the sustainability of human life and health and to ecosystems at all scales. The new knowledge changes possibilities and responsibilities, in terms of safety, performance, competitiveness, and costs. The policy challenges are numerous, and do not respect departmental or disciplinary boundaries.

The OECD has addressed aspects of the diffusion and application of modern biotechnology which have implications for public policy and are of international significance or common interest. Initially, in the 1980s, Member countries were largely concerned with safety issues relating, first, to laboratory work on genetically modified organisms and subsequently to industrial production using those organisms, and saw the need to develop appropriate guidelines. They also examined policy issues such as finance, university-industry relationships, patents, and the role of government. A series of policy reports followed, clarifying and addressing the new questions, and through the processes of dialogue involved in preparing these reports, helping to educate the policy-advisory circles concerned.

In the 1990s, as the products and processes deriving from modern biotechnology have been more widely commercialised, policy issues that bear more directly on sustainability are coming to the fore, with implications for a far wider range of policy-makers in ministries of agriculture, environment, industry and trade, as well as for research. As a result, the OECD, like many governments, has worked to develop horizontal mechanisms in order to maintain coherence, co-ordination, and transparency among the bodies working in this area.

Various facets of OECD work on biotechnology are relevant to sustainability. The OECD promotes the useful application of biotechnology. It provides a forum for exchanges among governments as a means of facilitating mutual learning and adaptation. It encourages policy co-ordination, particularly where its absence might lead to trade impediments or other obstacles, and to economic inefficiencies. Moreover, it continues to seek to develop consensus on concepts or principles for safety assessment and hence to facilitate the harmonization of regulations. Finally, it increasingly collaborates in "outreach" activities with non-member countries and UN agencies, by involving them, where feasible or appropriate, in the OECD's work, for example, on the development of publicly accessible databases, *e.g.* on bio-safety.

BIOTECHNOLOGY FOR ENVIRONMENTAL PROTECTION

Biotechnology can prevent or reduce local environmental damage in various ways. It is a means of developing added-value processes, which convert a waste stream into useful products, some of which can be used to help restore natural balances. Biological means can be used in ''end-of-pipe'' processes to purify the waste stream to the point where the products can be released without harm into the environment. Through biotechnology, new biomaterials can be developed, which can be used to manufacture materials and products with reduced environmental impact. Finally, new biological production processes can generate waste that is more easily managed.

At present, the main environmental use of biotechnology involves cleaning up pollution; the process is called ''bioremediation'' and it involves using micro-organisms to break down pollutants. An early application of biotechnology was clean-up of waste water, later followed by air and off-gas cleaning (biofilters). The focus in this area is now shifting towards treating contaminated soil and solid waste, an area which raises complex scientific and technical questions concerning the interactions of organisms with each other and with soil. Bioremediation is in the foreground today because countless polluted sites – which bear witness to the non-sustainability and the unacceptability of past and current practices – call for urgent remedial action and because of the improving relative cost-efficiency of biological clean-up methods as compared to the more traditional physical and chemical ones.

An ongoing series of OECD initiatives deals with the role and application of biotechnology (see Box 1). These started with a study of the use of biotechnology for environmental clean-up. The resulting report pointed to the existence of a large, unknown, and little exploited potential of naturally occurring organisms which can contribute to environmental restoration but also noted the need to use genetically modified organisms *in situ* to degrade recalcitrant pollutants, especially since natural evolutionary processes may be unacceptably slow. The report, *Biotechnology for a Clean Environment* (OECD, 1994), discussed the need for technical developments, and made specific recommendations on R&D for treating air, soil and land, solid wastes, waste water and industrial effluents, as well as for improved monitoring and environmental assessment. It also stressed the need for policy contexts that encouraged their application.

Box 1. **OECD proceedings on bioremediation/bioprevention**

- The latest scientific and technical advances are reviewed, with emphasis on long-term environmental protection and life-cycle management (Tokyo, 1994).

- Bioremediation of air and soil is an industry that might reach $75 billion by the year 2000. It is moving from scattered production of various technologies to an organised business sector (Amsterdam, November 1995).

- Techniques of modern biotechnology can contribute to water quality and conservation and improve both performance and cost-efficiency. The presence of pathogens can be recognised earlier than with current practices, and the outbreak of epidemics may be averted (Mexico, October 1996).

The depletion of aquifers, and the inadequacy – even the perversity – of current policies (*e.g.* under-pricing of water for agricultural use, statutory obligation to use obsolescent technology) show the need for technological innovation based on modern science and a rational policy framework that encourages sustainable use. The recycling of water in a crowded world poses continuing scientific and technical challenges which are central to the maintenance of public health and to agricultural productivity. The OECD is pursuing these issues in its work, for example, reviewing how modern, molecular techniques can give earlier, surer and more cost-effective surveillance of water quality.

However, biotechnology also has a protective role to play in industry and in agriculture, where it can be used progressively to replace certain unsustainable practices and processes and help integrate life-cycle concepts into industrial products and processes ("bioprevention"). In this respect, its function is not only to remedy existing damage to the environment but to prevent future damage. Indeed, the top priority for environmental biotechnology in the future will be to reduce and prevent damage and thus to enhance the sustainability of the processes and practices concerned.

In terms of the need to rethink industrial products and processes, the OECD has launched a major new project on the use of biotechnology to achieve cleaner industrial products and processes, with contributions from both academic and industrial experts. The project has a double focus: it seeks to define technologies for use in specific sectors, and more broadly the aim is to contribute to the redesign in the twenty-first century of industries that account for approximately half of gross manufacturing output. The sectors addressed include food and feed, chemicals, pulp and paper, textiles and leather, materials and minerals, and energy.

It is important for the findings of scientists to reach policy advisers and decision makers, particularly in government. Therefore, the OECD not only brings scientists together to discuss advances and results in biotechnology but provides the scientific communities concerned an opportunity for communication and dialogue with governments, whose actions (or lack thereof) can have a decisive influence on the behaviour of the private sector and on the creation and growth of new market opportunities. In this way, the OECD has been ensuring the discussion and diffusion of information on the usefulness of biotechnology for environmental protection and the need for appropriate policy. By understanding regulation-technology linkages, stressing performance, working with competitive mechanisms, and harmonizing internationally, governments can drive technology and innovation in constructive directions, not least towards greater sustainability.

FOOD AND AGRICULTURE

Products resulting from work in biotechnology have increasingly entered agricultural production and the food chain. The commercialisation of an agri-food product derived through biotechnology raises regulatory issues in terms of environmental biosafety, food safety, and varietal seed certification. In this area, Member countries have chosen to focus OECD work on certain topics requiring further work both in scientific and in policy terms, each of which is relevant to sustainable development:

- environmental biosafety: concepts and principles for assessing the safety of genetically modified agricultural crop plants or micro-organisms and developing a common basis for harmonization of regulatory issues;
- food safety: the development of consensus on concepts for assessing safety to underpin the development of national and international regulation;
- seed certification: especially for international trade in seeds or trials in different regions and countries;
- management of biological resources: the interests and needs of agricultural research, as it assimilates the tools and techniques of modern biotechnology;
- biotechnology and developing country agriculture: many biotechnology applications in the developed world do not address the needs of developing countries, where the needs and potential benefits are likely to be even greater.

ENVIRONMENTAL BIOSAFETY

The OECD pioneered the review of environmental biosafety aspects of agri-food products and, in the 1980s, developed an array of scientific concepts and principles to ensure the safety of biotechnology R&D related to plants and micro-organisms from the laboratory through field testing. In 1986, it developed the *Recombinant DNA Safety Considerations*, on the basis of which most Member countries have developed regulations for examining the environmental biosafety aspects of agri-food products.

As such products began to reach the commercialisation phase, OECD began work on harmonizing regulatory structures in Member countries to ensure product safety, to make regulations more transparent and efficient, and to facilitate trade. As a first step, a survey was made of national policies and regulatory regimes, including data requirements and means of assessing data. The survey showed that the scientific foundation for assessing risk was the same in all countries.

The OECD has therefore begun to develop consensus documents containing the technical information used in a regulatory assessment of the biology or the traits of a particular product. These documents, developed in this collaborative way, are used as tools for national regulatory activities. Through collaboration with United Nations agencies (UNEP and UNIDO), certain documents are forwarded to non-member countries for exchange of expertise and information.

In an effort to facilitate access to such information, BioTrack OnLine has recently been developed and made available as an Internet Web site (see Box 2).

Box 2. **BioTrack OnLine: An international resource**

Website: http://www.oecd.org/ehs/service.htm

Contains:

- Major legislative developments in OECD Member countries, including information on relevant regulatory authorities
- Field trials of transgenic organisms (on-line database)
- Products commercialised in OECD Member countries
- Links to related World Wide Web sites
- Biotechnology
- OECD's consensus documents containing technical information for use in regulatory assessments

---

FOOD SAFETY

New foods developed through modern biotechnology offer the promise of increased harvests, greater resistance to certain diseases, and thus reduced use of pesticides, thereby contributing to sustainable development. However, the safety of new foods or food components derived through modern biotechnology is both a scientific issue and a concern of policy makers. In 1990, the OECD began to elaborate scientific principles for assessing food safety, which were intended for use by evaluators. Scientific experts based these principles on the concept of "substantial equivalence": the new food is compared with a traditional counterpart having a history of safe use, and the procedures used in the past for accepting comparable innovations are examined and clarified. Case studies illustrate how to apply the concept of substantial equivalence to new foods (*Safety Evaluation of Foods Derived by Modern Biotechnology: Concepts and Principles, OECD* 1993). New foods of aquatic origin were not initially included. Subsequent work concluded that the concept could generally be applied to products of aquatic origin as well (*Aquatic Biotechnology and Food Safety*, OECD, 1994).

The next step was assessing the safety of new foods that lack a conventional counterpart and to which the concept of substantial equivalence cannot be applied. Testing methods and testing strategies for the assessment of foods developed through biotechnology and for irradiated foods have been examined (*Food Safety Evaluation*, OECD, 1996). This work is continuing, with particular support from Member countries having major food production sectors and a strong science base. Work on testing methods and strategies for the toxicological and nutritional evaluation of novel foods in 1997 will offer OECD Member countries an opportunity to share experience and explore possibilities for harmonization of their safety requirements. In preparation, surveys are under way on serum banks for testing allergenicity to new foods, on the use of data banks for assessing the safety of new foods, and assessing the safety of animal feeds.

The OECD's work on food safety is co-ordinated with the efforts of other organisations, such as FAO, WHO, and the Codex Alimentarius Commission for which they are jointly responsible.

SEED CERTIFICATION

Three criteria – distinctness, uniformity and stability – are the basis for identifying seed varieties and the backbone of seed development and commercialisation. They are also at the heart of the diversity of cultivated crops and the survival of wild strains. This puts seed varieties at the centre of the sustainability issue, especially when hybridisation and genetic modifications are involved.

The OECD Schemes for Seed Certification were developed to regulate international trade in seed as well as counter-season multiplication of seed between the northern and southern hemispheres. They have been implemented by a total of forty-five Member and non-member countries across all continents. Their essential purpose is to harmonize the assessment and certification of identity and purity of cultivars (cultivated crop plant varieties) – including genetically modified ones – and ecotypes (local cultivars). Most species, including all basic staples, are eligible and the varieties from all participating countries appear on an annually published official list: *OECD List of Cultivars Eligible for Certification*.

In conjunction with increasingly sophisticated laboratory analysis and the introduction of intellectual property rights regimes, the schemes can serve as guidelines to help modernise the seed sector. They also facilitate the improvement and dissemination of both local and imported varieties.

BIOLOGICAL RESOURCE MANAGEMENT FOR SUSTAINABLE AGRICULTURAL SYSTEMS

In recognition of the great importance of agriculture as an aspect of sustainable development, most OECD Member countries have agreed to participate in a co-operative research programme on biological resource management for sustainable agricultural systems. Scheduled to run from 1995 to 1999, it is organised around four scientific themes:

- the safe exploitation of micro-organisms in plant/soil systems;
- quality of animal production;
- utilisation and ecology of new organisms;
- surface and ground water quality and agricultural practices.

The programme's aim is to intensify fundamental research in biotechnology, with particular emphasis on more efficient use of input factors in producing plants and animals and on the quality of ground and surface water. It seeks to reinforce international scientific co-operation, and to facilitate the exchange of information on current research, in particular that of value to developing countries.

The programme has two major activities: scientists receive post-doctoral fellowships to work in laboratories in countries other than their own, and workshops are held on specific areas of research.

BIOTECHNOLOGY AND DEVELOPING COUNTRY AGRICULTURE

In the broader context of general technological change in agriculture, it is important for developing countries to create the conditions that will allow them to take full advantage of biotechnology's potential to contribute to more sustainable methods of agricultural production. Efforts have therefore been made through the work of the OECD Development Centre to determine the kinds of policies and institutional arrangements that are most likely to facilitate the technological change of which biotechnology is a part (*Biotechnology and Developing Country Agriculture: the Case of Maize*, OECD, 1991; *Integrating Biotechnology in Agriculture: Incentives, Constraints and Country Experiences*, OECD, 1996). Studies conducted in different parts of the world (including Brazil, Colombia, India, Indonesia, Kenya, Mexico, Thailand, and Zimbabwe) have looked not only at the nature and scope of biotechnology research but also at constraints and bottlenecks in the process from basic research to the marketing and widespread diffusion of a biotechnology product. The outcomes of agricultural biotechnology projects and programmes funded by bilateral and multilateral donor agencies have also been analysed (*International Initiatives in Biotechnology for Developing Country Agriculture: Promises and Problems*, OECD, 1994).

These studies have shown the need to compare the advantages and disadvantages of imported biotechnology techniques and/or products versus local development. In certain situations, it may make both scientific and economic sense to purchase, license, or import particular aspects of technology or finished biotechnology products. In others, however, products such as herbicide-tolerant crops developed in industrialised countries may not be the most appropriate for addressing, for example, the problems confronting low-input agriculture in developing countries.

Whether developing countries adopt products developed elsewhere or develop their own – and usually it will be a combination of both – they will need to build national capacity in terms of human resources, financing and institutions. In addition, they will need to improve their ability to address issues of biosafety and intellectual property rights. In some cases, only marginal changes will be needed in intellectual property laws, health regulations, testing procedures, and the like. In others, new structures may be required to deal not only with implementation, but also monitoring and enforcement.

Individual countries will, of course, formulate their own strategies or policies for developing biotechnology for use in agriculture. It is important, however, that biotechnology policies and programmes are closely integrated in the framework of the general problems confronting agriculture and agricultural research, with a clear sense of the specific problem areas to which biotechnology could best contribute.

Certain problematic situations arise where a restructured and reduced public sector no longer fulfils an earlier role of promoting technology diffusion, and yet efficient technology markets have not fully developed. In such cases, alternative transfer and diffusion mechanisms for agricultural technology may be required and would need to involve various public and private partners. This matter will require reflection on the part of developing countries, relevant non-governmental organisations, the donor community, and the international agricultural research community as a whole.

BIOTECHNOLOGY FOR SUSTAINABLE SOLUTIONS IN HEALTH CARE

Despite the great medical achievements of the first half of this century, many difficult tasks remain. According to the latest *World Health Report* (WHO, 1996), of the 52 million deaths in 1995, some 20 million were due to infectious and parasitic diseases. Tuberculosis killed about 3 million people, hepatitis B perhaps 1 million and malaria around 2 million. In 1995, there were over 24 million HIV-positive adults world-wide. Waterborne diseases continue to afflict many countries: in 1992, 72 500 cholera cases were recorded in Sub-Saharan Africa and more than 200 000 in Latin America. These figures reflect the fact that basic public health infrastructures and services are still lacking in many countries. They also indicate the need for cost-effective, improved diagnostic methods, vaccines and therapies, and in general, better knowledge of the disease agents. Medium or long-term solutions will require strategies based on environmentally friendly, sustainable technologies.

At the same time, OECD countries can no longer indiscriminately adopt new technologies. Slowing economic growth and the escalating costs (to government) of health services have led to this realisation and to efforts to reform the financing and delivery of health care. The difficult issue of rationing health care is also being felt by all countries, and is affected in particular by the changing demographics of most populations. World-wide, average life expectancy at birth in 1995 was more than 65 years, an increase of more than three years since 1985. Thus, ageing populations present large challenges to systems of health.

Biotechnology offers the promise of smarter solutions to health problems through deeper understanding of living matter and the disease process. It may be viewed as an integral part of a new rational approach to medicine and to drug development, production and delivery primarily based on two methods developed in the 1970s: recombinant DNA technology and monoclonal antibody technology, which make possible a more rational approach to vaccine design and thus better immunisation and prevention. In the past, for example, live vaccines were derived by purely empirical methods, but advances in molecular biology over the past 15 years have made it possible to create live vaccines with restricted growth potential or which undergo only partial replication in the host. Another very promising area of application of biotechnology is the use of improved diagnostics, both for human disease and for monitoring water quality and waterborne diseases, as more specific and rapid testing could have important epidemiological benefits.

Despite international efforts, current methods of determining water quality lack the precision and specificity to measure low levels of pathogens and contaminants and are ultimately inadequate as diagnostic tools. This implies the need for action at various levels. It was emphasized at the recent meeting in Mexico that medium- and long-term solutions will depend on new technological developments for improved surveillance. Biotechnology, combined with other chemical and physical methods as appropriate, is currently the most promising technology to address these needs.

The OECD first approached health matters from an economic perspective, developing the statistical tools and definitions which enabled discussion and comparison of expenditures for a sector that absorbs a growing proportion of national budgets. More recently, attempts have been made to review the efficiency and effectiveness of such expenditures, in response to the interests and needs of its Member countries. However, the diffusion of new scientific and technological developments, including biotechnology, is clearly world-wide in scope; as a result, the assessment and evaluation tools that are being reviewed or developed at the OECD have universal relevance, particularly when they concern the socio-economic implications of innovations.

Work on biotechnology for health care has tended to focus upon applications of interest to the developed economies, with the research priorities of the pharmaceutical industry naturally influenced by considerations of market potential. Yet the needs of the developing world, and the potential of biotechnology to address those needs in a cost-effective way, are enormous in diagnostics, prophylactics, therapeutics, and production technologies as UN agencies such as the World Health Organization have clearly recognised.

However, benefits from the introduction of new technologies will always depend on the availability of basic health services and infrastructures and will need to be evaluated against several variables, such as prevalence of disease, costs, and ultimately outcomes. How the management and adoption of new technologies can be improved is at the heart of most of the current studies on health and biotechnology at the OECD. The problems experienced in the evaluation of new biotechnology products are similar to those experienced in the evaluation of novel technologies in general, and are being reviewed with the aim of generating data toward sustainable solutions in health care.

EMERGING ISSUES

The knowledge and techniques of biotechnology are clearly relevant to sustainability. They will be essential to addressing the ever-changing problem of maintaining high productivity in agriculture, both to feed a population that is rising to over 10 billion, and to do so safely, without significantly expanding the existing cultivated areas, or increasing environmental pollution. They will be no less necessary for addressing two other major dimensions of sustainability – health care and protection of the environment.

As these technologies are developed and applied, there will be unforeseen consequences, side-effects, and policy implications. While the safety record of modern biotechnology has been excellent to date, any adverse events will interact with the suspicion and hostility which in some regions already delay the adoption of new techniques and products. Public perception, information, confidence in the industrial and governmental systems on which public safety depends, are sensitive topics, and policies that encourage transparency, education and comprehensible information will continue to be needed.

As information is central to science and technology, its management, diffusion and application will take on growing significance in the transition to a sustainable economic system. This will be particularly important in the sectors concerned with biotechnology. The mapping and sequencing of complete genomes will transform agriculture, food and health care into ever more information-intensive sectors. Already, the OECD Megascience Forum has started work on biological informatics, focusing on information infrastructure. This infrastructure is fundamental to the science and taxonomy needed for conservation and inventory of biodiversity. As bioinformatics also enters the commercial realm, there will be controversies about intellectual property in germplasm and copyright in scientific databases and literature. These are areas where international policy approaches will have to be developed.

Work undertaken by the OECD will need not merely to be communicated to, but conducted in co-operation with, other international agencies with corresponding responsibilities, interests and strengths. This recognition is already in part reflected in the programmes and projects mentioned above.

BIBLIOGRAPHY

OECD (1996), Integrating Biotechnology in Agriculture: Incentives, Constraints and Country Experiences, by C. Brenner.

OECD (1996), *Wider Application and Diffusion of Bioremediation Technologies: The Amsterdam '95 Workshop.*

OECD (1996), *Food Safety Evaluation.*

OECD (1995), *Bioremediation: The Tokyo '94 Workshop.*

OECD (1994), *Biotechnology for a Clean Environment.*

OECD (1994), *Aquatic Biotechnology and Food Safety.*

OECD (1994), *International Initiatives in Biotechnology for Developing Country Agriculture: Promises and Problems.*

OECD (1993), *Safety Evaluation of Foods Derived by Modern Biotechnology: Concepts and Principles.*

OECD (1991), *Biotechnology and Developing Country Agriculture: the Case of Maize.*

OECD (1986), *Recombinant DNA Safety Considerations.*

OECD (annual), *List of Cultivars Eligible for Certification.*

Chapter 15

ENVIRONMENTAL EDUCATION AND SUSTAINABLE DEVELOPMENT: TRENDS IN MEMBER COUNTRIES

by

Kathleen Kelley-Lainé

INTRODUCTION

The Centre for Educational Research and Innovation of the OECD has been involved in developing environmental education in Member Countries since 1986. During this time environmental education has changed fundamentally in character. It has existed traditionally as ''outdoor education'', ''nature studies'' and for many years has been considered as a marginal part of the curriculum. Increasing awareness of the problem of ''sustainability'' has had a significant effect on the issue of environmental education – making it more complex, and demonstrating the connections to economic, social and technological problems. As environmental consciousness increases in OECD Member countries, the question of environmental education becomes the question of how to reach a ''critical mass''. The challenge for OECD Member countries today is not only to transmit a body of knowledge about the environment to citizens but to educate for sustainable development, to change behaviour in students and to motivate them in developing personal responsibilities toward the environment.

From 1986-1994, the CERI worked with a wide range of teachers, researchers and administrators in nineteen OECD countries to explore how to set an agenda better adapted to today's needs. They identified two main approaches in vogue: environmental studies, which are cross-disciplinary, but do not necessarily involve an inter-disciplinary mode of knowledge construction aiming to inform intelligent action in the local environment; and environmentalism, which is when students take in ideas about the environment that are not based on their own experience, which incurs the risk of identifying with a committed teacher's dogmatic views. They found it preferable to focus upon the need for students to have experience-based curricula so that learning would not be a matter of simply taking in principles of environment-friendly behaviour without thinking; they stressed the need to discover the environment, study situations and carefully seek solutions.

A NEW ENVIRONMENTAL EDUCATION PARADIGM

This new challenge requires personal involvement and motivation, critical capacities, and the necessary skills to be able to identify and formulate problems. Through inter-disciplinary learning and research it gives students the opportunity to view environmental issues in their complexity rather than simplifying causal relationships. Being able to have an impact on matters of real social concern develops dynamic qualities in students, such as initiative, independence and responsibility.

According a formal place to "values" in the curriculum

The Australian Education Council, in its draft on *Studies of Society and Environment,* outlined three important ways that values play a part in the curriculum:

1. Values became an object of study as students investigate and analyse people's actions and the values and beliefs that influence society and the environment, against the backdrop of their own experience. It is recognised that values influence what is selected for study, and, given the diversity of values in Australia, it is important to reach agreement on what is selected; the democratic process of selection is considered important.

2. Social justice is a second area of study which includes concern for welfare, rights and dignity of all people; empathy with people of different cultures and societies; fairness and commitment to redressing demonstrated disadvantage and changing prejudicial and violent practices. Ecological sustainability is another strand in this area. It involves conserving the environment, maintaining the diversity of the species and enhancing economic productivity in order to avoid future generations being disadvantaged.

3. The promotion of certain values is considered a direct result of studying society and the environment: students come to value curiosity and questioning, thorough and balanced investigation and logically developed lines of argument. Students also develop shared values around concepts of democratic process, social justice and ecological sustainability.

Fostering such qualities has been an important challenge to schools. A promising route to achieve them is through school initiatives focused both on the environment itself and on building knowledge from concrete experience of the environment. Countries have documented the difficulties they have encountered in integrating this new paradigm of teaching and learning within the mainstream curriculum in schools.

One significant issue confronting schools has been the role of values, and how to tackle controversial questions. Many schools in the study found that an important condition to develop values which are environmentally sound is to involve students in projects where they feel that they can make a difference. If students are involved in initiatives they consider meaningful and which have beneficial effects on the environment, caring becomes a value.

EVALUATING THE QUALITY OF ENVIRONMENTAL EDUCATION

How to evaluate the quality of environmental education and the development of dynamic learning in students is gaining increased attention. This means not only evaluating the outcomes of the actions taken, but also of the teaching and learning processes that evolve as a result of the actions.

In some countries "action-research" is used as a tool to favour reflection and formative evaluation. Learning to act reflectively and intelligently in relation to the environment is not so much a process of acquiring information about the environment and then applying it in action, but rather a matter of learning to deliberate about the practical problems one experiences in relating to the environment. The capacity to deliberate involves the development of four basic intellectual qualities:

- cognitive initiative or the capacity to initiate a course of action to improve a situation;
- the capacity to diagnose, discern and discriminate the practically relevant dimensions of the problem situation;
- the capacity to empathise with the thoughts and feelings, the points of view of those who are involved in a situation; and,
- the capacity to self-monitor one's own actions and their consequences in the environment.

These could be called indicators of dynamic qualities, powers of understanding, which can be equally displayed by individuals who adopt different value positions on environmental issues and arrive at different conclusions about what ought to be done. A number of countries are developing quality indicators for environmental education. In the Netherlands, for example, quality criteria are being developed from Agenda 21 and the objectives for education contained therein, at the curriculum level, the school organisational level and the support level. In many countries, the development of research to evaluate the effects of environmental education on young people's behaviour and attitudes regarding sustainable consumption is seen as a priority issue, as environmental education becomes increasingly widespread.

TEACHERS' PROFESSIONAL DEVELOPMENT

Are teacher's being trained to meet the multiple challenges of environmental education? The results of the studies of environmental education policy show that the training of teachers in environmental education is the weakest point in all countries. Initial training is often non-existent and in-service training is too costly. CERI's work with school initiatives demonstrated the important potential of dynamic networks for professional development. Dynamic networks are a kind of joint venture wherein different partners create an active networking relationship to carry out a common goal. They facilitate effective utilisation of existing know-how, abilities and energies within the teaching profession for further education of teachers. However this implies a new concept of educational support; Member countries reported on how dynamic networks were used to foster professional development of teachers.

An Example of Dynamic Networking in Environmental Education

In a secondary school in Tyrol, Austria, a biology teacher started an "energy network" with a group of 14 year-old students. In a pilot phase they began by studying energy use in their school building and in their homes. A year later they tackled a major task: to analyse the use of energy in four small villages (the home communities of most pupils). The first step was the development of a questionnaire, with the advice of an energy expert, followed by an intensive learning phase to understand the issues and the practice of survey data collection. Students conducted the survey from house to house, which served as a useful process not only for gathering information but also to inform people about the intentions of the work. Nearly 70 per cent of the households completed the questionnaire.

Students produced a comparative analysis of each household's energy use and made suggestions for the use of renewable energies (such as biogas, wood and solar energy). The results were presented by the students at a public event. Two months later, a few pupils with their parents started to build sun collectors for their own houses. This stimulated the foundation of an association for renewable energy and within two years 700 installations for solar water-heating were built in the whole region. A number of other investments followed. In one village, for example, the school building was insulated to reduce energy consumption.

This project showed students and teachers that, with relatively little effort, a considerable amount of energy could be saved and public approval could be gained. The next step was to link up with other schools and to find solutions for a number of new questions: how to inform schools, how to identify persons and institutions who could provide financial, political and other kinds of support.

In 1994 the network reached beyond the school to find partners in the community. To foster ownership of innovations by the community, the network involved persons and institutions in the community having some influence or interest in energy saving. The network newspaper (originally school-based) became a newspaper of community environmental projects. Schools (teachers and pupils) were still involved but the community projects were no longer fully dependent on their participation.

GREENING OF SCHOOLS

An important international trend, which could be considered as part of the new environmental education paradigm, is that of greening schools. In German-speaking countries, this concept is known as ''ecologising schools''. This approach considers the school to be a holistic ecological learning place, involving the building itself, the natural, social, economic and technological environment as well as the processes of teaching and learning, management and organisation.

A survey carried out by the University of Klagenfurt showed that a number of middle and northern European countries are increasingly involved in the ''ecological redevelopment of the whole school''. Often schools start with energy saving, developing strategies for economising water, re-cycling waste, paper, etc. The raised awareness is often extended to the management and organisation of the school and its relationship to the community. Good examples of eco-schools demonstrate that sustainable strategies concerning the school's environment result in material benefits and actually make money for the school. Teamwork is an important factor and to create an eco-school means involving the whole school and the community. Over and above material benefits, it has been found that when students participate in ''greening'' their school, violence tends to decrease. Students take part in activities that give them a sense of accomplishment; the resulting self-esteem and pride in the outcomes make for less vandalism of school property.

The Eco-Stamp of Quality

An exceptionally ecologically aware community in Austria decided to include the "greening schools" in their communal Eco-Plan, wherein local citizens, entrepreneurs, local government officers and other staff, as well as politicians, plan and design environmental measures. Between 1992 and 1994 all twelve schools in the Weiz community underwent an eco-review which meant that the schools' environmental performance was closely examined. An assessment scale was developed by the teachers and experts to evaluate the "hardware" (energy, school equipment, office supplies, waste management, cafeteria and school design) and the "software" (teaching and in-service training).

Results showed that the most common features of environmental awareness were the use of recycling paper, waste separation, a toilet flush stop button to save water, the cultivation of indigenous plants on the school grounds, eliminating aluminium and plastic containers and using alternative sources of energy. The most important environmental problem of the schools was energy waste through the lack of heat control in the classrooms; there were no thermostats, no insulation or sound-proofing of windows.

The "software" side was more difficult to asses; there was evidence that the pedagogy did not leave much room for pupils' creativity in terms of changing the environmental situation of their own classroom, and that the real problems of the school were not tackled in class. However, the exercise stimulated interest in teachers and students, resulted in some concrete measures such as a seminar for janitors on the use of ecological detergents, as well as the creation of a network of eco-schools.

THE CHALLENGE OF A NEW CURRICULUM

Most countries now agree that environmental education is not only a question of transmitting pre-defined knowledge about the environment to students, but should involve them personally and mobilise their sense of responsibility for having ''sustainable'' lifestyles. The need is for a dynamic curriculum model of teaching and learning that engages the active qualities of students (problem solving, values and emotional investment, cognitive and social skills, etc.) and has the flexible capacity to adapt to local community conditions.

The tension between according a formal place for environmental issues in the core curriculum and providing the necessary pedagogical processes, resources and flexibility to encourage a ''new environmental paradigm'' in schools has not been resolved. Examples from countries illustrate how they are struggling with some of these contradictions: the mere presence of environmental education in the core curriculum is not a guarantee for raising student awareness for the environment and ensuring sustainable consumers for the future.

Examples from Finland

Finland, like most Nordic countries, began discussing the inclusion of environmental education in the curriculum as early as the 1970s; in 1977 the report of the Upper Secondary School Curricula Committee noted that *"today's living environment and life in contemporary society are based to a large extent on developing the content area of the natural sciences"*. In the curricular guidelines of 1985 environmental education was required by legislation. The development of a "new environmental education paradigm" has taken a more varied and complex route than formal curriculum statements; and Finland has taken part in a number of projects, including the OECD's Environment and School Initiatives Study to explore and develop new environmental education strategies.

Finland's participation in the OECD/CERI study on *Environment and School Initiatives* from 1986-1997 (financed jointly by the Ministry of Education, the National Board of Education and the Ministry of Environment) enabled the establishment of a network of schools carrying out practical research to identify local environmental problems and bringing about concrete changes by acting on the environment. Local decision-makers and the general public have been kept informed of the school's work by the media. Since 1992 schools have been developing criteria to evaluate environmental education including indicators to show whether the goals of EE have been reached.

In 1991-92 the National Board of Education launched a campaign called "Towards Sustainable Development by Consumer Education" in co-operation with the National Consumer Administration of the Ministry of Trade and Industry. The purpose of the campaign was to strengthen students' abilities to take on an active role as critical consumer. Many of the participating countries have used similar strategies to complement and expand the formal environmental education curriculum in schools in the effort to develop a "new environmental education paradigm".

EDUCATING CITIZENS FOR A SUSTAINABLE SOCIETY – A CHALLENGE FOR POLICY MAKERS

The necessity for ''sustainable development'' today is a challenge for policy-makers. Education is potentially one of the most powerful policy instruments for bringing about new ways of thinking, global as opposed to compartmentalised awareness, as well as developing the necessary skills, attitudes, behaviour, values and ethics for stewarding a sustainable world.

Despite the acknowledged need, the powerful potential, and the international agreements, however, environmental education still tends to remain a marginalised and compartmentalised part of most education systems. Looked upon by educators as an ''environmental issue'' and by environmentalists as an ''education issue'', environmental education tends to fall between the good intentions of two different Ministries and diverging logistics. Even when policy-makers mandate the inclusion of environmental education within the core curriculum, there is no guarantee that the relevant teacher training, resources and the necessary pedagogical tools will be made available to assure significant developments.

The outcomes of the OECD/CERI reviews of environmental education policies in six Member countries (Austria, Australia, Finland, Germany, Hungary and Norway) have highlighted many aspects of international developments. Experts identified advanced innovative practice in schools; the effective use of networking as a tool in education and teacher training; the use of action-research as a method of formative, ongoing evaluation for teachers carrying out community-based school initiatives; teachers, students and schools tackling controversial issues within their local environment.

However, if the need for a new "environmental education paradigm" throughout education systems were addressed, giving it wide political legitimacy, solid epistemological status, and the funding to back up research and teacher training, as in some mathematical and scientific areas, then present policy measures are not yet up to meeting the challenge.

The development of environmental education policies in participating member countries are set within particular social and cultural contexts. Governments are moved by grass-roots initiatives that are often conditioned by environmental accidents, threats, or the fragility of the land. Environmental issues are high on the agenda if there is sufficient grass-roots pressure. Institutions, universities and policy-makers do not seem to be initiating environmental policies or activities but are rather responding to the initiatives taken by schools, students, parents and other grass-roots organisations.

Environmental education policies tend to be voluntary and permissive rather than mandatory. Although environmental education appears in the curriculum guidelines, it is often considered with other "soft" issues such as gender studies, native populations or "man and society". In some systems, environmental education is still in its traditional place of "nature conservation".

In order that a new "environmental education paradigm" may develop, there is the need for the creation of a fresh knowledge base that can master the complexity of the inter-disciplinary nature of environmental issues. For this to occur there needs to be a significant investment on the part of universities, both in research and in the professional development of teachers. Governments need to invest funds to stimulate these activities, both at the higher education levels as well as in other institutions.

Part of the question of "legitimacy" is related to the fact that environmental education is seen as competing with economic development. It is both necessary and urgent to consider that economics is a very important part of environmental education, as are issues concerning values and investment of human resources. Some industries are in fact realising the importance of creating partnerships with schools in this area, since they are conscious of the need for the training of future workers and managers in environmental issues.

Education programmes need to be more long-sighted and recognise the intimate links between environment, economy, employment and education – the "Four E's".

In identifying the shortage of necessary competencies and the need for advanced education in the environment area, the United States Association of Environmental Engineers estimates that 5 000 new environmental engineers per year would be required, but schools of engineering produce one third of that amount. The potential is there for universities to create programmes not only in environmental engineering, but also in business schools, departments of public administration, and other professional education programmes.

Universities and Vocational Training Institutions can play a very important role in fostering environmental awareness in the community and society at large.

Employment, too, can be an important result of education related to the environment, not only in pollution prevention and control, but in many other fields, such as medicine, scientific and technological research, urban planning and so forth.

If "environment, economics, employment and education" could become part of a new, holistic policy paradigm, rather than being seen as incompatible, isolated and conflicting elements, the creation of a new "market" for public investment, significant potential for job creation and assured public awareness for sustainable development could result.

SUMMARY

This chapter identifies some of the major trends in environmental education in OECD Member countries as a result of the work of the CERI in this field for the past eleven years. Based on the experience of the Environment and School Initiatives network, the international curriculum development network set up and managed by the CERI between 1986 and 1994, the Centre was able to monitor grass-roots developments in nineteen Member countries. The network is now managed in a Member country – Scotland – in association with CERI's programme. Policy reviews in environmental education in six countries enabled participating countries to raise some of the major current issues in developing adequate policy strategies in environmental education.

Future education policy directions point towards the "Four E's": environment, economics, employment and education, and foresee the powerful development of a new "education market" for public/private sector partnerships investment in the area of sustainable development.

BIBLIOGRAPHY

OECD/CERI (forthcoming in 1997), *Environmental Education Policies in Selected Countries.*

OECD/CERI (1995), *Environmental Learning for the 21st Century.*

OECD/CERI (1994), *Evaluating Innovation in Environmental Education.*

OECD/CERI (1991), *Environment, Schools and Active Learning.*